P9-CKA-530

A
LIFETIME
IN EVERY
MOMENT

A LIFETIME IN EVERY MOMENT

JOSEPH F. LITTELL

HOUGHTON MIFFLIN COMPANY

BOSTON   NEW YORK

1995

All of the events described in this book are true. A few conversations, especially in the earlier time periods, have been re-created in order to convey more fully the spirit of what took place. The names, along with some places and dates, of a few individuals have been changed to protect their privacy.

Copyright © 1995 by Joseph F. Littell

All rights reserved

For information about permission to reproduce selections from this book, write to Permissions, Houghton Mifflin Company, 215 Park Avenue South, New York, New York 10003.

For information about this and other Houghton Mifflin trade and reference books and multimedia products, visit The Bookstore at Houghton Mifflin on the World Wide Web at http://www.hmco.com/trade/.

Library of Congress Cataloging-in-Publication Data
Littell, Joseph F.
A lifetime in every moment / Joseph F. Littell.
p. cm.
ISBN 0-395-73792-3
1. Littell, Joseph F.   2. Publishers and publishing — United States — Biography.
3. Textbooks — Publishing — United States — History — 20th century.
4. Children of missionaries — United States — Biography.   I. Title.
Z473.L558A3 1995
070.5'092—dc20
[B]   95-24395   CIP

Book design by Anne Chalmers
Text type: Electra (Linotype-Hell)
Display type: Escorial (Metamorphosis); Bodoni Black (Monotype)

Printed in the United States of America

QUM 10 9 8 7 6 5 4 3 2 1

Permissions for quoted material appear on page 303.

This book is lovingly dedicated

to my wife,

Joy.

Home is where one starts from. As we grow older
The world becomes stranger, the pattern more complicated
Of dead and living. Not the intense moment
Isolated, with no before and after,
But a lifetime burning in every moment.
And not the lifetime of one man only
But of old stones that cannot be deciphered.

           — T. S. Eliot, *Four Quartets*

CONTENTS

A
LIFETIME
IN EVERY
MOMENT

PROLOGUE

SEVERAL YEARS AGO, I was chatting with a friend of mine — the head of an accounting firm — in his Chicago home. Somehow the subject got around to my life and the unimaginable things that have happened to me over the years. As I unfolded my story, which I had never told before except in bits and pieces, my friend sat and listened as if in a trance. (Even his Yorkshire terriers, FIFO and LIFO, lay at his feet and paid rapt attention.)

Over a period of several hours, I told my friend what it was like

- being one of seven children born into a missionary family deep in central China.
- being brought up in Honolulu, where my father was the Episcopal bishop and where I had to cope with the suicide of a member of the family in the kitchen of the Bishop's House.
- being an exchange student to Hitler's Germany in 1939; going on war games with my German classmates; receiving my junior high school diploma from Heinrich Himmler, chief of the German Gestapo.
- being kept five thousand miles from home throughout my teenage years, lonely and homesick, while left to the mercy of a cruel and sadistic uncle.

- being called up by the U.S. Army at the age of eighteen and being wounded in the Battle of the Bulge; being captured by the Germans; escaping from a POW camp with two other Americans, only to be recaptured and nearly shoved in front of a firing squad; being imprisoned in a section of Buchenwald, to be liberated at last by General Patton's Third Army.
- being estranged from my parents for twenty years until I discovered a surefire way to replace anger with love.
- discovering that marriage and the job can have earthshaking effects on each other, for better and for worse.
- being co-founder of McDougal, Littell & Company, a firm that is today one of the top half-dozen educational publishers in the nation.
- returning to the scenes of my childhood in Honolulu   where surprise and anguish awaited me.

All of the events that I related to my friend, and am about to relate to you in this book, are true. Although some may appear extreme — even bizarre — they are only reminders of the boundless range of human experience. The strengths and frailties we all possess simply take a variety of forms and disguises.

In essence, this is a story of survival. It is a story of devotion and alienation, of acceptance and rejection, of love beyond understanding, and ultimately of a final, heartfelt homecoming.

HANK GOES TO CHINA

THE DELAWARE HELLION

"Prankster!" "Scamp!" "Hellion!" they called him. "Someone ought to take a hand to his backside!"

That was the well-earned reputation of my father, who, as a boy in the 1880s, was never without a plan for mischief. Known as Hank, he was the son (or, as some said, the "despair") of the Reverend Thomas Gardiner Littell, rector of St. John's Episcopal Church in Wilmington, Delaware. Although never mean or malicious, his mischief-making would raise eyebrows, even havoc, at times among the staid and God-fearing gentry of this highly proper and law-abiding community. It was the talk of the town when young Hank

- took his pals skinny-dipping in Brandywine Creek. Completely in the pink, they splashed around in full view of the carriages rumbling over the Brandywine Creek bridge.
- took his chums to the local park and lobbed firecrackers into groups of Sunday picnickers, watching from behind the bushes as, in panic, people screamed and ran for cover. Picnic tables collapsed! Plates full of ham and potato salad clattered to the ground! Glasses of sarsaparilla went flying and soaked everyone!

- when the coast was clear, smuggled his friends into the kitchen of his house to make white sugar sandwiches. They each took two slices of bread, troweled gobs of soft butter on them, then piled a half inch of refined sugar on each slice. Finally, they slammed the two slices together and — what a feast! "Yummy!" they all exclaimed.
- found his father's portable Communion set in a downstairs closet and passed the bottle of Communion wine around to his pals. They all giggled as they sipped the forbidden drink. But "ugh!" they said. "What a terrible taste!"

Hank's older brother, John, was usually away in boarding school in Philadelphia, while his younger brother, Elton, who lived at home, never got into mischief. "He's a 'goody-goody,'" said Hank's friends. "He's always boasting that he's going to be a doctor. What a bore!" Hank said *he* wanted to be a privateer, steering his sleek four-master through mountainous waves to hunt down foreign vessels whose captains hated the United States. "Any ship's captain who refuses to swear allegiance to our country," he told his friends, "will be blindfolded and made to walk the plank." To get his friends to sign on to his future voyages, he gave them all sorts of inducements. "If you get captured," he promised them, "I'll slip ashore in a rowboat in the dead of night and free you from your rat-infested dungeons."

Also in the family were two younger sisters, Helen and Mary. Whenever a boy teased one of them or threw something at her, he was always sorry. Hank, their protector, boxed his ears roundly. The word got around that it was best to leave Hank's sisters alone.

As the boys entered their teenage years, their father taught them to be strong swimmers and tennis players. The Reverend Dr. Littell was himself quite an athlete. He even encouraged Hank to join a boxing club in Wilmington, where Hank regularly pummeled the stuffing out of teenage opponents who were taller, had a longer reach, and outweighed him by as much as twenty pounds. Hank was a scrappy kid!

Somewhere along the line, as he matured further, Hank became intensely religious. It may be that he wanted to grow up to be like his father — a man of deep compassion who revealed a loving heart and who set for his children a daily example of Christian charity and godliness. Hank's mother, Helen Harrington Littell, a strong-willed matriarch with fierce ambitions for her children, encouraged him to emulate his father.

And this he did. By the time he enrolled at Trinity College in Hartford, Connecticut, Hank had decided to enter the ministry. After graduating in 1895, he spent a year at Oxford University, then three years at New York's General Theological Seminary.

OFF TO CHINA, WHERE THE ACTION IS

At that time, thousands of missionaries from many lands were fanning out all over China, determined to make Christians out of a people who comprised a quarter of the earth's population. They were eager, too, to bring education and health care to a country ravaged by famine, poverty, disease, and ignorance. Fired with zeal, sure of their faith, they were positive they knew what was best for China.

Prominent among them was the Episcopal bishop of Shanghai. One day this dedicated man paid a visit to the General Theological Seminary, where Hank was a third-year student, and made an impassioned plea for missionaries to China. "Go ye unto all the world and preach the gospel to all nations," he implored his audience of young seminarians, borrowing all the marching orders he could find from the New Testament. "Go ye and bring light to those who walk in darkness."

Hank was smitten. As a boy he had whetted his appetite for adventure with books such as *Treasure Island*, *Kidnapped*, and *The Count of Monte Cristo*. He now had a chance for a two-fer: doing important religious work while enjoying a rip-snorting life of adventure. By graduation time, Hank knew he had to go to China.

On hearing his decision, his parents beamed with pride, embracing him warmly. "Go with our blessings, son," they said. "Make China a better place for all mankind."

But his sisters, Helen and Mary, listened to his news in shock and disbelief. Since early childhood they had adored him, depended on

Hank, while a student at Oxford.

him, and now he was leaving for the opposite side of the globe. All they could do was pray that they could persuade him to stay in America.

Clasping her hands in supplication, Helen cried, "Dear, dear brother, do you really want to throw your life away in a godforsaken land swarming with filthy and ignorant heathen? Do you want to be another Father Damien, laboring until your death — not from leprosy, but from smallpox, cholera, dysentery, typhoid, or Lord knows what else? And you'll get to die of one of those diseases *only* if Chinese bandits don't slit your throat first!"

And Mary, dabbing her eyes with a lace handkerchief, sobbed, "Oh, Hank, dear Hank, can't you just take a New York pulpit, where a speaker of your eloquence will quickly achieve prominence? Do you want to waste your God-given powers of persuasion on a people who won't understand a word of what you are saying? I can't bear the thought of seeing you only once every five years when you're home on furlough!"

After listening to his troubled sisters, Hank gave the thoughtful reply: "It is true that I have no idea what lies ahead — whether I will be happy in China, whether I can make any kind of real contribution. So many doubts have I had, in fact, that I've notified Church Missions Headquarters that I will go to China only on condition that I be allowed to pay my own fare. I want to feel free to return home after a year if things don't work out. But being a man of adventurous spirit, I know only this: If I go to China I may be able to affect the lives of tens of thousands, perhaps hundreds of thousands, of human beings — people who need food, medicine, education, and a knowledge of Jesus Christ. By contrast, how many lives can I affect if I stay in America and become rector of some church like St. Swithin's-in-the-Swamp? So you see, my dear beloved sisters, I must go."

Helen and Mary finally resigned themselves to the reality that their brother would be absent from home for years at a stretch. Neither of them could have imagined that, from this time forward, Hank's home would be Hankow, China, where he would take a wife, raise a family, and work for thirty-one years among the Chinese.

On graduating from the seminary, Samuel Harrington Littell (for that was Hank's real name) boarded a train for San Francisco, then a ship to Shanghai, and finally a river packet for the last six hundred miles up the Yangtze to Hankow, a throbbing city of almost a million souls. Ranking tenth in size among the cities of the world, together with the adjoining cities of Wuchang and Hanyang it made up the sixth-largest accumulation of human beings on our planet.

I'LL HAVE THE SEA SLUGS
AND A SIDE OF COAGULATED PIG'S BLOOD

Hank spent the first two months in Hankow taking a crash course in Mandarin from a Chinese convert who spoke English. He was then assigned a mission in the walled city of Wuchang, across the river from Hankow. There he held services each Sunday and made converts by the dozen.

One Sunday after services, a wealthy Chinese Christian named Soong Yee invited him to his home for a Sunday feast. For Hank, the meal was a gastronomic horror! The main dish was river and sea slugs, served in an ornate porcelain bowl and brought in by a silk-robed servant who, with majestic aplomb, placed it carefully on the teakwood table. Gingerly Hank tasted the slugs while his host watched to see his enjoyment of them. They were sweetened, about the consistency of rubber, and very sticky. Hank nobly ate a polite amount while Soong Yee popped scented jellyfish skins into Hank's mouth from the end of his own chopsticks. By now, Hank was close to gagging. He hid all signs of distress, however, for he knew that in China good manners demanded that politeness supersede honest comment or display of feelings. The next alimentation, which had the smell of fireplace ashes doused in sulfuric acid, was a five-year-old black egg that had been buried in lime. He managed, somehow, to get that down. The final challenge, met with equal valor, was coagulated pig's blood, cut into squares and stir-fried with onions.

"*Ding hao, ding hao!*" ("Very good! Very good!") exclaimed the proud host, smacking his lips. "*Ding hao, ding hao!*" echoed Hank with the bravest of smiles.

That evening, having recovered from the feast, Hank wrote his usual Sunday-night letter to his father and mother in Wilmington. "I would partake of a feast like that every Sunday," he wrote, "if I could convert as many heathen as we did today: twenty-one in all! What a glorious day this has been!"

"KILL THE FOREIGN DEVILS!"

For all foreigners in China, the close of the century spelled trouble. A secret society called the Society of Righteous and Harmonious Fists (the "Boxers") was fanning hatred of foreigners because of their efforts to Westernize China. The prime targets? Missionaries and their Chinese converts. To make matters worse, that xenophobic old woman, the empress dowager, gave her solid support to the Boxers, even decreeing that all foreigners were to be killed. The year was 1900. Wearing their characteristic red turbans, the Boxers broke into the homes of Chinese Christians in Peking and massacred them by the thousands. Emboldened by their swelling numbers, the Boxers also murdered many missionaries and surrounded foreign legations, laying them under siege.

Shock waves from the outbreak reverberated throughout Wuchang, where Hank had his mission. Tensions reached a dangerous level. The Episcopal mission was a small compound of stone and wooden buildings, including a church and infirmary, near the west wall of the city. One evening, at ten o'clock, all out of breath, two of Hank's Chinese clergy rushed into the compound and banged on his door.

"T'an Hsien Sen!" ("Mr. Harrington!") cried one, so frightened he could barely speak. "The Boxers have broken into the houses of the Swedish missionaries and are butchering them in their beds! They're killing Chinese Christians, too! Protect us! Protect us!"

Cried the other: "They are only five *li* [two miles] from here and are headed this way! They may be here by tonight! And the city gates have already been shut for the night! Help us, T'an Hsien Sen!"

Trying to calm them down, Hank ordered: "Go and find the Christians who live in this vicinity. Tell them to come here immediately and to leave their possessions behind. Everyone is to wait here in the compound. I will soon be back and will try to help you." Hank then disappeared into the dispensary.

Soon, twenty converts ran into the compound, all of them excited and spouting words noisily. "T'an Hsien Sen!" shouted one man to Hank, who had just returned. "The Boxers are coming! They are less than two *li* from here and are putting the sword to the English missionaries! They're slaughtering the converts, too! They're headed this way!"

Hank and Dr. Borland, a medical missionary, had found a crude rope ladder in the corner of an abandoned building. Its wooden rungs were just long enough to reach from the top of the city wall to the ground. There was not a minute to lose. "We're all going to let ourselves down the wall and get across the river to Hankow, where we will be safe," Hank told the anxious group clustered around him. "Now follow Dr. Borland and me." Then he and the doctor led the two dozen Chinese — including ten women with painfully bound feet — across the roof of one of the mission buildings to the top of the wall. As the two men let the ladder down on the other side, Hank shouted, "Turn around, all of you, and climb down right away. No more than two people — hear me, *two people* — on the ladder at one time. When you reach the bottom, stay there. Do you hear me? We'll find a way to get across the river. As you climb down, *hold tight!* God will be watching over you."

It was a scary drop — about forty feet from the top of the wall to the ground. A man started down first. When he was halfway down, a woman began her descent. The man reached bottom. The woman's bound feet, however, would not adhere to the rungs of the ladder. In panic, as she struggled to hang on, her head got squeezed between a wooden rung and a piece of rope that was holding it in place. Gagging, she could not move. Then, in their frenzy to escape, two more men climbed down the ladder, ignoring the woman and forcing themselves around her body. Then a freak accident occurred. The men's combined weight at the bottom pulled the rope — pulled it so taut around the woman's neck that it blocked her breath. As several more men climbed down, the rope was pulled ever tighter. A minute later the woman had strangled to death.

In desperation, Hank twisted the ladder so that the corpse would hang on the inside, next to the wall, thus allowing the others to descend without having to climb over the back of the dead woman. This worked, except that those people descending — including the woman's husband — had to pass within an inch of her face, her glassy eyes popping out at them and her long tongue dangling out of her twisted, gaping mouth.

When the last person had reached bottom, Hank paid a coolie to take everyone across the river in his sampan. This took three trips. At last the Wuchang Christians were gathered around a fire in the Hankow mission, gradually becoming warm and dry, but still too confused, too exhausted, to talk. In a voice choked with emotion, Hank asked them to kneel in prayer: "O God, we thank Thee that Thou hast delivered us from the forces of darkness and terror. We pray for the soul of Thy faithful departed servant, Wang Ling. Grant to her husband, Thy servant Wang Pei, the faith and strength to sustain his loss. We ask this in Thy name. Amen."

Eyewitnesses later described the barbaric rampage of the Boxers as they invaded Wuchang. Wielding lethal weapons, they axed to death three converts, whose hiding place was pointed out by their non-Christian neighbors. One of them they found in a backyard privy, immersed up to his head in fecal matter, urine, and lime. With a heavy pole they battered his head until he sank and drowned. They then pulled out a woman hiding between two stacks of firewood, hacked her to pieces, then stacked her arms and legs neatly on a pile of wood. Laughing uproariously, they departed.

A month later the hostilities and bloodshed came to an end when an international force of British, French, American, Russian, German, and Japanese troops fought its way into Peking. The Boxers' siege of the legations was lifted. The foreign powers forced the Manchu government to sign the Boxer Protocol, which imposed severe penalties on the Chinese. And so, for their violent attempt to achieve independence in their own land, the people suffered paralyzing punishment. But at last the Boxer Rebellion was over.

From that day forward, except for an occasional "Down with the Foreign Devils" demonstration and a few scattered outbursts of violence, the missionaries were allowed to go about their work. But Hank himself had already found much more adventure than he had ever bargained for.

MARRIAGE, CHILDREN, AND PERSONAL LOSS

In 1902, now assistant to the bishop at St. Paul's Cathedral in Hankow, Hank began to hit his stride. Bubbling with enthusiasm for his work, he was such a spellbinder in the pulpit that Church Missions Headquarters in New York began to assign him to special tours of the United States. Here was no ordinary preacher. This was the Reverend S. Harrington Littell, fund-raiser extraordinary!

It never failed. Each time he was guest preacher at St. John's Church in Wilmington, where his father was the rector, Hank preached with such vigor, such passion, on the subject of China — on the need for funds for churches, schools, hospitals — that the collection plate bulged with bills of sizable denominations. But the best part came when Hank spotted a certain family, long time members of that parish — the du Ponts. Quick to bring them to their knees, he would say, "Let us pray!" And then: "O Lord, grant that those who have been more fortunate in Thy bounty than others [and here he would look the du Ponts straight in the eye] may be moved by Thy Spirit to help the millions of Chinese who suffer the scourge of famine, flood, disease, and ignorance."

Jackpot! Following the service, the du Ponts would line up to hand him their checks.

On Hank's very first tour of America, he reaped an unexpected bonus. In Detroit, he met a most engaging young woman, Charlotte Mason. Unable to get her off his mind, he wrote her a letter from China. Her response was enthusiastic. The correspondence became ever more sizzling so that soon he sent her a cablegram — a proposal of marriage. Overjoyed by her acceptance, he arranged her voyage to Hankow, where, in the Cathedral of St. Paul, amid scores of well-wishers, the ceremony was performed by Hank's "boss," the Right

Reverend Logan Roots, bishop of Hankow. In time, to the happy couple, two sons were born, John and Edward, and a daughter, Charlotte.

In 1911, there occurred a memorable event — a "happening" of momentous significance to the history and future of China.

It started with an explosion. Just two blocks from Hank's house in Hankow, at ten P.M. on October 10, a bomb rocked the city and touched off an uprising so powerful that the people overthrew the ruling house of China, the Manchus, and established a republic — the Republic of China.

This uprising has since been celebrated as the Birthday of the Republic — the Double Ten (the tenth day of the tenth month). Just how the Revolution of 1911 affected Hank's life we do not know. But we do know that for his work as chairman of the China-International Famine Relief Commission — for organizing widespread relief from famine, drought, and flood conditions — he was chosen by the new regime to receive a prestigious medal, the Order of the Felicitous Grain. With great ceremony, this medal was presented to him in person by Dr. Sun Yat-Sen, the first president of the Republic of China.

Two years later, in 1913, a son, Harrington, was born to Hank and Charlotte. However, a dark shadow clouded the home on the birth of this fourth child. Just when mother and child seemed to be doing well, very suddenly Charlotte died. It was a pulmonary embolism.

Assuring himself that "God has called her to a higher purpose," Hank still had to summon all his strength to deal with the shock of her death. He was now in crisis. "Who will care for my four children?" he grieved, "especially those helpless infants, Charlotte and Harrington?" Praying for guidance, he apparently received a fast response. He fired off this telegram to his unmarried sister, Helen:

TO: MISS HELEN LITTELL, WILMINGTON, DELAWARE

URGENT YOU COME TO HANKOW IMMEDIATELY TO CARE FOR FOUR MOTHERLESS CHILDREN. AFFECTIONATELY.

HANK

Happy to answer the call, within six weeks Helen was in Hankow, managing that large household of four children and four Chinese servants, relishing the chance to bustle about, to make a "blessed home" for her beloved brother Hank. This, she presumed, was to remain a permanent position.

In only two years, however, the rug was yanked from under. Hank introduced his sister to Evelyn Taber, a pretty young missionary just arrived from Baltimore. Like a protective lioness with nostrils flaring, Helen sensed the threat. And right she was. For this vivacious young woman, seventeen years younger than Hank, would win his heart, marry him, and share his life for the next fifty-two years. She would also become my mother.

2

WHO SHOULD SHOW UP IN HANKOW BUT EVELYN!

E(VELYN) = MC²

My mother was a continuous explosion of energy. And what a grand way she had of meeting life head-on! Such gusto, such enthusiasm! You had to get out of the way! She was forever plunging into something "edifying," as she called it — whether it was midnight study, lecturing on Italian art, running charity bazaars, hostessing lawn parties featuring watermelon-spitting contests, or managing all the comings and goings, all the shenanigans, of our large, unruly family. God, what a personality!

Throughout her life — from early adoption, to her years in China, to her role as bishop's wife in Honolulu — Mother had her ups, yes, but also her downs, which were also met with emotional intensity. Looking back, I see that, by any standard, hers was a difficult existence, filled with what to most women may have seemed to be insurmountable obstacles. But Mother was healthy, strong as a workhorse, and certain, as she used to say, that "life is a many-splendored thing." And so it was tragic that in her final years she was overpowered, prematurely and avoidably, by forces not of her own making.

My mother was born Evelyn Alma Taber, in Baltimore, Maryland. Her father, Edward Taber, was a poet and dreamer who for years collaborated with John Philip Sousa, writing lyrics for his marches. When the two men quarreled and split up, Edward took to heavy drinking. After a few years his wife, Ann Moffett Taber, became so fed up with his absences, slovenliness, and under-the-table blackouts that she did the unthinkable — in those days the unacceptable: she divorced him. At this point, heartsick and penniless, Ann gave up her daughter for adoption by a well-to-do sister. Evelyn, then twelve years old, went to live in Washington, D.C., with her aunt Henrietta Fletcher and her husband, the Reverend Joseph Fletcher, canon of Washington Cathedral.

Evelyn was never close to her own mother, for they had different outlooks on life. Often the two would rehash, reclash the Civil War, Evelyn being from Maryland and her mother from Tennessee. Ann Moffett Taber was no intellectual, and Evelyn would become exasperated by her "lack of logic" and her "ignorance."

Nor did Evelyn feel close to her adoptive parents. Joseph Fletcher was a quiet, absentminded intellectual befuddled by the daily events that swirled around him. Henrietta was a blustering harridan who, it was observed, did all the talking except from the pulpit.

A BROKEN PROMISE — A SHATTERED DREAM

I ache to think of it, but there was one incident in Evelyn's early days, when she lived with her aunt and uncle, that had a powerful effect on her life and a profound influence on the way she brought up her own children, including me.

When she was twelve, her aunt Henrietta promised her, as a high school graduation present, a Grand Tour of Europe. Ecstatic, Evelyn dreamed of this trip and studied for it diligently, burying herself in the histories and cultures of England, France, Spain, Italy, and Germany. She kept pinching herself. "A voyage abroad with Aunt Henrietta and Uncle Joseph! What bliss! In all the world, isn't this the most thrilling gift a girl could ever receive?"

As June approached, it was time for preparations — for hauling trunks out of the attic, purchasing travel clothes, buying tickets. Evelyn's pulse quickened as she pictured the R.M.S. *Lusitania*, whistles blowing, funnels spouting, poised to slice through the waters of the Atlantic.

Then came the bombshell. Two weeks before departure time, Evelyn's aunt took her aside. "Listen, dear," she said. "Your uncle Joseph and I have decided that it would be best if he and I went on this trip by ourselves. You'd not be interested in the same things as we. You're only eighteen. You'd enjoy such a trip when you're older and more mature."

"Oh! Oh! Oh!" was all Evelyn could manage to say as she buried her head in her hands. Her world had collapsed. How can one describe her feelings of disbelief, desolation, and betrayal? Thus it happened that from a New York dock, amid tossed bouquets, colorful streamers, and joyous shouts of "Bon voyage" from friends ashore, the prestigious Fletchers sailed off, minus Evelyn, to begin their Grand European Tour.

THE MAN WITH THE FAN

It was a hot summer day, one year after that cruel experience. Still smarting from the wounds of rejection, Evelyn was sitting in a Baltimore church listening to a talk by a zealous missionary from China. Deeply moved by his eloquent plea for recruits, she was equally charmed by an exotic Chinese hand fan he waved through the air as, vigorously, he pleaded, "Go ye into the world and preach the gospel to all nations" (the exact words that, years earlier, had smitten him as a seminarian). It was perfect timing! For now, at nineteen, young Evelyn was ripe for the picking. "Even though China is not the Europe of my dreams," she mused, "it sounds like a place of high adventure."

After the service, she approached this handsome man of the cloth. With eyes radiating, she burst forth: "I'm going out there *this instant!*"

Touching her shoulder to calm her, the Reverend S. Harrington

Evelyn, at age twenty-two, just before she left for China.

Littell warned: "Not so fast, young lady. You need to make solid preparation for the task that the Lord has revealed to you. First, you must pray diligently, asking God if it is His will that you go so far from home. Second, you must go to the Baltimore Deaconess School for two years of training. Third, you must take a course in nursing. By then you will know if, for your life, this is the appointed calling."

"I'll see to all of that!" exuded Evelyn. And so she did. And go to China she most certainly did. Then, recalling Mr. Littell's invitation — "Get in touch with me if you go out there" — that she also did, right away.

Two years later, her girlish crush having blossomed into mature love, she married this fascinating man with the fan. In a letter to her mother she wrote: "Mama, I've never seen Hank preach without the aid of that dazzlingly bright bamboo fan. With it he chops the air, flashes it in all directions to make a point, and abracadabra — he bewitches his congregation — just as he did *me!*"

WEDDING BELLS FOR HANK AND EVELYN

Dawned the happy day, May 19, 1915, when, at the Hankow cathedral, Hank pledged his troth to Evelyn Taber. As the towering organ pipes poured forth the stirring Mendelssohn wedding march, down the aisle walked the bride, lovely in Chinese silk and lace, while before her, adorably dressed in white linen, marched Hank's children — John, Edward, Charlotte, and little Harrington. As the couple exchanged rings, one could hear from far above the rafters the joyous peal of the bells of St. Paul's, proclaiming the event.

Perhaps they chimed, as well, to foretell the future — the arrival of three additional missionary kids ("mish-kids," as we would be called): Morris, Nancy, and Joseph. I am Joseph, the youngest of the seven, born in 1924 to become the recorder of the extraordinary events described within the covers of this book.

It was from this background that Evelyn was plunged into the family of Littells. Amid laughter and tears, she had colossal adjustments to make — not only to the confounding Oriental culture, but

The wedding of Hank and Evelyn in Hankow. At Evelyn's right is Hank's sister Helen, soon to become Evelyn's arch rival for control of the household. At Helen's right is Hank's son John and at his right, Edward. At Evelyn's right, below her bouquet, is little Harrington. The second from right in front row is Charlotte, and directly behind her is the bishop of Hankow, the Right Reverend Logan Roots.

in marrying a widower seventeen years her senior. Added to that, she had to mother four rambunctious, ready-made stepkids. And, as if all that were not enough, she had to suffer the stress of coping with an in-law firmly implanted in the household — her husband's hefty, domineering sister, Helen. And bless her stony heart, Helen utterly failed to grasp the fact that now, since the sound of wedding bells had died down, her presence was superfluous, that now it was time for her to relinquish the throne to her rightful successor.

Two strong-willed Amazons running the household? *Two* women managing the children and the Chinese servants? Imagine the conflicting commands, the clash of child-rearing concepts, the jealous vying for Hank's attentions. Bewildered, the new bride felt trapped as, on both sides, hard feelings surfaced. At long last, and in a huff, Helen packed her belongings, made a melodramatic exit, and returned to Delaware — there to unleash her lamentations on the family. All of that explains why the Littell relatives remained forever aloof, forever critical of Hank's beloved soul mate. Their unaccepting, disdainful attitude was picked up — easily sensed — by us children whenever we visited them in Wilmington.

Although enjoying her expanded role as a mother, although performing faithfully such matronly duties as "socks and sweater knitter," Evelyn could never overcome the blow dealt to her by Aunt Henrietta in denying her the Grand Tour of Europe. She continued to dream of those lands of enchantment, determined that someday she would achieve her prized goal — not only to get herself, but to get her children as well, to make that splendid voyage. "Not one of my children," she vowed, "will ever have to suffer the heartbreaking experience of a broken promise."

If China was Mother's first taste of world travel, it was, in fact, just a starter. During the next forty years she branched out to as many countries, as many continents, as possible, stuffing us all with culture, exposing us to great theater, grand opera, concerts, ballet, museums, scenic beauty in the great world capitals. Yes, she made good her vow that the Littell clan would never know the shock of deprivation that she herself had once endured.

3

MY EARLY YEARS
AS A "MISH-KID"

OUR HOME IN HANKOW

Wistfully I look back to the late 1920s. I can see Hankow, that sprawling international city, with its busy port of oceangoing ships that steamed six hundred miles up the Yangtze from Shanghai. I can hear the chugging of the Peking-Hankow-Canton railroad, pouring commercial goods into the area. I can picture the Bund, that wide strip of concrete stretching mile after mile along the riverbank, dotted with stately foreign consulates, each flying its national flag.

Divided into "concessions," the Bund was owned not by the Chinese but by their foreign "benefactors," mainly the United States, Great Britain, Germany, France, and Russia. Strolling along the Bund, thousands of people daily enjoyed the sights, sounds, and smells of sampans, houseboats, and tugboats. By contrast, in plain sight on the river, were the red-sailed junks where the most destitute of families dwelled. How clearly, too, I remember gaping at the fleet of combat-ready, steel-gray gunboats, ominously patrolling the Yangtze to "protect the rights of foreigners."

Hankow was also an international center for missionaries. The Americans lived within a walled enclosure, the well-guarded U.S. compound. Some families lived in row houses, but we Littells, perhaps because Father was assistant to the bishop, lived in grander style

Our faithful servant Liao Lai-Lai helps me walk at the age of one.

in a two-story stone house, the facade adorned with Corinthian columns. Next door, in a similar house, lived Bishop Roots, a pious saint if ever there was one. Right next to his home stood the large Gothic cathedral where Father and Mother were married and where, in the sweltering heat of summer or the bleak cold of winter, Father conducted services. Quite adaptable to freezing temperatures in an unheated church, the Chinese congregation came to worship armed with foot-warmers, tin hot water bottles, padded clothing, and buckets of snacks and toys for their restless children as all present tried, politely, to listen to the three- or four-hour sermon!

Morris, Nancy, and I in front of our Hankow house. In central China, extremes of temperatures are so great that palm trees and snowstorms are simultaneous elements of the landscape.

Like most foreign families, we had four devoted servants for whom we provided living quarters behind our house. How my sister Nancy and I loved to sneak back there, against Mother's orders, to watch our amah, Liao Lai-Lai, oiling her black hair, flattening it back from her forehead with a curved ivory comb, then rolling the long tresses into a tight bun at the back of her head. It was she who would tuck us kids into bed, make sure the mosquito nets were firmly draped around the four-posters, and get us up in the night by candlelight to "go potty." Poor Liao Lai-Lai, with her painfully bound feet. I remember how, without ever complaining, she would tote heavy buckets of water to the second floor, to be poured into the tin tub for our Saturday-night baths. Then there was her much older husband, Liao Tze-Fu, who served as handyman and waiter, while Da Tze-Fu (*Da* meant "big" — he was "big boss" in the kitchen), highest in the pecking order, kept things organized back there. One of our culinary delights was his roast turkey. He slaughtered the bird with his own hands, roasted it, then smothered it with giblet gravy, peanuts, and raisins. Ceremoniously, this festive dish was brought into the dining room, the silver platter placed in front of Father, who, having honed his carving knife, was prepared to violate all the rules of artistic carving. And Mother, sighing heavily, looked on and scolded, "Dear, that's *not* how it's done — you're butchering that bird!"

The fourth servant we seldom saw — this was the one we called the Popo Woman. It was her job, hobbling on bound feet, to empty the chamberpots as far away from the house as possible, then scrub them with something like Lysol.

HOW TO CATCH A BUSY FATHER

We Littell kids were always asking, "Where's Father?" Always we got the same answer from Mother: "He's up the Yangtze on mission business — helping victims of disasters, converting the heathen." And so we presumed, since his offspring were healthy and since he'd already converted us all, that he was more sorely needed "up the Yangtze."

At times, though, we did succeed in catching him to read to us aloud. But why did we always have to settle for *his* choice of literature? Sometimes it was Dickens — *that* we liked. But mostly it was his grand passion, the Old Testament, especially the Book of Esther. My, how Father would beam as he relived the adventures of Esther and of that ruler of Persia, King Ahasuerus! And oh, how he loved to roll his tongue over that delicious word, "A-HAS-U-AIR-US," repeating it endlessly to embed it firmly in our little heads. I vowed that if I ever heard the name again, I'd go out and chew mud! Surely there must be such a thing as overeducating one's offspring, filling their minds with trivia, such as the names of dead, buried, ancient kings of Persia.

Somehow we learned to cope, seeking whatever good might result from these Esther-Ahasuerus readings. I guess we were glad to get even a small slice of Father's time. So thank you, Honorable Ahasuerus, for helping to make those "togetherness" sessions possible.

How else did we get Father to notice us? "Come on, Father," we'd beg. "Let's have a sing-song. Play us some hymns on the piano." (His repertoire excluded all else.)

And so he'd try. I say "try" because his broad hands, his stocky fingers, couldn't help but mash several keys at a time — it's what they call "all thumbs!" Concentrating on singing and playing at the same time, Father would keep hitting the wrong notes. Chaos and disharmony reigned as with powerful vigor he'd keep right on performing, unaware that, one by one, we kids were silently stepping back and vanishing from the scene.

Lucky the neighbors if they owned earplugs!

"GET OUT OF CHINA — FAST!"

Periodically, the Chinese populace protested the intrusion of foreigners. Sometimes their protests took the form of violent uprisings. On one occasion, during a "Down with the Foreign Devils" demonstration, we missionaries received a warning from our consulate, delivered by courier: "GET OUT OF CHINA — FAST!" Leaving behind all our possessions, we boarded a gunboat and steamed toward Shanghai as rifle shots ricocheted off the armored sides of the vessel. Soon afterward, a gang of bandits swarmed aboard, overpowered our captain and crew, and were about to take us passengers hostage when suddenly — we never knew how — the tables were turned, our crew regained control, the bandits were brought to their knees, and, one at a time, dumped overboard. It was not until six months later that we were officially notified at our refuge in Japan that it was safe to return to Hankow.

Fortunately, life in Hankow was not all bandits and unruly mobs. My mind is flooded with happy memories of events that to a child back home would seem strange, scary, even preposterous. For example, going to school was not like riding a bus and being deposited at the door of the school. When there was peace — that is, an absence of mob rule — it was deemed safe to walk to school past the sentries who guarded our compound. Where there was a street to cross, we were escorted by a six-and-a-half-foot-tall, black-bearded, red-turbaned Indian Sikh policeman. It never occurred to us to fear him as we looked up to his face in the sky. He was our protector.

"May I take your hand, Mr. Policeman?" I often asked, whereupon this gentle giant would bare his flashy white teeth to smile down at me, his huge black eyes sparkling, and with his heavy British accent respond, "This way, little boy." With him I felt so safe! I liked the feel of his massive, white-gloved hand as it enveloped mine.

At the Hankow British School we had the usual lessons in reading, writing, and arithmetic. In addition, the girls learned to weave baskets and the boys, how to play cricket. Every school day began with the singing of "God Save the King."

CULTURE, BY THE CRATE, ARRIVES BY OXCART

Twice a year our Hankow home was ablaze with excitement. That was when our mail-ordered supplies arrived from Woodward and

Lothrop, the big Washington, D.C., store. Groceries, books, toys, Victrola records, clothes — they all came in huge crates, delivered to our door in an ox-drawn wagon.

"Now we can hear the voice of Enrico Caruso!" proclaimed Mother.

"And now we can be the best-dressed kids in the compound!" exclaimed Nancy.

"And now I can read *David Copperfield!*" said Morris.

"And *I* can read *Alice's Adventures in Wonderland!*" added Nancy.

"And *I* can read *The Story of Dr. Doolittle!*" I shouted, not to be upstaged.

"And oh, boy," Morris said happily, "now we can drink milk from a can!" (In China, fresh cow's milk was a deadly no-no.)

"And don't forget," added Father, "that the milk makes ice cream in our hand-churn freezer. Then whoever does the churning gets to lick the dasher!"

For several days, euphoria prevailed as we reached down to the very bottom of the crates, discovering such goodies as canned peas, canned peaches, and canned apricots. But alas, there was one fruit that we could not order from Washington or buy locally. That was our favorite, the watermelon. Because the natives sold it by the pound, they had discovered a way to make each melon heavier: just bore tiny holes in the rind and soak the whole thing overnight in some contaminated stream or river. Ay-ya! Good thing old Liao Tze-Fu gave us due warning!

Something else happened twice a year — only this, for us, was a dreaded occasion. It was the appointed day when, punctured by those sharp needles, we were vaccinated against smallpox, diphtheria, dysentery, cholera, and typhoid. In addition, we had to take an antiworm medicine, Santinen. Ghastly! Then, as if that were not torture enough, we were served that panacea for all ailments, a hearty dose of castor oil. (Mother actually fancied that she could disguise the taste by adding orange juice.) Anyway, except for that nauseating guck we had to swallow twice a year "for our own good," we found China to be an exciting place in which to grow up as, with the above precautions, we remained robust and vibrantly healthy.

I must mention the water. In China, almost before a newborn starts to breathe, he or she is taught — *must learn* — this most important lesson: all water is contaminated. Here, you never, ever drink water that has not been boiled, upon pain of everlasting extinction from this planet.

CHRISTMAS IN HANKOW

Christmas! Without question, that was the most exciting time of the year. We had the same Santa Claus, the same "stockings hung by the chimney with care." On Christmas morning, however, Father suddenly became cold and cruel. Just as we were wild to open our presents, he made us go to church. How restless we were as those darned hymns and prayers took up our precious time! Wouldn't our souls survive if, just this once, we skipped a service?

To make matters worse, as later we tried to make a mad dash for home, we were again stymied, this time by our pitiless mother. Almost dragging us by the collar, she insisted we make a slight detour to peek in on the Russian Orthodox church, to savor the ornate, eye-dazzling decor, the scarlet and gold vestments, the powerful, thunderous male choir, to smell the intoxicating clouds of incense being batted around by thurifers, and, finally, to hear the great organ as it swelled in magnificent crescendos. Despite my impatience to get home, I admit I was overwhelmed by the drama, the majesty of those great Russian rituals.

After dinner on Christmas Day, Father would summon all the servants to the living room and make them bow their heads as, enthusiastically, he would offer a prayer of thanks to the Lord, "for that Thou dost fill all things living with plenteousness." (*Here*, in this famine-racked country?) Next, he would hand each servant a crisp one-dollar bill. (In those days, that provided a whole month's supply of rice.) Gratefully, they would bow to us, retreating backward out the door as they murmured, *"Do shei, do shei"* ("Thank you, thank you"). I suspect they were also breathing a sigh of relief that this patronizing

ordeal was over — albeit appreciating the well-meant motives behind the act.

OUR SERVANT LIAO TZE-FU IS DRAGGED AWAY

None of us ever knew when there might be an uprising or when a
mob might force its way into the compound. I recall with anguish the
time a band of picketers stopped in front of our house, having pushed
their way around the guards at the gate. The ringleader demanded
that our faithful servant Liao Tze-Fu, who had been with us for more
than fifteen years, come out and join the march. The old man refused, whereupon he was grabbed, brutally pummeled, dragged to
the line of marchers, and forced to carry a "Down with the Foreign
Devils" placard.

As our family and servants, especially his wife, watched in horror,
we saw him look back at us, great tears flowing down his cheeks.
Father nodded to him to comply with his captors — a matter of his
very life. Straining a second time to look back at us, he was jerked out
of our sight. Dear old Liao Tze-Fu — we never saw him again.

"THERE'S A LONG, LONG TRAIL A-WINDING"

Oh, that sizzling 104-degree Hankow heat! In summer it was enough
to drive many missionaries up the mountains to Kuling, in Kiangsi
Province to the south. There my parents owned a rambling bungalow. The trip, however, entailed great perils. I cannot understand
why we were not terrified by these hazards, which seemed not to faze
any of us stalwart missionaries. From Hankow, we had to embark on
a boat for an overnight sail down the Yangtze to Kiukiang. Then
followed a long rickshaw ride to the mountain foothills, at which
point we were accosted by a crowd of clamoring coolies, all vying for
our sedan chair business to haul us up the mountain. Here's where
the danger began. To reach Kuling the coolies, with their passengers,

To get up to our bungalow in Kuling we had to be carried up the treacherous "Thousand Steps Path" in a sedan chair. The most nerve-racking bit of the trail was the "Coffin Corner," shown here.

In Kuling, in 1925, outside our bungalow. Seated (left to right): Mother (holding me), Charlotte, Morris. Standing: Nancy, John, Father, Harrington. Edward was away at Harvard.

had to climb a steep trail and, ultimately, a long, narrow, hazardous path consisting of a thousand steps ("the Thousand Steps Path"), high above precipitous cliffs. At several points, where there was a hairpin turn, our chairs actually swung out over the edge. Think of it — one misstep by a coolie and you would plunge hundreds of feet to the bottom of a deep ravine! It was amazing what faith our parents placed, not only in these coolies, but in the Lord! When the path became ever steeper, the coolies, instead of slowing down, would initiate morose chanting — "Ya de hey hoe, hey ya de hey hoe" — and begin to run, the sinews in their legs bulging like rocks. Year after year we made this scary journey — yet lived to tell the tale.

Upon our arrival in Kuling, the coolies set down the sedan chairs to deposit us at one end of town near the Gap (between mountains). There, gathering our luggage, cats, dogs, and personal belongings, we marched a mile or so to our bungalow — a welcome sight. Such relief — the long, perilous journey was over.

Up here it was cool! And we had the whole summer to look forward to.

THE GREAT LEAP FORWARD

One day, Father and Mother rounded up Morris, Nancy, and me and herded us into the living room. (The older children were in schools in America.) Once we were settled in our chairs, Father announced, "I have important news. I've just received a cablegram from church headquarters in New York." Beaming he said, "I've been elected bishop of Honolulu by the House of Bishops of the Episcopal Church." He paused for a moment, then went on: "After giving the matter much thought, your mother and I have decided to accept the call. This means that very soon we'll all be moving, bag and baggage, to the beautiful, warm, sunny Hawaiian Islands. I know you'll love it there."

"*Pu hsing! Pu hsing!*" ("Not so! Not so!") we cried out.

Morris was the first to speak. "Does this mean we'll all have to leave China, the only place we've ever known?" he asked, visibly upset.

Nancy was next: "Does this mean we'll have to leave all our friends — never see them again?"

I was last. "I'm staying *right here!*" I announced, folding my arms in front of me in bold defiance. "Liao Lai-Lai can take care of me. The rest of you can all go if you want to. I'm staying here!"

To their great surprise, my parents now had another uprising on their hands — not a rebellion by the Chinese, if you could believe it, but by their own children! Only gradually, over a period of days and with continued assurances from our parents that we would find a happy life and new friends in Honolulu, did we become reconciled to the idea of leaving China.

Now came the hard part: how to tell Liao Lai-Lai and Da Tze-Fu. The news was bound to shake them badly. We Littells had always been their "family." Leave them behind? Unthinkable! And poor Liao Lai-Lai, who with horror and anguish had witnessed her loving, faithful husband, Liao Tze-Fu, being dragged away, never to be seen again! In the end, but with painful outpourings on both sides, Father promised Liao Lai-Lai and Da Tze-Fu a new, loving family right there in Hankow — financial security and all.

And now the packing! Six carpenters packed our precious Chinese teak furniture, rose medallion dishes, and scrolls into wooden crates for shipment down the Yangtze to Shanghai and from there to Honolulu. They carefully wrapped the two-hundred-year-old Chinese hand-made wool rug, the centerpiece of our living room in Hankow and soon to be the highlight of our living room in Honolulu. That rug now lies in my own living room in Lake Forest, Illinois, still vibrant, still almost alive. It is a rich black except in the middle, where black gives way to a shimmering medallion of ever-changing blues. The entire rug is patterned with a mosaic of budding and full-blown peonies in shades of beige and pink-beige laced with touches of pale greens, rosy pinks, and soft lavenders. There can be no more beautiful rug in the world.

February 1, 1930, was the day of our departure for Honolulu. As our beloved servants, our Chinese and foreign friends, waved their goodbyes from the dock, we tearfully pulled away in our riverboat bound for Shanghai. Settling into our cabins, each of us kids felt the strain of it all — the feeling that we were leaving behind everything we had ever known. Down deep in our hearts, though, we knew we would come through. We mish-kids had learned well that we could be survivors in this world of just about everything and anything.

And so —

Viva our memories!

Viva our happy, crazy, unnerving childhood!

Viva fascinating Hankow, Kuling, and our beloved China!

4

THE BAREFOOT
YEARS IN HONOLULU

DISCOVERING THE ALOHA SPIRIT

Our ship, the *President McKinley*, slid through the silver-blue waters, nearing the island of Oahu. Father, Mother, Morris, Nancy, and I all hugged the rail, marveling at the distant skyline with its steep mountains wearing so many shades of green. The city of Honolulu sparkled in the sun as it moved toward us, spreading out along the shore and spilling over to the ridges and valleys of the ranges beyond. The air was warm, almost fragrant. The city moved closer. "There's the Aloha Tower!" cried Morris, pointing to the famous landmark. "Look — the big clock! I can almost see the hands!"

Directly below us, brown-skinned divers, like dolphins, flip-flopped in the glistening water, clamoring for coins. "Yo-ho — here's a dime!" called Father, and one of them slithered into the deep and reemerged with a grin, only to beg for more.

I cupped my ears. "What's that — music?" I called out. The sound grew louder. Soon we could tell it was the Royal Hawaiian Band playing the hauntingly lovely "Aloha Oe." Our excitement was almost unbearable!

Suddenly the music was drowned out by a thundering *bo-oo-oo-om* from our ship's funnel — a protracted, low-pitched blast. Any louder and it would have knocked us down! Now we could see, lining the dock, hundreds of blurred faces seemingly merged into a profusion of multicolored flowers — the tropical fragrance being carried up to us by the gentle breezes. What a picture! So this was the famous Aloha spirit!

Bump! Our ship hit the heavy protective tires hanging from the dock. Deckhands scampered around every which way, securing heavy ropes to the moorings. As a ship's officer gave the "Go ahead" signal, we hurried down the gangplank, despite our wobbly sea legs, to be greeted by a wildly waving contingent of people from the Episcopal Diocese of Honolulu. In a moment we were loaded up to our eyebrows with leis — plumeria, orchid, hibiscus, gardenia — leaving just enough room for us to peek out without strangling. Newspaper reporters popped up from nowhere, grabbed our attention — "Look here, let's have a nice smile!" — and snapped our arrival for the next day's paper (which, we later noted, showed only the hair and foreheads of "the Episcopal Bishop-elect and his family, just arrived from the Orient").

We piled into a waiting limousine and a chauffeur drove us straight to our new home in downtown Honolulu, the Bishop's House on Queen Emma Square. Finally, breathless, we had arrived! What a welcome!

So this was the Bishop's House! Our new home was a rambling, two-story, seven-bedroom mansion, impressive with its high, arched front lanai (porch) and more lanais above and to the back — wide and spacious. The front lawn, lush and verdant from the predictable daily showers, provided a rich carpet for stately Royal Hawaiian palms. Around the house — everywhere you looked — were poinciana trees with their fiery-red flowers! And fragrant plumeria trees with their creamy-white blossoms!

As we circled the outside of the house — surprise! Out back was growing a single, lonesome tree. But what a work of art, that giant, sixty-foot tree — there was hardly room for another one! "It's a bread-fruit tree," shouted one of the greeters. "See those branches weighted down with that round, grapefruit-size fruit? It's edible!" Over the

Queen Emma Square. At left, the Bishop's House. Center, St. Andrew's Cathedral (with bell tower). At right, the edge of the great banyan tree.

years, our Japanese cook, Hisayo, would delight our palates with her breadfruit casseroles — that is, if and whenever I climbed the tree and snatched the breadfruit off their moorings.

And so it evolved that, for years, the Bishop's House would bustle with activity with its threefold purpose: as home for our family, as office for Father, and as command post for my pranks, scams, and shakedowns. (Father's legacy to me, of course!)

Right next to the Bishop's House stood St. Andrew's Cathedral, the seat of the Episcopal Church in Hawaii and one of the finest examples of Gothic architecture in the Western Hemisphere. Its soaring bell tower was the tallest structure in Honolulu — with the exception of the Aloha Tower.

The cathedral has a remarkable history. Early windjammers, making the long, suicidal trip around Cape Horn, carried loads of limestone from English quarries as ballast. Upon arrival in Hawaii, the rock was dumped on the beach to make room for the ships' stores and cargo. From this English stone much of the cathedral was built. The cornerstone was laid in 1867 by King Kamehameha V, who had been converted by English missionaries to the Anglican faith. It was in this cathedral that Father would preach his interminable sermons and that I would sit in the choir stall praying that he would find a way to bring them to an end.

Both the cathedral and the Bishop's House looked out on Queen Emma Square, a spacious park that had as its centerpiece an enormous banyan tree. Have you ever seen a giant, tropical banyan tree — its awesome, flat-topped crown so spread out that it hides the sky? Have you observed the many trunks, the myriad ropelike fibers that descend from its branches to embed themselves deep in the earth? A tree so colossal that it resembles a small forest? Well, it was this very wonder of nature that occupied center stage in Queen Emma Square. How we marveled at its majesty from the windows of the Bishop's House! And what a super hide-and-seek spot it was for us kids — except that the seeker always knew that my hiding place was somewhere inside that mammoth maze! Of all the trees I had seen anywhere in the world, this was the one, this was my absolute favorite — and it still is!

CULTURE SHOCK!

It was only one day after we arrived in Hawaii that I got into a frenzied fight with a boy my age. Billy Stokes, who lived at the other end of Queen Emma Square, came over to see the new kid on the block. We played around in the banyan tree and then climbed a plumeria tree in our front yard. Because the day was warm, I soon felt parched. "I'm thirsty," I said to Billy. "I'll go into the kitchen and get us a drink of water. Be right back — you wait here."

"No need," said Billy. "Here's an easier way." Reaching for the garden hose, he brought the end piece to his mouth.

"No, no!" I screamed. Making a lunge at him, I jerked the hose out of his hand, pushing him so that he fell flat on his back. "*You crazy?*" I yelled.

Panting, sputtering, furious, he jumped up, shouting, "You idiot! What's the matter with you?" He took a hefty swipe at me with his fist. I punched him mercilessly, then we wrestled each other to the ground. "I'll *never* come over here again, NEVER!" he gasped and ran home to tell his mother: "There's a darned-fool idiot-kid just moved into the block!"

Hearing the commotion, Mother called me into the house. "Did you start a fight with Billy?" she demanded.

"No," I answered, still seething. "Do you know what he did? Something horrible! He started to drink the water from the garden hose! It wasn't boiled! He could have died of cholera or typhoid!"

"Oh!" said Mother, thoroughly relieved. "Well, Joe, I should have told you that here in Hawaii you can drink in safety any water from any tap anywhere. It's pure rain water. It isn't like the water in China, which has been contaminated by polluted rivers and streams."

"You mean people here can drink water right from a garden hose?" I asked, dumbfounded.

"Yes," she answered. "Now why don't you go over and tell Billy you're sorry."

"Aw, Mom, do I have to?" I sighed. "I was only trying to save his life. It isn't my fault that the water here is clean and pure."

"Well, go see him anyway," she said, laughing. "I'll call his mother and explain everything."

I went over to Billy's and we quickly made up. From that day forward, we became the best of friends as, over the months, he helped me to survive various other episodes of what Mother called "culture shock."

Thinking about that incident later, I realized how easy it is for individuals, and even nations, to go at one another's throats before a serious attempt is made to study, understand, and, above all, respect cultural and other differences.

FATHER BECOMES BISHOP OF HONOLULU

Two weeks after our arrival in Honolulu, Father was consecrated bishop. The *Honolulu Advertiser*, the Islands' morning newspaper, went to impressive lengths to capture the pageantry and solemnity of the occasion.

NEW BISHOP CONSECRATED
IN IMPRESSIVE CHURCH SERVICE

In the presence of the most distinguished assemblage of clergy and laymen of the Episcopal Church ever known in the Islands, Samuel Harrington Littell was consecrated Bishop of Honolulu at St. Andrew's Cathedral yesterday. The solemn rites of the Church, which have come down the ages from Peter the Fisherman, were celebrated by four bishops, one of whom, Bishop James D. Perry, is at present supreme head of the Church in America. He was the consecrator while the co-consecrators were the Rt. Rev. John McKim, Bishop of Tokyo, and the Rt. Rev. Henry B. Restarick, retired Bishop of Honolulu. The preacher on the historic occasion was the Rt. Rev. Edward L. Parsons, Bishop of California, who was also the presenting bishop, and reader of the certificate of election. Yesterday's ceremonies were deeply impressive and the noble, yet simple ritualism of the ancient Catholic faith has never before been so effectively made manifest in this community. At the con-

Father, after being consecrated bishop of Honolulu.

clusion of the service, which began at 10 o'clock and continued for two hours and a half, Dr. Littell, with the laying on of hands, became the fifth Bishop of Honolulu. Most appropriately, since he came to his high station after thirty years as a missionary priest in the Orient, the Bishop-elect's attending presbyters were the Rev. Y. Sang Mark, of St. Peter's Chinese Church, and the Rev. Philip T. Fukao, of the Holy Trinity Japanese parish. . . . The beautiful nave of St. Andrew's was thronged to its capacity. . . . In a reserved pew were Mrs. Littell and her children, Morris, Nancy and Joseph. With her also were her sisters-in-law, the Misses Helen and Mary Littell of Wilmington, Delaware. . . .

Yesterday afternoon from 4 to 6 the new Bishop and Mrs. Littell held a reception at their residence which was attended by hundreds of persons.

So began Father's ministry in Hawaii. His twelve years as bishop would be years of great fulfillment for him and for Mother. They would also be years of great happiness for the rest of us — their children — during those brief, treasured periods of time when we were home from boarding school and college.

IF YOU'VE GOT A GOOD THING, GO WITH IT!

"Children!" called Mother. "Morris! Nancy! Joe! Guests again for dinner tonight! Get yourselves cleaned up and put on your best clothes!"

Whenever we had dinner guests, it was a wonderfully festive occasion. They came with such frequency and in such variety that we kids never knew who was coming. It might be friends or relatives from the mainland. It might be a Chinese-American clergyman and his family from Maui. It might be, as on two occasions, Thornton Wilder, the novelist and playwright. (His father had been in the consular service in China and had known Father; Wilder himself grew up in China.) It might be Henry Luce, co-founder and publisher of *Time* magazine. (*His* father had been a Presbyterian missionary in China, and

Luce himself was born there.) It might be the violinist Yehudi Menuhin, then in his teens, playing on a world tour. Or the contralto Marian Anderson.

Through her friend Fritz Hart, conductor of the Honolulu Symphony, Mother was able to invite various musicians to our home. No matter who came to dinner, Mother often included Mrs. Clancy, a disabled resident from a nearby nursing home, or some other lonesome soul she had casually met on the street. And what about us kids? Well, we were always made to feel a special part of that important social ritual known as dinner. We might be banished to another continent for years at a stretch, but never to the kitchen.

For such occasions, Mother knew exactly what to serve. She had only one specialty: a superb Indian curry laden with chicken, spices from the Orient, mangoes, ginger imported from India, and cashews, all served with steaming hot, fluffy rice. (The only variation she would ever allow was peanuts instead of cashews.) When Hisayo made the curry, Mother would supervise its creation and eventual presentation without ever peering directly over her shoulder. (Local Japanese cooks would often balk if watched while they worked.) What a sumptuous delicacy it was — this luscious curry dish, served on our Chinese rose medallion platter!

Mother quickly came to a practical conclusion. "Since I have a recipe that makes a dinner party memorable," she told Father, "I really should capitalize on my good fortune and serve my curry and rice at every party. After all, the guests are different at every dinner, so what difference does it make? Back at Carnegie Hall, does Yehudi say to Marian, 'You mean you had curry, too?'" And so for years we had curry as often as twice a week.

Whenever Mother announced to us kids that guests were coming to dinner, Morris, never the soul of tact, needled her mercilessly. "What's for dinner?" he'd ask. "Same old thing with cashews, or same old thing with peanuts?" And Mother, stung to the quick, would jump to her own defense: "Well, I'm having a *nice curry* tonight. And the curry will have tender, tasty pieces of chicken, spices from the Orient, and fresh mangoes that Mr. Eigenbrodt brought us yesterday from the other side of the island. You remember Mr. Eigenbrodt, don't you, Morris? And ginger made from wonderful candied ginger roots imported from India. And to cap it all off, I'm having Hisayo add peanuts — nice, plump, fresh-roasted ones. So the whole thing is going to be perfectly scrumptious — I'm sure of it — and I know you're going to just absolutely love it!"

As Mother predicted, Morris always found the curry to be perfectly scrumptious. While everyone else was still nibbling politely on a first helping, Morris was packing away a second or third.

Just as Mother learned to go with a good thing, so did Father. He loved to tell humorous stories. When he found one that was sure to get a good laugh, he told it again and again. Since he had a different audience each time, what difference did it make?

Here is one of Father's favorite stories, which he told in the company of close friends and after the younger children had been excused from the table.

In a small town in medieval Europe, a poor peasant earned his living by carting loads of goods for people. But after many years his old horse died, and the peasant was in despair. He went to his priest, who said, "Never mind, all will be well. Just come with me."

"Oh, can it be so easy?" asked the peasant.

"Yes," said the priest. "Just come up the hill with me."

So they walked up the hill to the baron's estate and right into his magnificent stables. There was a splendid array of horses. The priest said, "Take your pick."

"What?" said the peasant. "That would be stealing from the baron!"

"Never mind, everything will be all right. Take your pick."

So the peasant chose a splendid draft horse and led it down the hill. The priest, meanwhile, went into the horse's stall and fell fast asleep.

An hour or so later, the baron came to the estate and decided to look over his horses. He was amazed to see the priest sleeping on the straw in one of the stalls. "Father! Father!" he said, waking the priest up. "What are you doing sleeping in my horse's stall?"

The priest looked bewildered and then sat up, exclaiming, "A miracle! I must have been forgiven!"

"What do you mean?" said the baron.

"I will explain," said the priest. "When I was a young priest, I used to hear the confessions of a very attractive young woman, and, well, one thing led to another and, we uh, well, you know what happened."

"Yes, yes," said the baron. "But why are you sleeping in my horse's stall?"

"Because God punished me," said the priest, "and reincarnated me as a horse, a beast of burden. But now, here I am a man again! Oh, what a miracle! God is good!"

The baron was amazed and bade farewell to the priest, who walked down the hill with a glad expression on his face.

Meanwhile, the poor peasant was happy, doing well with his splendid new beast. One morning a week later, the baron went into town and saw the peasant carting a load. The horse somehow looked familiar. The baron stopped the peasant, who was now trembling. He saw his own brand on the horse. He examined the horse's teeth. Yes, there was no doubt, it was his horse.

The baron backed off a bit, looked severely at the animal, and said, "Well, Father, I see you've been at it again."

Whenever Father told a funny story, he would tremble with mirth. Then, just before the punch line, he would become convulsed with giggles. His body shook. Tears streamed down his cheeks. Finally, after he had somehow managed to spew out the punch line, he would shake his head from side to side and launch into paroxysms of laughter. His story, together with his way of telling it, would send his guests into such protracted fits of hysteria that they had to keep dabbing their eyes with their napkins.

Father had another habit at dinner parties — one that drove us kids crazy. Whenever he told a story, he would lift a forkful of curry, or whatever, and suspend it, poised halfway between his plate and his mouth for minutes at a time. Finally, instead of putting the forkful of food into his mouth, he would set it down neatly on the far side of his dinner plate. After two or three stories, he had managed to relocate his entire dinner to the other side of his plate.

Morris, Nancy, and I would stare at this whole operation, transfixed. One time Morris whispered to me, "Why doesn't he just turn his plate around once every ten minutes? He could save himself a heckuva lot of work!"

During many a party when I was but seven or eight, Father would give me the cue that it was my turn to shine. "Joe, do you have a limerick to tell?" he would ask. And I would shyly, but happily, recite my limerick:

> There was a young man from the West
> Who loved a young lady with zest —
>   So hard did he press her
>   To make her say "Yes sir,"
> He broke three cigars in his vest!

— whereupon Father would burst into fits of laughter that never gave the slightest clue that he had heard the limerick dozens of times before.

In those days, did we eat a lot of curry? Did we hear a lot of stories we had heard a zillion times before? Sure as I'm sitting here. But, again, what difference did it make? We were all having such a good time.

After a party, Father could be counted on to exclaim: "That was a bully evening!" And Mother, just as exuberant, would slap her thigh and say, "Didn't we have a Littell of a time!"

CONFESSIONS OF A CHOIRBOY

At the tender age of ten I became a choirboy. "No big deal!" I thought, unaware of the impending threat to my youthful dignity. "All you do is put on your white outfit and sing each Sunday." If only things could have been that simple!

St. Andrew's Cathedral had a well-trained choir of twenty men and women and fifteen boys. Of course we were appropriately attired for

On the lanai of our house, at the age of seven, I appeared to epitomize the Age of Innocence. While it is possible that I was contemplating what good deed I might perform that day, it is more likely that I was deciding which of my father's visitors' gas tanks I should fill with root beer.

this honor. The adult choristers wore, over their regular clothes, their long purple cassocks covered by short, lacy white surplices. We boys wore the same, but with the addition of starched white collars plus, bulging from our Adam's apples, those big purple bow ties. If only we'd been supplied with wings and halos, we'd have resembled innocent cherubs from on high!

Before Sunday services, we were groomed and fussed over by the ladies of the Women's Auxiliary. "We must make sure you boys look your best for the Lord," they would say. "Are your shoes nicely shined?" At this point I would groan. Shoes? Those awful things? I never had to wear shoes — not downtown, not to the movies, not to the Chinese restaurant, not even to school. I hoped the Lord appreciated my wearing them on Sundays, for oh, how those oxfords pinched my spread-out feet!

Well, anyway, to look our Sunday best and be properly attired, we had to be nicely fitted around our necks with those stiff white collars. This meant we had to remove our shirts. That was no problem for the other fourteen boys. But for me it posed a serious predicament. Unlike the others, who wore trousers that were separate from the shirt and held up by a belt, I always wore a combination cotton shirt and short pants, with the pants held up solely by buttons on the shirt. I couldn't get my shirt off without dropping my pants. And I couldn't keep my pants up without keeping my shirt on. And I had nothing on underneath. The ladies had to devise a scheme for getting my shirt off. They would throw my cassock over me loosely and then let me drop my pants so that they could get me out of my shirt while, at the same time, allowing me to preserve my angelic modesty. After putting me through a number of contortionist's moves that made me look like a festooned pretzel, the ladies succeeded in getting me into my vestments.

For a whole year I sang with no pants on. If I looked angelic, I sure didn't feel it. I was squirming inside, dead sure that my vestments were transparent, positive that all eyes in the congregation were rigidly fixed on me in outright condemnation. Years later, my fears were verified when I learned the awful truth. Said Henry, son of the presi-

The choirboy. Everyone in church had always known that underneath that cassock I was as naked as a newborn babe (and I had always thought it was a well-kept secret!).

dent of the Women's Auxiliary: "Joe, the whole parish knew it all along — had always known that underneath your cassock you were as naked as the day you were born!"

My special friend in those days was a fellow choirboy named Hamlin Day. When things got slow, we had a way of cooking up mischief, especially after the Sunday service, when parishioners were socializing in the parish hall. Hamlin and I would stroll over to the church parking lot and let the air out of a few tires. After a few Sundays we became bored with that, too. I then had an idea. "Hey, Hamlin," I said, "we're wasting our time. Instead of just fooling around like this, why don't we do something that earns us some money? I need a few dollars to buy model airplanes."

"Me, too," replied Hamlin. "I need money for chewing gum cards and Big Little Books."

And so we devised the wickedest of scams. On Saturdays, when parishioners or clergy came to Father's office, parking their cars just outside the Bishop's House, Hamlin and I would remove the car keys from their ignitions, then hide them. (In those days, people never locked their cars or their homes.) Then, when the visitor emerged from the bishop's office, we would giggle silently as we watched him search frantically for his keys. After a while, we would stroll over to him and ask, "Something wrong?" When the frustrated person declared that his car key was missing, one of us would say, "We'll help you look for it. If we find it, will you reward us each with a quarter?" The distraught man would agree, and in less than a minute — what luck! — Hamlin and I would find his key behind a palm tree in the front yard!

For weeks our pockets jingled with the profits from this enterprise — until some fink in the parish ratted on us and told Father. Upon learning of our shameless scheme, Pop was livid. He already knew that I was a mischievous imp, but, until now, he had refrained from putting his hefty hand to my backside — probably because he well remembered that he himself, at my age, had also been a mischievous imp. But this was different — something not too helpful to his image as a father and a bishop!

I was happier than it appeared when my sister Charlotte returned home after a series of piano recitals on the East Coast.

This time he charged out of the house, grabbed me by the ear, hustled me upstairs, and whacked my fanny to within an inch of its life. Before consigning me to solitary confinement, he armed me with a Book of Common Prayer as well as a Holy Bible — ostensibly to assist in the "repentance of a contrite heart," and in the reinstatement to Grace of a "miserable sinner."

Who would have imagined that, after all this, an unexpected benefit would result? Father had forgotten something. He had neglected to make us hand over the proceeds from our nefarious venture. To my delight, I was able to add handsomely to my collection of model airplanes (Fokker Triplanes, Sopwiths, and Spads). Hamlin was able to add similarly to his collection of chewing gum cards (famous Indians and Chiefs) and Big Little Books (*Dick Tracy*, *Popeye*, and *Terry and the Pirates*). What a haul! "Crime does pay," I said to Hamlin with a roguish look. "Sometimes, anyway!"

One day, when it dawned on Father that I was getting as much as seventy-five cents a week for singing in the choir, he sprang into action. "Son," he said, "singing in the choir should be an act of praise, not a source of gain. Early in life you should get into the habit of giving a part of what you earn to church missions. For that reason I think you should put half the money you earn each week into the mite box sitting on the dining room table." I obediently dropped thirty-five cents into the box every Sunday. However, I very quickly learned how to take it out again! I simply slipped a dinner knife into the coin slot, turned the box on its side, and jiggled it until the coins slid down the knife into the palm of my hand. Thus what I gaveth to the Lord on Sunday I tooketh away on Monday. I was careful, though, never to take more money out of the box than I had put in, because I didn't think that would be a very nice thing to do to all those missions that Father was always preaching about and that needed so much help.

Being told that I had to give half of my earnings to missions was my introduction to the concept of taxation. The future looked ominous. Here I was, only ten years old, and already in the fifty percent tax bracket!

ROTTEN EGG BEHIND EAR!

From his office in the Bishop's House, Father published a monthly newsletter called "The Hawaiian Church Chronicle." Providing church news of all the Islands, the "Chronicle" was his pride and delight. He would go into ecstasies on the day of publication. "Have you seen this?" he would exult, accosting anyone within earshot. "This is really a 'bully' edition!" His enthusiasm was catching.

My brother Morris caught it and announced, "I'm going to start a paper of my own." Although only fifteen years old, he turned out a rather sophisticated, if naughty, publication called "The Littell Family Chronicle," which in all likelihood was the forerunner of our current tabloids. Through painstaking investigative reporting, his paper exposed family gossip, secrets, and misadventures and brought closet skeletons out into the open. For a weekly price of "five cents a peek," Morris circulated this five-column, handwritten newsletter to family, neighbors, and clergy.

As an aspiring journalist, Morris reached the peak of his profession on the day he overheard Father whispering to Mother, "Confidentially, dear, I'm planning to relieve the canon of the cathedral of his duties. We don't see eye to eye on church policy." Days before Father was scheduled to break the news to the unsuspecting cleric, Morris beat him to it. In bold script, across all five columns on page 1, appeared what was to become his most notorious headline: *BISHOP FIRES THE CANON!*

While many of Morris's headlines had a spicy, sensational ring to them, others, such as the following, were more homespun:

BISHOP CONFIRMS EIGHTY, THEN SPRAINS ANKLE

200 APPEAR TO ENJOY CHARLOTTE'S PIANO RECITAL

MRS. LITTELL GETS SICK AFTER SEEING POPE

MORRIS DEMANDS NEW PIANO TEACHER

It wasn't long before competitors appeared on the scene. A neighbor boy, Fred Hinckley, also aged fifteen, came out with his "Emma Square Gazette." At once his publication became the object of Morris's scorn, the target of acid editorials. In one of them he wrote, "'The Emma Square Gazette' is of inferior quality, a rag of no imagination and boring content — certainly not worth the five cents Fred is charging. The 'Gazette' is a swindle!"

"Enough is enough!" fumed Fred after reading that editorial in "The Littell Family Chronicle." Storming mad, he went after Morris, chased him all around Queen Emma Square, then up the spiral staircase leading to the roof of the cathedral bell tower. "Ha-ha — *trapped!*" yelled Fred as he landed a swift punch in the nose to Morris, whereupon blood shot from his nostrils, splattering his face and shirt with blotches of bright crimson. As Fred dashed to escape down the stairs — mission accomplished — Morris grabbed a large pigeon egg from an abandoned nest atop the tower and hurled it, full force, at Fred. Bull's-eye! The egg landed squarely behind Fred's left ear, making a gooey mess that flowed down his neck and inside his shirt. The next headline in the "Chronicle" was destined to become Morris's most famous: *ROTTEN EGG BEHIND EAR!*

I still have fond recollections of Father sitting at his desk, leaning back in his brown leather chair, howling with glee. Of course he was reading "The Littell Family Chronicle."

Just as Morris had been inspired by Father's journalistic enthusiasms, so, too, was I. And when Morris was packed off to boarding school in the East, I inherited his "Littell Family Chronicle." Although only ten years young, I was determined that my version of the paper would not be handwritten. Heck no. I'd make it look more like a *real* newspaper! It would be typed on a machine. So how about that Underwood typewriter in Father's office? There it sat every evening after business hours — useless. Who would know if I sneaked in there, adopted it, and then brought fame and fortune to the family with a brand-new kind of neighborhood newspaper?

Well, doggone it, Father found me out one evening as he walked past the office door. Hearing the *tap-tap* of the keys, he poked his head into the office. He looked amazed! I looked even *more* amazed! To my surprise, however, rather than bawl me out, he said, "Go ahead, son. You may use my typewriter. Putting out a newspaper is a worthy activity."

And so for two years I used the office typewriter at night — with Father's blessing. He probably never noticed that the very first thing his secretary, Mrs. Aitken, did upon arriving at the office every morning — even before removing her hat — was to rethread the twisted ribbon in the typewriter. Nor, probably, was he aware of the frequent visits of the typewriter repairman, summoned by Mrs. Aitken to fix the stalled carriage, the bent letters, and the other ravages wrought upon the machine by his ten-year-old son. Father dwelt on a spiritual plane far removed from the mere tangled wreckage of an office typewriter. As far as I know, never once did Mrs. Aitken complain to him about the threat I posed not only to the episcopal correspondence but to her own sanity. Good Christian that she was, she bore her cross in silence. Bless her heart, that woman was a saint!

Another staunch supporter of my newspaper was my sister Charlotte, who often asked, "When will your next issue be out, Joe? I have my five cents ready." That gave me an idea. Why not include a guest editorial in each month's issue, beginning with Charlotte? When I asked her, she readily complied with a nice piece entitled "Thoughts on the Birthday of King Kamehameha." I then asked Nancy to do an editorial. Wish I hadn't. She wrote a not-so-nice one called "Thoughts on Kid Brothers Who Pester Their Sisters for Editorials." I must have learned something about freedom of speech from Father, for I printed every word of her humiliating harangue.

Although a couple of competitors to my newspaper sprang up in the neighborhood from time to time, I had the circulation in Queen Emma Square pretty well locked up. I had learned a valuable lesson in marketing: if you try to put out a newspaper that is well written and illustrated and then market it aggressively in a neighborhood comprised mainly of Episcopalians, you will outsell your competitors five to one if your father is the bishop.

DANGER — EPISCOPAL BISHOP AT THE WHEEL!

If, in China, Father was "all thumbs" at the piano, you should have seen him in Hawaii in the '30s, trying to drive a car! Thumbs? Why, he must have had forty of them. When our 1935 Chevrolet coupe went cruising down Beretania Street, Father behind the wheel, look out! It was the terror of the town. From a distance, policemen shook their fists at this oncoming menace. But — presto! Their ire quickly turned into broad grins of forgiveness as they noted that here was no ordinary drunk at the wheel; it was none other than that revered man of the cloth, Bishop Littell of St. Andrew's Cathedral. How can you apprehend a saintly man on a saintly mission?

In those days, since traffic was light, Father got away with untold violations; several times a policeman, without a word, winced as the good bishop rolled through a stop sign.

One day, Morris and I cornered Father on our front porch. "Come on, Father," we begged. "Take us over to Kailua Bay for a swim." No one loved to swim more than Father, and he jumped at the idea. "I'll see if your mother can go along, and then I'll be ready in ten minutes." So off we went for a swim on the island's north side. Father took the wheel, Mother got into the car beside him, and Morris and I climbed into the rumble seat, not suspecting the crazy mishap that was to befall us. To get to Kailua Bay, we had to take a narrow, twisting road over the Pali, a twelve-hundred-foot cliff that drops almost vertically to the plains on the island's north side. Halfway down the Pali was a treacherous hairpin turn, a turn so sharp the road nearly doubled back on itself. As it happened, Father could not quite negotiate this turn, and the car sideswiped some bushes growing out of the cliff. Immediately, an avalanche of red clay and tropical vegetation tumbled down on Morris and me, the debris burying us up to our laps in the rumble seat. For the rest of the trip we remained planted back there like two small palm trees, our parents, up front in the cab, totally oblivious to what had happened to us.

When we reached Kailua, Morris and I struggled out of the rumble seat, our heads, faces, necks, shirts, pants, and shoes caked with clay and grime. Mother stared at us in horror. "Morris and Joe!" she bellowed. "How on earth did you get so much filth all over you? Can't your father and I leave you two to yourselves for five minutes? *This very instant* I want you both to stop being such wild, unmanageable hooligans!"

It was never clear to any of us how Father ever passed his driver's test. One day, he decided he would drive to the hospital to see a sick friend. Sitting at my upstairs window, I suddenly heard what sounded like a bulldozer — a *squeak*, a crackling *crunch*, and a *thud*. Looking out, I saw that the left door of the garage had been wrenched from one of its hinges and was hanging loose at a cockeyed angle. I watched as Father got out of the car, surveyed the damage briefly, and then got back into the car to proceed on his pastoral mission. Backing out farther, he turned the wheel to the left instead of to the right and slammed into the trunk of our breadfruit tree. The left rear fender was now history, and the entire back bumper was lying on the ground.

That was the last time Father was ever seen behind a wheel, to the blessed relief of his family, his parishioners, and, of course, the entire Honolulu police force.

WHAT'S GOING ON IN THE BEDROOM?

On many a night, when I got out of bed at one or two in the morning to go to the bathroom, I could see soft shafts of light playing on the walls of the upstairs hall. The light moved up and down, up and down, slowly and rhythmically, and came from Father and Mother's bedroom.

One night, it suddenly hit me. "They're doing it!" I murmured. "Father and Mother are doing it! I've never seen anybody do it. This is my chance. I'd better have a look." Ever so quietly, ever so stealthily, I tiptoed up to the door of my parents' room and peeked inside.

"AW, NUTS!" I said to myself, thoroughly disappointed. "They're not doing a thing." All I saw was Mother sitting up in bed, Father sleeping soundly beside her. She was reading by a little portable light she had perched on her stomach, along with the book she was holding. As Mother breathed, her night light heaved up and down on her stomach, casting those eerie lights and shadows around the upstairs hall.

Although Mother never went to college, she used to sit up until all hours of the night studying books on art, music, literature — everything she considered to be "constructive" (her favorite word). She told us children, whenever one of us misbehaved, to "go do something constructive." So here was a self-taught woman, educated to the point where now she was capable of lecturing on such subjects as French architecture, Italian art, classical music, and the Bible.

One day, the *Honolulu Star-Bulletin* announced that Mrs. S. Harrington Littell would be giving a series of three lectures at Tenney Auditorium on the subject of Italian Renaissance art. Most seats were quickly taken, for she had already developed a reputation for being a fascinating speaker. She had a sense of drama, a feel for the artistically perfect stage decor, the use of music of the period under discussion, and the importance of bringing the eye, the ear — all the senses — into play. She moved about the stage, spoke with intense inner excitement, her eyes sparkling, her enthusiasm contagious. Three hundred people attended the first lecture in the series. When the time came for the third, people stampeded the auditorium, stood ten deep in the back, and clogged the aisles. According to the news report, more than a thousand people attended that last lecture.

The same thing happened at the Honolulu Academy of Arts, where she gave a series of subscription lectures, "The Cathedrals of France." She packed them in. Her lectures always received rave reviews in the *Star-Bulletin*.

It was revealing to thumb through the myriad books she studied, to see phrases underlined, handwritten notes in every margin, dictionary definitions everywhere. As Tyndall observed, "Knowledge once gained casts a light beyond its own immediate boundaries." Most certainly my mother, Evelyn Littell, endowed with high-voltage magnetism, not only cast her light but beamed it far beyond its immediate boundaries!

HOW TO BUY A HAT

Nobody ever called Mother a fashion plate or a clothes horse. That unselfconscious, precious woman, with her beautifully chiseled Grecian nose, sparkling eyes, erect carriage, and famous dimples — what a shame she had no sense of style, no idea of how to dress to enhance her natural good looks. Either that or she was too busy to bother. Nancy told me what it was like to accompany her to the Liberty House, Honolulu's only department store, and watch her purchase a hat or a dress.

She would walk to the nearest discount rack, grab at any dress her size, hold it up to her body, refuse to try it on, and tell a salesgirl, "I'll take it." And when back home she put it on — never mind if her slip showed, never mind if the waist was too high, never mind if her heels were run down or if her stockings were rumpled — she was dressed and ready to meet her public, whether it was a derelict at the back door or the chancellor of the University of Hawaii. Nobody minded. Mother's charm surpassed all other mundane considerations.

And oh, to watch her buy a hat — it was unbelievable! She would spy a hat in a shop window, dash in, grab it off the rack, jam it on her head with no thought of checking it in a mirror, and sometimes with the tag still dangling or even wearing the hat backward, she would pay the cash and head back home.

Quite unconscious of the impression she made on others, Mother was always her own charming self — that was how her magnetism worked. I see in some of her early China snapshots that her slip shows or her stockings are pulled haphazardly over her lovely, slim ankles. And her hair? Oh, my. Even way back then she wore it in a heap around or atop her head, all stuffed into a hairnet, and let it go at that.

No, Mother, we didn't mind. We gave up trying to remake you — finally didn't want to — for that was who you were — your own unique, effervescent self. Yet sometimes we couldn't help but cave in to such secret thoughts as: "Oh, Mother, you could have looked like a queen — you had all the makings!"

OH, GOD, I CAN'T STAND SUCH BEAUTY!

"Nancy! Joe! Come here — quick! Exciting news!" Mother was ecstatic over one of her impulsive decisions. It was on a spring day in 1936 that she made her dramatic announcement: "Children, I simply *have* to go to Europe — I have to go *right away*. I need the change and stimulus, and I've decided to take you two along. We'll visit England, France, Germany, and Italy on a three-month trip. Now isn't that thrilling?"

"Of course," said Nancy, "but what about school? I'm supposed to graduate from high school in two months."

"Well, dear," she answered, "I'll talk to Punahou School and explain the cultural advantages of your going. Same with you, Joe. I'll talk to Iolani School and overcome their objections, too. And we'll be off!" (Because Nancy didn't graduate that June, she had to take a whole year of high school equivalency courses to get her diploma.)

It was right about then that I began to get the feeling that Mother was running away from something. What it was, I didn't know, and wasn't to find out, either, for nearly twenty years. Dismissing my half-formed hunch, I went about packing for our sudden trip.

From the day Mother set foot on European soil, she became a person possessed! Her confrontations with the magnificent art, architecture, and music of those countries became experiences of such emotional intensity that she was sometimes overcome to the point that she was close to fainting.

How could I ever forget that day in France when Mother entered Chartres Cathedral? No question, this is a once-in-a-lifetime emotional experience. But for Mother it was too much. As her eyes adjusted to the dimmer light, she reeled, had to steady herself against the shock of the overwhelming aura of the place. Glancing at the stained-glass windows — at their gloriously deep mystical blues with flamelike touches of red — she nearly fainted. Flopping on a pew, trying to catch her breath, she gasped, "O God, I can't stand such beauty!"

A similar incident occurred in London when we attended a Beethoven concert at Royal Albert Hall. The music was straight from the portals of Heaven. For a while Mother sat, enraptured. But soon, as the music of the Seventh Symphony overpowered her, tears streamed down her cheeks. Pulling at my sleeve, she choked and said, "Let's get out of here — I simply can no longer stand it!" And so we walked out!

Another time, at the Lido resort in Venice, Mother acquired too much sunburn. That evening, after we had returned to the hotel, her skin looked scorched and she seemed to have developed a fever. "Call a doctor," she commanded Nancy and me. "I know I'm going to die. And quickly call Father in Honolulu — tell him my will is in the back of the top drawer of my desk and that I love him very much and I love you all and I will miss you terribly, and Nancy and Joe, you keep calm — people here will tell you what to do when I am gone. Ohhhhhh dear!" By morning Mother felt fine, had forgotten about the whole thing, and was leading the charge to St. Mark's Church, the Palace of the Doges, and the Bridge of Sighs.

On our trips to Europe, Mother did everything on a shoestring, or even just the aglet of a shoestring. She made Scrooge look like a wild spender. On ocean trips, we always traveled third class; to anyone who had never seen the elegant dining rooms, spacious salons, and staterooms in first or second class, third-class passage would have seemed fine enough. And so it was to us.

In almost every large city in Europe, there was a small, clean, modest hotel that became our pied à terre. In London it was the Celtic Hotel, a family hostelry on Russell Square near the British Museum. In Paris, it was the Hôtel Greffulhe, on the Rue Greffulhe, a block from that magnificent Parthenon-styled church, the Madeleine. Mother deemed a hotel suitable if the stairs leading up to our rooms creaked and groaned and the hallways sagged underfoot. In Fontainebleau we stayed at the home of John Baxter, an American friend who had been in the consular service in Hankow and was now with the American Embassy in Paris. (Because the French pronounced Baxter "Back-stair," we called him "Monsieur Escalier de Service.")

Mother's penny-pinching reached its peak when we traveled across the United States by train. She always got tickets for the San Francisco–Chicago run on the *Challenger*, a reduced-fare train. For the three-night trip, instead of getting a lower berth for herself and an upper berth for me, she would get just a lower for the two of us. For three nights we would sleep together, my head at her feet and her head at my feet. All night long, each of us would keep pulling the blanket up — back and forth, back and forth — exposing first her feet and then mine. Several times a night I would wake up with her toes twitching in my face.

Mother, you really knew how to save a buck!

Something else about her. Mother was never above pulling rank. There was the time that she and Nancy and I crashed a party — an unusual kind of party. For nearly three centuries, the Three Choirs Festival, which celebrates the English choral tradition, has attracted tourists from all over the world. It is a spectacular event in England, held annually, in turn, in the great cathedrals of Worcester, Gloucester, and Hereford. That year the festival was being held in Worcester.

We had not heard of the festival until, arriving at a nearby town, we saw posters announcing the gala event. We hurried to Worcester only to find, as we arrived at the cathedral, that great throngs had already gathered. Long lines of music lovers waited to show their tickets. Not a seat remained.

Well, along came that indomitable Evelyn Littell and her two straggling children, Nancy and Joe. And no, this lady would not abide any lip from a pipsqueak young usher who told us "the cathedral is full — no one else will be admitted."

"Look here, young man," bellowed my mother, eyes flashing. "I've come all the way from Honolulu to hear this concert. You *have* to let us in. I am the wife of His Lordship, the Bishop of Honolulu! Take us at once to a front pew."

The poor man, completely cowed, bade us follow him, pushed his way through the maze of people, and finally got us to the chancel, where he told several people they would have to move over to make room for the wife and family of His Lordship, the Bishop of Honolulu.

As we sat down, Mother whispered to us, "Say, children, we didn't even have tickets!"

That was my mother for you!

DO GIRLS REALLY HAVE THREE *PUKAS*?

Never once did my parents discuss with me the secret, mysterious, forbidden topic of sex. Nor did they get a teacher, priest, counselor, or any other adult to enlighten me. Everything I learned about sex I learned on the playgrounds at school. And since I attended four different schools during my prepubescent years in Honolulu and graduated from four different playgrounds, can you imagine what wild and fanciful tales I picked up?

From one boy I heard: "If a girl stands on her head for half an hour, her 'thing' will grow out instead of in, and she will become a boy. Her mother will have to run right out to the store and buy boys' clothes."

From another boy: "Every girl born on the Islands has three *pukas* [holes] — one for *haolis* [whites], one for *kanakas* [Hawaiians], and one for everyone else." That was my introduction to the concept of racial segregation.

When I was ten, I decided that after all the talk and fuss I had heard on the playgrounds, I would find out for myself what girls *really* had. I told an eight-year-old girl (whom I'll call Mary), "I'll give you fifteen cents if you'll pull down your underpants so I can see what you have."

That turned out to be an offer too enticing for her to refuse. "Okay," she said, "but I want my money first." After I had given her three shiny nickels, she led me behind a banyan tree and pulled down her underpants. I had about two seconds to look at her before she pulled them up again. After I had looked at what she had, I was gravely disappointed. I was disappointed not so much in what girls had as in what they *didn't* have.

"That's all you have?" I asked Mary. "That's all there is? It's not worth the fifteen cents. I want my money back."

"A deal's a deal," she said haughtily, and walked off. Before my eyes, this shy, quiet child had transformed herself into a hard-nosed, hard-core business girl!

Mary had now turned her first trick (so to speak), at the age of eight, for fifteen cents. Did her newfound awareness of the salability of her body and the easy money to be made plunge her, in later years, into the life of a *fille de joie* living in the nether shadows of society? The answer is no. I'm happy to say that she entered the worthy teaching profession, became an English teacher, and went on to become the dean of a well-known college on the mainland.

It wasn't until I left the playgrounds of Honolulu and went away to boarding school, at the age of twelve, that I received a sex education I thought to be reliable. There, at least, my schoolmates' descriptions of things that happened during the sex act seemed to fall within the realm of anatomical possibility.

Still, was there anything in the world that was harder to do than getting a straight story on sex? Trying to climb Mount Everest? Probably not. Trying to climb Mount Everest with roller skates on? Maybe.

THE MYSTERIOUS DEATH IN THE BISHOP'S HOUSE

The strange and disturbing events I am about to relate occurred in August of 1936, in our home, the Bishop's House. I was eleven years old. Living in the house at the time, along with my parents and me, was my sister Charlotte, who was in her late twenties.

Charlotte was a tall, slender woman with a classic, sculpturally chiseled face, soft green eyes, and blond hair curled in bangs over her forehead. To many, she seemed a perfectionist — to some, too much so in her careful planning of everything she undertook, in her close attention to every detail, and in the strict demands she made on herself. To me, she was a warm, caring big sister, and I loved her dearly.

Charlotte was a concert pianist — one who was gaining an increasingly fine reputation. A music major at Vassar, she had given a number of highly acclaimed recitals in New York and other East Coast cities. And now, in the coming month, she was scheduled to make her debut with the Honolulu Symphony Orchestra as soloist in the Beethoven C Minor Concerto. In preparation, she was practicing ten hours a day, at home and in her studio.

On this particular day in August, I had just returned home from a Cub Scout camping trip to Maui. To my surprise, Father met me at the front door and hustled me into the house. He set down my duffel bag, led me onto the lanai, summoned Mother, and bade us kneel with him in prayer. For over half an hour — for what seemed to me an eternity — he offered up prayers from his prayer book. I had no idea what was going on, but when I began to catch words and phrases like "thy departed servant Charlotte" and "grant thy servant Charlotte an entrance into the land of light and joy" and "take thy servant Charlotte into the fellowship of thy saints," it began to dawn on me that my sister Charlotte had died. At the end of the prayer session, though, I knew nothing more than that, and I left the room thoroughly confused.

For a week, Father and Mother didn't mention Charlotte in my presence. I knew she had died, but I didn't know how or why. I missed her terribly. As I rode my bike and worked on my stamp collection, the grief in my heart knew no outlet, and the questions on my mind found no answers.

The next week, school started. As long as I live, I will never forget that first day of school. No sooner had I joined the other boys for recess than one of them pointed to me and, in a taunting voice, announced to the group: "His sister committed sewer pipe!"

No words can describe my reaction to that announcement. For a second I was simply angry with that boy for ridiculing me in public, for trifling with my inner pain. Then suddenly I realized what he had said. *He had just revealed to me how my sister had died. She had committed suicide!* I hadn't known. Heaped now upon the anger I already felt were feelings of shock, anguish, bewilderment, and grief — engulfing me all at once, rendering me unable to speak, unable to think. I was numb. My mind and body were paralyzed.

Charlotte's suicide had been front-page news in all of the Honolulu papers, but I had known nothing about it.

Two more days went by. I still knew no details about how Charlotte had died — and my parents still weren't talking to me about Charlotte at all. Then Jimmy Eckert, a neighbor boy about my age, came over to see me.

"Want to play?" he asked.

"Sure," I said.

"I brought over the latest issue of my newspaper for you to look at," he told me. (He and I had an agreement to buy each other's paper every week.) He then handed me his paper, "The Jimmy."

I glanced at page 1 of "The Jimmy." At once something leaped out at me. Pasted up on the first page was a clipping with the screaming headline: DAUGHTER OF BISHOP FOUND DEAD IN KITCHEN. It was the Honolulu Star-Bulletin's front-page article reporting Charlotte's death. I took the copy of Jimmy's paper and sat down with it on the front lawn. Slowly, agonizingly, I read the entire article.

Charlotte Littell, 28, daughter of the Rt. Rev. S. Harrington Littell, Bishop of Honolulu, was found dead shortly before 9 this morning in the gas-filled kitchen of the Bishop's residence adjoining St. Andrew's Cathedral on Queen Emma Square.

The body was found by Miss Mabel Polson, temporary secretary to the Bishop.

Two minutes later an undisclosed woman reported to police that the body had been found. Detective Thomas P. Quinn of the homicide squad and the Deputy Coroner Isaac Waiolama went to the scene. The driver of an ambulance from the emergency hospital judged at 8:56 that Miss Littell had been dead for about an hour.

Miss Littell lay face down with her head within the gas oven of the kitchen. Her body was supported by the opened oven door. She was clad in a nightgown and kimono. Her feet were bare.

The body was taken to the morgue about 10 this morning. . . .

After I had finished the article I said to Jimmy, "I can't stay out and play. I have things to do. I'll see you later."

"Okay," answered Jimmy, "but don't forget you owe me a nickel for the paper."

"Oh, that's right," I said absently, fishing in my pocket and pulling out a nickel. Then I went into the house and stayed in my room for I don't know how long. All I remember is that I was sick to my stomach and deeply troubled.

That's how I found out how my sister Charlotte died.

Why did Charlotte do it? Why? Over the years, down to the present, that question has been the subject of speculation on the part of many people both inside and outside the family. The more that people have speculated, the deeper the mystery has grown.

Some conjectured that Charlotte had been nervous about her responsibility as soloist for the Honolulu Symphony Orchestra concert. Yet she was a seasoned soloist who, from all reports, had carried off every performance up to that time with grace and style.

Others hypothesized that Charlotte had cancer. Some time after her death, Mother told Nancy and me that Charlotte had been depressed after learning that she had two cysts in her ovaries. However, Dr. James Morgan, the family physician, steadfastly maintained to my brother Harrington that the autopsy had revealed no such malignancy nor any other abnormal physical condition.

Several members of the family recalled that Charlotte had often spoken of Gerald Saunders, a man from New York whom she had known for a long time and who was now married. They suspected that she may have been hopelessly in love with Gerald, judging by the cautious excitement she showed when she mentioned his name. Gerald and his wife had visited Honolulu earlier that year, and the three of them were inseparable. Nancy's gut feeling has always been that Charlotte really cared for that man and agonized over the hopelessness, the futility, of the situation.

To this day the shock of Charlotte's death is still with us, and to this day none of us really knows why this sweet, gentle, bright, talented young woman — our beloved sister — snuffed out her life just when it held so much promise.

.   .   .

Attending the funeral service for Charlotte were many Island notables, including the governor of Hawaii, Joseph B. Poindexter, and his
family. To the surprise of some, Father conducted the service himself.
A few voiced the opinion that he should not have done so. Said one,
"His taking the service himself was much too dramatic a gesture.
Why didn't he just sit with his wife and children in the front pew and
let the dean of the Cathedral take the service?" But handling the
situation as he did was just like Father — bold, strong, steadfast in his
faith, indomitable in his hour of sorrow. Said Father, "I wanted to be
there for Charlotte at the most important time in her existence . . .
the time when she needed me most . . . the time when she could
receive my most precious gift: a proper send-off on her glorious
passage to Heaven."

5

BANISHED TO
BOARDING SCHOOL

THOSE HAPPY YEARS growing up in Hawaii — they couldn't last forever. When I was twelve, my parents packed me off to boarding school in the East. To them it was unthinkable that their children could obtain a good education outside the northeastern corner of the United States.

The "gateway to opportunity," perhaps, but to us children there was a downside. Each of us endured a gnawing inner ache, an excruciating pain called homesickness. For years at a stretch, not one of us got home to see our parents. My brother Edward, for example, absent for six straight years at boarding school and college, experienced unspeakable trauma when he arrived for his freshman year at Harvard unaccompanied by any relative. Intimidated by the tall wrought-iron fences surrounding Harvard Yard, he was afraid to enter for fear he might be trespassing. It took him two hours, saddled with baggage, to locate his assigned room.

The boys in the family went to Kent School in Connecticut. John and Edward went to Harvard, Charlotte to Vassar, Harrington and Morris to Trinity, and Nancy — breaking the northeast "tradition" — to the University of Heidelberg.

Thousands of us "mish-kids" attending U.S. schools and colleges suffered severe transplantation shock. We spoke and dressed differently. We were misfits. We couldn't make friends. We saw life from an entirely different perspective. We had no understanding of the social issues and other matters that were discussed all around us. It was so bad, in fact, that some colleges provided counselors for us BICs (born in China) to help us adjust to college life and to American customs. Even so, some, like my brother Morris, fell by the wayside.

It was fall 1937 when I entered St. Andrew's School in Middletown, Delaware. Founded by Felix du Pont, it offered a rigorous curriculum for boys headed mostly for eastern colleges. Besides taking the usual courses in math, science, English, and history, we were expected to take four years of Latin and French. "Well, now," I thought, "after being batted around like a Ping-Pong ball, after attending four different elementary schools in Honolulu, I'm finally settling in for five uninterrupted years at St. Andrew's."

Or so I thought. Glad I didn't bet on it.

"FROG NIGHT"

St. Andrew's was a cluster of stately, ivy-covered limestone buildings designed in the Gothic style. Beside the school, and winding around the back of it, was a serpentine lake called Noxontown Pond. The school and grounds, except for a stand of woods on the far side of the lake, were surrounded, as far as one could see, by fields of corn and clover. It looked as if someone had picked up one of the colleges at Oxford and dropped it into the middle of absolutely nowhere.

The school had an enrollment of about 120 boys from all over the country, ranging from second-formers (eighth-graders like myself) to sixth-formers (twelfth-graders). Because I had been born in China, it was inevitable that my classmates would find a suitable nickname for me. From day one I was known as "Chink."

On weekdays we had classes from eight A.M. to two P.M., athletics in the afternoon, and study hall in the evenings. Saturday nights were supposed to be free time. But not for us second-formers, as it turned out. On those nights, if we valued our hides, we slipped away from the dinner table without even waiting for dessert and headed for the woods, for we knew that as soon as dinner was over a group of third-formers would form a posse and hunt us down like frightened possums. To escape whatever terror they had planned for us, we hid in branches of trees, or on the ground covered with leaves, or in holes formed by uprooted trees.

Soon enough, however, they approached. Long, bright flashlight beams crisscrossed each other in the black night. Twigs snapped and crackled. Urgent voices became louder and closer. I shivered with fear. For, as always, they would track us down.

The third-formers rounded us up one by one. Beaming their flashlights into our eyes until they had practically blinded us, they proceeded to put us through the tortures they had cooked up for that particular Saturday night. Especially gruesome was the hazing that occurred on "Frog Night" — a night *not* to remember, if only I could blank it out from my mind. It was their idea of fun to take a group of us to the side of the lake farthest from the school. Then Basil, their leader, commanded: "Now strip down to your skins and jump into the lake." We obeyed. "Now swim around in a circle, croaking like frogs." We did that, too.

Suddenly I saw that a boy ahead of me was gasping and unable to keep his head above water. I yelled out, "This kid can't swim!" and got a classmate to help me pull him out of the water. Said a third-former: "Oh, let the sissy sit down and catch his breath." But then they attacked the two of us who had pulled him out and gang-whacked us with sticks and branches until our backs and backsides were raw and bloody. I sensed that we got it because momentarily we had deprived them of total control.

Basil then ordered: "Okay, now, everyone out of the lake and put on your clothes. We're going to have a frog race. The frog who jumps to the finish line first wins the prize. The prize," he announced with a sardonic grin, "is to drink a twelve-ounce bottle of Pepsi-Cola filled with half Pepsi and half piss." Since none of us wanted to win the race, our jumps were mostly vertical, and we thus provided our tormentors with more than ample time to whack our fannies relentlessly with their rough-hewn sticks. We frogs were forced to make croaking sounds as we jumped. I can't remember who won the race, but it wasn't me.

Basil then gave us still another order: "Now everyone line up in a row, squat down like frogs, and catch flies with your tongues. I warn you — don't stop until each of you has caught a fly." Then, while we were all making our tongues dart in and out of our mouths, the third-formers disappeared, their leader calling back over his shoulder, "We'll be back to check on you!" Although they never returned, we were so afraid of being caught disobeying them and being put through even worse tortures the next Saturday night that we stayed there past the eleven P.M. school curfew. As a result, we received demerits for returning late to our dorm, with added punishment in store.

Friends, what a way to spend my special day! It happened that this was my thirteenth birthday.

How could such things go on, year after year, with second-formers being terrorized by third- and fourth-formers almost from the day school opened? There were two reasons. The first was fear. No second former dared to tell Walden Pell, the headmaster, or any of the faculty what was going on. Repeatedly, upperclassmen had warned us that things would go far worse for anyone who squealed. As a third-former, with clenched fist, scowled and said, "Chink, if you say *one word* about this to anyone, some night you'll find yourself tied up in a gunny sack being hauled off to a dark, secret place where no one will discover you for years. Anyone who does find you will find nothing but a tattered sack of dry bones." The image I conjured up of myself decomposing in a dark cave was enough to keep my mouth clamped forever.

The second reason these barbaric abuses continued unchallenged was, in my opinion, Walden Pell's fiercely guarded naiveté and denial of what was going on in the school. He had no street smarts — or if he did, he resolutely suppressed what they revealed to him.

I never told my parents about my Saturday nights at St. Andrew's — they were still in far-off Hawaii. How does a thirteen-year-old boy who is trying to become a man put those things into a letter, anyway?

Besides, at that age I thought everything was preordained, everything charted out for me. I had no sense whatever of options or alternatives. "This is what life has to offer me this year," I said to myself. "If I can't take it, I don't measure up."*

---

*St. Andrew's discontinued the second form in 1984. Practices such as those described here no longer occur.

GALLIVANTING IN
GESTAPO-LAND

SUDDENLY, I'M AN EXCHANGE STUDENT
TO GERMANY

One December day in 1938, in the middle of my second year at St. Andrew's, I got the surprise of my life. Mr. Pell called me to his office and said, "Joe, I have some wonderful news for you. I have chosen you to represent the school as an exchange student to Germany. That means that for the next six months — from January to June of 1939 — you will be attending a German boys' school. It's an honor and a privilege to be chosen as an exchange student, and I hope you'll be proud that I have selected you."

"I *am* proud, sir," I replied a bit uncertainly. "It sounds like an exciting adventure."

Within four weeks I was wearing a khaki uniform with a black leather belt and shoulder strap — and, yes, a crimson-red swastika armband! Not only that, but marching in step, singing in cadence, and Heiling the Führer of the Third Reich! "What goes on here?" I said to myself. "I thought I was hunkering down to five years in prep school, uninterrupted, and getting my feet on the ground. *Gott im Himmel!*"

How did it happen that a fourteen-year-old American prep-schooler, with little on his mind except getting decent grades, making the sports teams, and maybe finding out about girls, suddenly found himself spending the first six months of 1939 (that threatening prewar year, of all times!) in a prestigious German boarding school dedicated to the training of future leaders of the Third Reich?

An organization called the American Schoolboy Fellowship had worked out exchanges between thirty German and thirty American schools to promote better understanding between the two countries. Tensions had arisen between them because of Germany's seizure of Austria and the Sudetenland and U.S. allegations that Germany was persecuting Jews — sending thousands to forced labor camps and thousands more to concentration camp gas chambers. The American Schoolboy Fellowship hoped that educational and cultural exchanges between the two nations would enable them to "get to know each other better" and would lead to mutual friendship and lasting peace.

Walden Pell chose me to represent the school because I spoke some German and was a conscientious student. He quickly obtained my parents' permission for the trip, and off I sailed to Europe. Did I say "it sounds exciting"? It was to be that and much, much more.

The German school was in the town of Köslin, about two hundred miles east of Berlin on the Baltic Sea. The name of the school was — are you ready for this? — the Nationalpolitische Erziehungsanstalt, which means something like National Political Educational Academy. Even the Germans must have thought that a mouthful! They referred to the school as the NPEA.

The NPEA was one of ten such boarding schools for grades seven through twelve scattered throughout Germany. These institutions were set up to educate the elite, the cream of German youth, for leadership in government, the armed forces, the professions, and industry. They combined the academic rigor of a fine American prep school with the stern discipline of a military academy.

My assigned school was a massive, four-story brick monstrosity that occupied a full block. With about seventy other boys, I slept in a large dormitory where row upon row of white metal beds made the place look like a gigantic hospital ward. The only decor was a giant swastika banner at each end of the room. At precisely five A.M., an instructor in full military uniform, including high, shiny black boots, threw open the door and at the top of his lungs shouted, *"AUFSTEHEN!"*

("GET UP!"). Scrambling out of bed, we had fifteen minutes to wash, dress, make our beds, and be at the breakfast table for sweet rolls and cocoa. Then from six A.M. to three P.M., classes: German literature, German history, English, French, geometry, biology, and chemistry, with a short noontime break for a meat sandwich, an apple, and a glass of milk. From three to five, sports: soccer on the athletic field or swimming in the Olympic-size pool. At five-thirty, a substantial dinner. From six-thirty to nine-thirty, study in the Great Hall. At ten P.M., lights out. On Sundays we had parade drill, orchestra practice, crafts, then free time. It was during those free periods that my fellow ninth-graders surrounded me and peppered me with questions:

"Why did America betray Germany after the World War? Why did the U.S. Senate turn its back on Woodrow Wilson's Fourteen Points, which would have brought lasting peace and stability to Europe?"

I didn't have the faintest idea why. I'd never even heard of the Fourteen Points.

In English class, we were beginning a study of Shakespeare's *Julius Caesar*. We read it in English beside a German translation. The class looked to me for insightful comments on the characters of the play.

I had never read *Julius Caesar*. In fact, I had never read any of Shakespeare's plays. What shame I felt! In a state of depression, I thought, "I am an utterly unworthy ambassador of my country."

It was overwhelming. Much of my bewilderment was due to the exceptionally rigorous nature of the curriculum, and much, also, to my lack of fluency in the German language. In any case, sensing my dilemma, the instructors mercifully transferred me from ninth back to eighth grade, where I suffered far less pressure. Even so, in trying to adapt, I felt a continuous tug on my nerves. "Why am I here?" I kept saying to myself. "Why did I consent to leave St. Andrew's or, for that matter, even Honolulu?"

I SINK THE *BISMARCK!*

In March, a flu epidemic swept through the school, and along with about twenty others I landed in the infirmary. In the bed next to mine was a tall, skinny tenth-grader named Rolf Sander. To help pass the time, Rolf taught me how to play Battleship.

Battleship is a game in which each player tries to sink the other's navy. Rolf, commander of the German fleet, made up a grid with twenty squares across (numbered 1–20 across the top) and twenty squares down (lettered A–T down the side), on which he plotted the locations of German ships without letting me see them. (Battleships were five squares long, cruisers three squares, and subs one.) I made up a similar grid and plotted the location of the British fleet under my command. The winner would be the one who had the last ship to remain afloat.

Rolf started the game. "A-7," he called out.

"*Nichts*" ("Nothing"), I said. It was my turn.

"F-14," I called out.

"*Treffer!*" ("A hit!"), he acknowledged.

"F-15," I continued.

"*Treffer!*" he again acknowledged.

"F-16."

"*Treffer — versunken!* Prinz Eugen!" ("Hit and sunk! *Prinz Eugen!*")

And so the game continued. H.M.S. *Prince of Wales* — sunk! H.M.S. *Gloucester* — sunk! *Scharnhorst* — sunk! H.M.S. *Duke of York* — sunk! *Bismarck* — sunk!

Finally, only three ships were left afloat — three German submarines. "I won!" exclaimed Rolf. "The German Navy has sunk the British Navy! Now shall we play again? This time you can use American ships and it will be the German Navy against yours."

"No," I said. "I'll take the British Navy again."

"Do you think the American Navy is as good as the Germans'?" he asked.

"I can't answer that," I said with a sly smile, "but if you happen to bump into Admiral Raeder, you might tell him he would be wise not to mess with the U.S. Navy."

Rolf laughed, if a bit nervously. "Your battleships are named after states, like *Nevada* and *Missouri*, aren't they?" he said. "And your cruisers after cities, like *Indianapolis*? [He pronounced it "Indiana-police."] And your subs after kinds of fish, like *Shark*? Right?"

"How do you know so much about U.S. warships?" I asked him as nonchalantly as I could.

"I've read a lot about various navies," said Rolf. "It's a hobby of mine. After I graduate from the NPEA, I want to fulfill my military obligation in the navy."

We played Battleship every day for a week, and every day Rolf sank the British Navy. Thrown together in the infirmary for all those days, he and I got to know each other quite well. To my surprise and disappointment, he was the only German in the school who ever asked me questions about life in the United States. Some of his questions I found intriguing.

"What are schools in America like?"

"Why don't more Americans study German? Most American tourists speak no German at all."

"How many Americans are millionaires?"

"Why don't Americans like football [soccer] the way other countries do?"

"How often do Americans go to the movies?"

"What percentage of Americans are Negro?"

"Is President Roosevelt Jewish? Is his real name Rosenfeld?"

Friendly as everyone was, none of the other students — or faculty — made any attempt to turn my six months at the NPEA into any kind of real cultural exchange. Wasn't that my whole reason for being there? It may be that they were all too pressured, too caught up in their own nationalistic fervor, to take time for trivialities like that. Too bad, because from the questions Rolf had asked me, it seemed obvious that the Germans had much to learn about the United States.

Several years later, after our two nations had become locked in deadly conflict, I thought again of Rolf and wondered what had happened to him. It wasn't until after the war that I found out. His fate had what struck me as an ironic twist. From a prewar exchange student at St. Andrew's I learned that Rolf's submarine had been blasted to the bottom of the Atlantic by the British Navy.

"*Treffer — versunken!*"

"HEINRICH HIMMLER'S COMING TO MY SCHOOL!"

In May, a month before graduation day, the school administration transferred me from eighth grade to ninth so that I could graduate from junior high school with my original classmates. At about the same time, the school superintendent posted a surprise announcement on the bulletin board that set off bursts of frenzied excitement among faculty and students:

IT GIVES ME GREAT PLEASURE TO ANNOUNCE THAT REICHSFÜHRER HEINRICH HIMMLER HAS AGREED TO BE THE SPEAKER AT OUR GRADUATION CEREMONIES ON JUNE 14TH. THE REICHSFÜHRER WILL ALSO AWARD THE DIPLOMAS TO THE GRADUATES PERSONALLY AND WILL SIGN THEM. . . .

"Heinrich Himmler!" I gasped. "The chief of Germany's Political and Criminal Police! The most important man in the Reich next to Adolf Hitler! I can't believe it. Wait till the people back home hear about this! He's not only coming to my school — he's going to award me my diploma!" I could hardly contain myself.

Then came the letdown. Just a week before the big day, the superintendent posted another notice:

I REGRET TO INFORM YOU THAT REICHSFÜHRER HIMMLER HAS BEEN DETAINED IN BERLIN AND CANNOT BE PRESENT FOR OUR GRADUATION CEREMONIES. HOWEVER, HE PLANS TO SIGN ALL THE DIPLOMAS AND HAVE THEM READY FOR GRADUATION DAY.

The message was met with disappointed groans from faculty and students. I myself was crestfallen. "What a feather in my cap it would have been to receive my diploma from such an important personage!" I mused. "Well, at least he'll sign my diploma. That's almost as good, now that I think about it."

At any rate, on June 14, 1939, in a gala outdoor ceremony attended by a thousand students, faculty, and parents — a ceremony for which German flags hung from school windows; the school orchestra played magisterial selections from *Tannhäuser*; faculty and students, including me, wore immaculately pressed brown uniforms complete with swastika armbands; and everyone *"Heil Hitler"*-ed everyone else to death — I graduated from the junior high school division of the Nationalpolitische Erziehungsanstalt. My diploma, with the name "Josef Littell" inscribed in Old German script, was signed by Heinrich Himmler.

I'm afraid I can't show you that diploma because in the confusion surrounding my hasty departure from Germany at the outbreak of World War II in September, I lost my trunk and all of my belongings. Later on, back in the States, I concluded that I didn't need that diploma anyway, especially in view of what I'd found out about Himmler. I began to realize that few, if any, employers would be willing to hire me on the spot on the basis of evidence that my junior high school education had been attested to and approved by the chief of the German Gestapo. Nor, once hired, could I expect that a certificate of satisfactory performance from Himmler — even if handsomely framed and hung on the wall behind my desk at the office — would give me the quick edge I sought for advancement up the corporate ladder.

It's just as well that I lost it.

ON WAR GAMES WITH THE GERMANS

There is still more to tell you about life as an exchange student in Hitler's Germany — for example, the extraordinary week I spent on war games with my German classmates.

It was the custom at the NPEA for all the boys to take one-week field trips several times a year. They might go glider flying in Bavaria, skiing in the Sudetenland, or sailing on the Baltic Sea. Or they might go on war games somewhere in the Reich.

In early June, in this fateful year of 1939, all the ninth-graders, myself included, went to southern Austria for a week of war games. A caravan of buses took us to wooded hills near Klagenfurt, where we linked up with four thousand ninth-graders from the other NPEAs in Germany. Yes, four thousand! We were all led immediately to a large clearing, where an NPEA instructor (who was also a captain in the Wehrmacht) got up on a stool and, shouting into a bullhorn in an earsplitting voice that echoed throughout the hills, addressed the four thousand fourteen-year-olds in front of him.

"German youth!" he bellowed. "I am Captain Klemperer. You are here for five days of military maneuvers. Welcome! You will be divided into two armies — two thousand Blues and two thousand Reds. The Blues and the Reds will engage each other along a two-kilometer front. The weapons you use will not be guns, but hands, arms, and legs. The Blues will wear blue cloth wristbands, and the Reds, red wristbands. The side that captures the greater number of enemy wristbands over a five-day period will be the victor. Anyone who has his wristband taken from him loses his life but may obtain a new wristband and a new life. But *Achtung!* You must take care not to maim the enemy or break his bones or injure his eyes as you grapple with him for his wristband. You must all remain healthy and strong, for in a few years you will serve your nation in the Wehrmacht. So fight hard in these maneuvers and prepare yourselves for the future. Prepare yourselves! And now, let the war games begin! *Heil Hitler!*"

For the first four days, each side engaged in thrusts, feints, frontal attacks, night raids — every action it could take to outwit the other. For each side, a general staff consisting of both boys and NPEA instructors masterminded the military strategy.

I was on the Blue side.

At the start of the games, I got to know Benno Nagorsen, a Norwegian exchange student from Brazil. Benno was a tall, lanky, fun-loving boy who spoke German, English, and Portuguese in addition to his native Norwegian. He and I became fast friends.

And did Benno have fun with the German language! How he

loved to string long German words together into a never-ending sentence, making the whole thing sound like a fifty-car freight train rambling along a track backward! And how he loved to roll those words off his tongue! As we struggled to get out of our sleeping bags for a day of maneuvers, Benno would say to me:

"*Guten Morgen, mein General. Sind Sie heute der volkssturmführende, feindschlagende, säbelrasselnde siegesdurstige Oberster-heeresstratege?*" ("Good morning, my general. Are you today the battalion-leading, enemy-smashing, saber-brandishing, for-victory-thirsting master strategist?")

"*Nein, mein Leutnant,*" I would reply. "*Heute bin ich bloß eine eimer-schleppende scheuerlappenschwingende durch-ein-Kopftuch-guckende Putzfrau.*" ("No, my lieutenant. Today I am just a bucket-dragging, mop-swinging, through-a-shawl-peeking cleaning lady.")

And so, on and on we went. The fun we had helped to keep our minds off the unpleasant fact that at any moment we could get our Blue butts kicked by marauding Red raiders.

Then it happened. On the third day, Benno and I had the misfortune to be part of a small patrol that walked right into a Red ambush. Seven Reds — all huge, hulking specimens of the Master Race — jumped us, pulled us to the ground, and rolled us in the dirt for what seemed an eternity as we ferociously resisted their efforts to get to our wrists. Finally in possession of our wristbands, they waved their trophies triumphantly in the air and hurried off to do battle somewhere else. Benno and I just sat there, too dazed and demoralized to inspect the cuts, scrapes, and bruises on our arms and legs.

Our fortunes improved almost immediately. In order to lick our wounds after the beating we had taken from those enormous bruisers, Benno and I repaired to a small thicket. Immediately we saw that we had company.

"Can I believe my eyes?" I said to Benno, licking my chops. "Do I see before me, wearing red wristbands, two *little* Nazis?"

"Yes, my colonel-general," said Benno, suddenly coming to life. "Two tiny *Meistersingers.* Shall we have a go at them?"

We beat the crap out of them and took their wristbands. A small victory, perhaps, for the Blue side — but oh, such a satisfying one!

What took place on the fifth and final day I can only describe as a sort of Teutonic Armageddon. On that day, all two thousand Blues and all two thousand Reds collided headlong in the middle of a wide clearing in a frenzied, hour-long free-for-all that is still as fresh in my mind as if it had happened yesterday. After the battle, the Blue side, able to display the larger pile of captured wristbands as evidence of its military superiority, was declared the winner.

Once again, Captain Klemperer got up on his stool. "German youth!" he bellowed. "Today the Blue side is the winner. In the larger sense, however, all of you are winners. All of you have passed the three tests of perseverance, endurance, and bravery. Congratulations! You have fought for the everlasting glory of Greater Germany! *Heil Hitler!*"

As soon as our war games were over, we set out on a day-long hike to meet the buses that would take us back to our school in northern Germany. That part was fun, too, for as we hiked along we sang popular German songs — happy, carefree songs like "Monika" and "Hop-Sa-Sa." Fun, that is, until we started singing a few that didn't fall so trippingly off my tongue — songs about the coming Nazi conquest of the world! Here are the choruses from two of those songs:

> *Heute gehört uns Deutschland*
> *Und morgen die ganze Welt!*

> Today we own Germany
> And tomorrow the whole world!

> *Denn wir fahren,*
> *Denn wir fahren,*
> *Denn wir fahren*
> *Gegen England!*

> We'll be moving,
> We'll be moving,
> We'll be moving
> Against England!

I felt edgy and uncomfortable singing songs like that. "Why are we singing those menacing songs?" I asked my two closest friends, Dieter and Sepp. "What is a non-German supposed to think when he hears them?"

Both boys shrugged off my questions. "The songs are just songs," said Dieter. "Just songs — they don't mean a thing."

I believed those boys were being honest. In the six months I had known them, they had never given a hint that they saw a real war in their nation's future. But again I wondered out loud: "Why have they been taught to sing such warlike songs and to sing them publicly?" In the end, I decided not to make any waves. The next time the singing started, I joined in as lustily as the others.

For a teenager, peer pressure is not just an influence, it's a force so compelling that it can transcend nationality and politics. It's hard to challenge your peers — whoever they are — unless you've had some experience or guidance in doing so. I had had neither. For me not to have sung along would have been taken as an insult.

All of this happened just three months before Adolf Hitler sent his panzers roaring into Poland — a move that surely foretold his intention to go *"gegen England"* and to take over *"die ganze Welt."* Like the German people as a whole, these boys were self-confident, happy, even exuberant. The idea of Germany ever really having to go to war seemed far from their minds. After all, hadn't Hitler, their *Führer,* always helped himself to everything he wanted — the Rhineland? Austria? The Sudetenland? Czechoslovakia? "No problem — he can just keep right on going," I'm sure they were thinking.

And so the prospect of war was far from their minds. Even farther from their minds, I'm sure, was the notion that within five years, many if not most of those boys would be dead.

THE SUMMER BEFORE THE STORM

In June of 1939, with the close of graduation ceremonies at the NPEA, I said *"Auf Wiedersehen"* to Dieter, Sepp, Rolf, and my other friends. Would we ever meet again? Even under these strange circumstances, I had developed a fondness for many of those boys.

I was headed for Heidelberg, in southwestern Germany. There I could stay with my sister Nancy, a student at the university who had a small apartment. My plan was to enjoy a relaxing summer before returning to St. Andrew's in September.

Heidelberg — that dreamy old city nestled among forested mountains at the edge of the winding Neckar River! Heidelberg — that place of total enchantment! We strolled around the rose-pink castle towering above the brown roofs of the town. We enjoyed evening concerts in the castle courtyard. We hiked up the Philosophers' Way, halfway up the mountain on the side of the river opposite the town, and picked strawberries, raspberries, blackberries, and currants.

Summertime in Heidelberg, according to the song from the Romberg operetta *The Student Prince*, is the time for music and romance. At fourteen, I was too young for anything but the music, but Nancy, at the age of twenty, was ready for both.

Nancy was a stunning young woman with long jet-black hair, large dark eyes, and a flashing white smile. She loved every moment of life, and when she laughed she threw back her head and laughed uproariously. In Heidelberg, who could cut a more romantic figure than a beautiful American from the fabled Hawaiian Islands, one who spoke German and French, loved literature, music, and sports, and could throw her head back and laugh like that? German men pursued her in droves. Not just university students but professors sought her company. Nancy hated to leave me behind all the time, especially during the day, so sometimes the price of a date with her was that her escort take me along. On more than one afternoon, in an elegant café, I ate cheesecake and drank orangeade with the compliments of her escort, who doubtless would have liked nothing more than to slip me a few marks and tell me to get lost.

Then it happened — that magic moment a young girl dreams of. Nancy met Fritz Esser, *the* man to give meaning to her life. A tall, strapping fellow in his late twenties, Fritz was a native of Heidelberg and a physician at a sanatorium in the spa town of Bad Orb, fifty miles to the northeast. His blond hair and blue eyes, his chiseled profile, matched perfectly that of the ideal "Nordic model" depicted in propaganda posters all over the Reich. Very soon,

Nancy, das deutsche Fräulein (complete with braided hair), at the edge of the Neckar River in Heidelberg. This photo was taken in August 1939, three weeks before the outbreak of World War II.

my sister and Fritz fell crazily in love and became engaged to be married.

That summer I had some memorable days with Nancy and Fritz. They took me along with them on canoe trips up the Neckar River, to serenades and concerts in the castle courtyard, and to *Wienerschnitzel* dinners at the restaurant Zum Ritter, where a string quartet played "Tales from the Vienna Woods," "Vienna Life," "Voices of Spring" — Strauss waltzes so liltingly, so hauntingly beautiful that they created goose bumps on my arms.

My chats with Fritz were always fun. He praised me for my fluency in German but threw up his hands in mock horror when I made a grammatical mistake. Keenly interested in all things American, he loved to talk about American movies. "Do you think they will make a sequel to *King Kong?*" he asked.

"Definitely," I said. "The next one will be called *King Kong Goes to Heidelberg.*"

"Really?" He laughed. "I doubt that King Kong would be very happy in Heidelberg. None of our buildings are over four stories high."

"Doesn't matter," I said. "Hollywood plans to build a *Wolkenkratzer* [skyscraper] right here on the banks of the Neckar. What do you think of that?"

"A *Wolkenkratzer!*" He laughed again. "Ha! You are a *Spaßvogel* [jokester]!"

In ways like that, I tried to tickle Fritz's funny bone — which was hard to do because Germans don't have a funny bone. It's called the *Musikantenknochen* (the musician's bone) for some reason — I never found out why. At any rate, Fritz and I got along famously.

"He's going to make the best brother-in-law I could ever have!" I said to Nancy happily — and then, as an afterthought, "and a great husband for you!"

September 1. Germany invades Poland. It's war! It's World War II, in fact, as two days later Britain and France, horrified by this latest of Hitler's aggressions, finally decide to draw the line.

The outbreak of war posed no personal problem for me because I was about to return to school in the States. But what a dilemma it created for Nancy! Here she was, passionately in love with a wonderful German to whom she was engaged to be married. Over and over she asked herself, "Should I stay in Germany and marry Fritz? If I do, won't I have to forsake my family and country? If America enters the war, surely she will do so on the side of Britain and France. What to do? What to do?"

For two months, Nancy took long hikes up the Philosophers' Way and bit her fingernails to the quick as she tried to make a decision. In the end, reason ruled. Bidding a tearful, heart-wrenching farewell to Fritz, she returned, across two oceans, to Honolulu. Within eight months, she was married to a captain in the U.S. Marine Corps.

But the astonishing story of Fritz Esser had only just begun to unfold. You haven't heard the last of him by any means.

Now as for *me* — how do *I* get out of Germany? Five hours after the outbreak of hostilities, I find the German-French border totally blocked. Distraught, I grab a train from Heidelberg to Basel, in neutral Switzerland, then head straight for the American Consulate. Calming my palpitating heart, those good people provide me with tickets to Paris and Le Havre, with guaranteed passage back to the States. Two days later, minus baggage, minus my toothbrush, minus even my diploma from Heinrich Himmler, I board the *Manhattan* (which is jammed with cots like a troopship and carries twice its normal complement of passengers, mostly Americans fleeing the war zone) and speed across the Atlantic to New York. By September 19 (again a memorable birthday), I am not in a celebrating mood. I am, in fact, in a daze. And now, back at St. Andrew's, I'm about to start my fourth-form year.

The "sounds exciting" adventure is over — my rub with the Third Reich, my gallivanting in Gestapo-land! I flop into a chair, sweep my forehead with the back of my hand. All I can say is "WHEW!"

CRYING UNCLE

RELATIVES FOR GOOD AND ILL

I never got home to Honolulu again. Through five long years at St. Andrew's, until Father retired and moved with Mother to New York City, I never ceased to feel the agony of alienation — the only boy around without a home, without roots.

Only once did my parents come to see me — just once, for half a day — on a hurried trip elsewhere. I remember that visit vividly. For most of the time they were preoccupied with a cluster of clerics who showed them around the school. "It's just lovely here — such a nice atmosphere for your studies!" said Mother to me as we were surveying the campus. "Good to see you, dear boy!" added Father — these remarks being about the extent and depth of our conversation. Their attention was usurped by others who, at great length, described for them the history, architecture, and philosophy of St. Andrew's School. Despite the presence of my parents, the old feeling of emptiness prevailed, worse than ever. I didn't feel "visited" at all.

I was grateful, though, that hardly a week went by without my finding an affectionate letter from Mother tucked in my mailbox. Sharing news of family and friends, she always ended with "Father sends his love." Her letters made me feel even more homesick, so that at times I thought, "I simply cannot stand one more day in boarding school!"

Though I hardly saw my parents during those years, I did, from time to time, see Father's sister Mary and also his brother Elton, staying with one or the other when school was out for vacations. Aunt Mary proved to me what a wonderful aunt could do to make me feel special. Uncle Elton, on the other hand, proved what a straight-laced, humorless martinet could do to plunge a lonely, homesick nephew ever deeper into the Slough of Despond. As you hear in more detail about these two opposites, you will see how worlds apart two siblings can be.

Last I spoke of Aunt Mary, she and Aunt Helen were pleading with their brother Hank, my father, not to throw away a promising future as a clergyman by taking a missionary career among the "filthy, ignorant, heathen Chinese." Since neither sister ever married, the two shared a home — a red brick Colonial house on a lovely elm-lined street in Wilmington. Aunt Helen died in her fifties, felled by carbon monoxide in their garage. Aunt Mary lived on for fifty years in that house, taking in a niece for companionship.

A warm, kindly, fair-haired person, Aunt Mary centered her life around charitable work and presiding over the Women's Auxiliary of the Episcopal Diocese of Delaware. Never too busy for me, she encouraged me to have friends over for meals. Although herself childless, she seemed instinctively to understand us young people — our messy ways, our boisterous talk, our loud radios, our self-centered agendas, our sudden movements in a house filled with antiques.

My uncle Elton, by contrast, was a horse's patoot. Last I mentioned him, he was a boy growing up in Wilmington, too much a "goody-goody" to mix with his brother Hank's high-spirited, mischievous chums; forever boasting, "When I grow up, I'm going to be a doctor." Uncle Elton grew up, as I suppose he had to, and did become a doctor as promised. A graduate of Trinity College and Columbia University's College of Physicians and Surgeons, he settled in Yonkers, New York. Underneath that mantle of respectability as a doctor and pillar of the church, however, lay an ominous trait — one that I had dimly heard about from others in the family but which, when I

My uncle, Dr. Elton Gardiner Littell, my unofficial guardian while I was away at school. He grabbed the reins and cracked his whip over my young life.

showed up in his life, erupted full force — that inflexible nature, that
domineering top-sergeant syndrome. Well, perhaps "tyrant" is not too
strong a word for this bespectacled, mustachioed redhead — this
banty-rooster of a man straight out of Charles Dickens. I often wondered if his being childless, then finding himself my guardian, might
have provoked secret hostilities toward me. Hard to say. But whatever
his hangup, he found in me the ideal scapegoat; and I know that
whoever made the following observation must have been well acquainted with Uncle Elton: "Some people don't form relationships;
they just take people hostage."

In a moment, more on this strange case history — I say "strange"
because of the stark, almost ludicrous contrast not only between him
and his sister but also between him and the lady he married.

He and Aunt Nancy lived in an aristocratic section of Yonkers,
their large stucco home adorned with authentic treasures from Europe.
As you entered the drawing room, you caught your breath — the
effect was startling. The walls, all four of them, were papered in a
rich, antique gold, a perfect backdrop for the Medici-period decor —
the massive mantelpiece, ornate candlesticks, Savonarola chairs, tap-
estries, and other Florentine antiques. The ambiance of the room
bespoke the very essence of Aunt Nancy — that regal, to-the-manor-
born matron with the piercing, azure-blue eyes — her halo of naturally wavy, silver-streaked hair lending added distinction to her noble
profile.

I can still see "Her Ladyship" holding court, seated in her impos-
ing, thronelike chair and arrayed in a deep burgundy velvet hostess
gown. With a warm *"Bienvenue"* she welcomes her courtiers to the
inner sanctum — only those guests of significant social status; only
those who, like herself, can roll their *rs* like a Parisian, spice their
conversation with a *bon mot* or an occasional *"Mais oui ma chère, je
suis enchanté!"* One must be "culturally correct," according to the
philosophy of this woman of immense personal charm, intellect, and
discrimination in the world of literature and the beaux-arts.

There you have her. That was my aunt Nancy. But now comes the
jarring note. Just how could her "consort," my uncle Elton, even

begin to fit into such a cosmopolitan setting? (He was always quick to excuse himself from her soirées on grounds of "professional urgency.") If she could talk Monet, Savonarola, and Rembrandt, he could only talk mumps, septicemia, and rectums; if she could talk Italy, Versailles, and Paris, he could only talk ischemia, vaginas, and polyps. And so when there was company, he couldn't talk at all — he just took off. Disappeared. And how incongruous, his affectionate nickname for this aristocratic queen — a name bestowed upon her, perhaps, as compensation for her barren state. How she must have winced each time he addressed her as "Little Muv"!

Thus, while Father and Mother felt a kinship with people from all walks of life — people of all nationalities, races, and creeds — Uncle Elton and Aunt Nancy had no such feelings. They peered down their noses at people they thought were beneath their station and took pains to avoid them. Actually, of the two, Aunt Nancy was the full-out, card-carrying snoot. Uncle Elton, who was crazy about her, simply carried out her wishes with a fawning servility.

For years they had a black servant who did the cooking and served the meals. When they hired him, Aunt Nancy made him change his name from George to Whittington. I can still hear her calling him: "Oh, Whittington! Whittington!" How that name resonated, especially in front of guests! My aunt and uncle used personalized stationery that bore the address Yonkers-on-Hudson rather than just Yonkers. It sounded better, and it helped to erase the image of Yonkers as a factory town, home of the Otis Elevator Company and Alexander Smith Carpet Company. Uncle Elton and Aunt Nancy were Victorian relics.

Uncle Elton's and Aunt Nancy's prejudices flew straight in the face of everything my father and mother had worked by example to instill in us children. How Father and my uncle Elton could be brothers required a leap of the imagination that I was never able to make. And how the two of them managed to retain an affectionate regard for each other throughout their lives placed an even greater burden on my powers of comprehension. Brotherly love runs deep, I concluded, but Christian love surpasses all understanding.

THE BALTIMORE FLOPHOUSE

At age fifteen, in my fourth-form (tenth-grade) year at St. Andrew's, I blundered into a hopeless predicament. It was late March. All the students were headed home for twelve days of spring vacation. But, for me, home was Honolulu — a bit far away. Usually I vacationed with Aunt Mary in Wilmington, but this time she had the flu. Instead, I accepted an invitation to spend the first three days of vacation at the Baltimore home of a schoolmate, George Thornburg. But this failed to take care of my remaining nine days. "Well," I figured, "something will turn up." Well, something *did* turn up — something disconcerting, to say the least!

Meanwhile, my three days with the Thornburgs were great fun! They lived in a large Colonial house in horse country, surrounded by trees and a gentle slope overlooking acres of land. Nearby was their stable, full of horses. We played chess and Monopoly and spent hours on horseback, riding the trails that wound through their property.

"Today there's a dog show. Let's go!" said George's mother, so we all piled into the car. At lunchtime, when she pulled out a ten-dollar bill for hot dogs and hamburgers, I made the fatal mistake of offering to get them. On my way to the food stand, I either dropped the money or I was cleverly pickpocketed. Too embarrassed to tell her, I used my own money — all but a few cents — knowing that now I'd be bankrupt. What was I to do for the next nine days? Fortunately, I couldn't foretell, or the horrors would have been too depressing to contemplate.

My three days were up. At the train station, I said good-bye to my friends. Never did they suspect the sorry state of my finances — never would I have had the nerve to tell them! No money for a ticket, no place to stay, no means of getting a meal. Wandering around the heart of Baltimore, I wondered what a homeless, hungry, penniless boy was supposed to do for an entire dismal week!

Soon I found myself walking down a street crowded with bars, nightclubs, and strip joints. All around me, neon signs and marquees throbbed and vibrated. This was the notorious Baltimore Street. I spotted a rundown hotel that displayed the sign: "Lodging — 25¢ a night."

"Only twenty-five cents!" I murmured, my spirits rising. "With a few dollars I could make it through another week! If I pawn one of my suits for three dollars, then sell the pawn ticket for another three, I should have money for food and lodging and for train fare back to school." I pawned the suit, entered the dingy hotel, and paid for the first night's lodging.

Oh, but when I saw the accommodations, my heart stalled! A seedy, unshaven character came up to me, saying, "C'mon — this way." He took me into a darkened room that contained sixteen tiny cages. Each cage, six feet by four by four, was made of chicken-wire and held together by a flimsy wooden frame. Was I supposed to enter that contraption? Yes, I was. To do so I had to get down on my hands and knees and crawl on all fours through the chicken-wire opening!

Seven nights I spent in that flophouse! Seven nights next to other cages filled with vagrants, drunks, and dope addicts who kept up a night-long chorus of muttering, coughing, and cursing. Each night, one of them would discard an empty wine bottle by heaving it up against the ceiling and sending a shower of broken glass down on the room. All night long I kept a watchful eye open, terrified that one of those weirdos would break into my cage to rob or stab me.

What to do with my daylight hours? Easy. Just as Mother had always taken refuge in literature, I hiked over to the Baltimore Public Library and buried my head in Charles Dickens's *Tale of Two Cities*. I left the library only to get a bite to eat. During that week, I made a conscientious effort to vary my diet: whereas one day my dinner might consist of a White Tower hamburger and a Hershey bar, the next day it might well consist of a White Tower hamburger and a Baby Ruth.

One night, after an overdose of Dickens, I had a hideous nightmare. Here's how it went — surely a revelation of my state of mind. Two men break into my cage. Shouting, *"Tyran! Ennemi de la France! Vous allez à la guillotine!"* ("Tyrant! Enemy of France! You're going to the guillotine!"), they drag me out to the street, feet first, and toss me onto a tumbril in which a dozen other condemned prisoners sit in silent despair. As the cart rolls down the street, I suddenly become crazed, physically shattered, and so drunk with horror that I sing and try to dance. Clattering down the cobblestone street, we reach the Bastille, where a great crowd awaits our execution. Numb with fright, I watch as each prisoner, in turn, is taken from the tumbril and thrown onto a board in a prone position, his neck in the exact spot where the knife will fall. The last thing each person sees before death is the basket, directly in front of his eyes, into which, in a few seconds, his head will drop. Each stares wildly ahead as a heavily weighted knife, cut on a slant, drops on his neck with a mighty crash! The crowd roars its approval.

Now, finally, it is my turn! I am strapped to the board, numb and silent, and I await the end. CRASH! I am done for!

But no — that's not the solid sound of a knife descending on my neck — it's the piercing, splintery sound of a hurled bottle, a bottle slamming against the ceiling and sending a shower of broken glass falling to the floor. I blink my eyes and discover that I am in my flophouse cage. I quickly reach up to see if my head is still attached to my neck. *Remercier le bon Dieu!* — it is still there. However, my heart pounds wildly, my body shakes nonstop, and my shirt is cold and wet. I try desperately to settle down once again for a night of watchful rest, and finally I doze off.

Eventually, just as I feared, real disaster struck. Two days before I was to return to school, a big hulk of a man with red eyes and blue tattoos on his wrists cornered me in the tiny bathroom of the flophouse. He put his hands up to my face and twisted his wrists menacingly in front of my eyes to simulate the wringing of a chicken's neck. Then, baring his tobacco-stained teeth, he clamped his great hairy paws around my throat.

"I need money, boy," he croaked. "How much you got?"

"Four dollars," I said, quaking with fear.

"Gimme the dough quick!" he demanded.

"Can I keep two dollars for train fare back to school?" I sputtered through the vise tightening around my neck.

"No!"

"Please? Just *one* dollar so I can buy food tomorrow?"

"No! Gimme it all! Now! Quick, or I'll choke you till you turn blue and then stuff your head down the toilet and flush you into the next world!"

"Okay! Okay!" I gasped. "Here's the money."

While the man kept his tight grip on my neck, I fumbled in my pocket and pulled out the four dollars I had left. Grabbing the money, he stumbled out of the bathroom, leaving me not so much shaken up by the episode but actually ecstatic that my neck had not been wrung like a chicken's. But now, again, I was dead broke. I couldn't even spend my last night in that horrible place.

I spent that night on a bench in the train station. Early the next morning I hit the road and hitchhiked back to school, arriving just in time for dinner. The other boys were already back, and, at the dinner table, I heard their animated boasts about their holiday fun.

"I went to the New York World's Fair!" exclaimed one.

"I saw the Rockettes at Radio City Music Hall!" chimed in another.

"I watched the Rangers beat the Bruins at Madison Square Garden!" whooped a third.

Oh, oh! — I could see it coming. One boy turned to me and said, "So, Joe, tell us what you did."

I knew right off that I couldn't say, "Well, I spent seven nights in a Baltimore flophouse in a hideous wire cage surrounded by a dozen writhing, retching drunks and derelicts who spent their nights smashing empty wine bottles against the ceiling and showering me with broken glass while they considered the proper moment to break into my cage and crack my head open." No, I knew I couldn't cut it with a vacation like that.

So I improvised. "Guess what!" I told the boys in a burst of bravado. "I spent the week at Granogue, the du Pont mansion near Wilmington. My aunt Mary is a friend of the du Ponts — they go to the same church.*

---

*I actually had spent a weekend at Granogue. The du Ponts were members of St. John's Episcopal Church, where my grandfather had been the rector, and the relationship between the two families went back more than sixty years.

"The du Ponts have so many dozens of bedrooms, they have to name them. I stayed in the Blue Room. Next to the telephone in my room was a list of the other rooms: Pink, Yellow, Purple, Green, Chartreuse, Mauve, and so on. My aunt said that if there hadn't been enough colors in the spectrum, the du Ponts would have had to call upon God to create some more so they could name the rest of their bedrooms.

"The du Ponts have garages full of antique cars. Their son Irenée was home from college, and every morning he took me out for a spin in one of them. A 1908 Pierce-Arrow touring car. A 1908 Packard runabout. A 1913 Cadillac roadster with an electric starter — no hand crank!

"One morning he drove me down Market Street in a 1914 Stutz Bearcat. It's a wide-open car with no doors. We sat high off the road, in bucket seats, way above the trolleys and the new cars. Irenée lent me goggles, fur gloves, and a red woolen scarf. Everyone around waved at us. Boy, I felt like a monarch on his throne!

"Next morning we drove around town in a 1910 Rolls-Royce Silver Ghost. It was the finest luxury car in the world! It even had a mahogany dashboard. It was called the Silver Ghost because of its ghostlike quietness and shiny, aluminum body."

"Gosh!" came the chorus from my wide-eyed admirers. "Tell us more."

"Okay. Every day we took a different car out. Unfortunately, with only twelve days of vacation, there was only time to ride around in twelve different antique cars. Pretty exciting, fellas, but [sigh!] it all had to come to an end. So here I am." In the space of five minutes, I had put Baron von Münchhausen and Pinocchio out of business.

"Wow!" exclaimed one of the boys. "You had some vacation!"

"Yeah," I replied. "*Some vacation.*"

That night I rested on my laurels, but the next day, having to keep the truth to myself, I began to feel more and more cast adrift — a boy without roots, without a home, without anyone around who really cared. I sorely needed to find a way to turn my life around. I found that way eventually, but — alas! — not in time to forestall the following escapade.

AT THE BURLEY-QUE IN PHILADELPHIA

My uncle Elton and aunt Nancy had a daughter named Ashley. When I learned she was an adopted daughter, that cleared up a lot of my questions about Uncle Elton. Many times I had tried to visualize him making love to Aunt Nancy, but each time I failed the test. For me, he demonstrated the ultimate truth of the Darwinian theory of natural selection that I had just been learning about in biology class. What was it the textbook said? "Those individuals who are strong and are capable of adapting to their environment will survive, reproduce, and pass their favorable characteristics on to their offspring" — to which I added, *"The rest have adopted daughters."*

One spring day during my fourth-form year at St. Andrew's, I received a note from Uncle Elton. "Ashley is to be married next month," he wrote, "and all of the Littells are being invited — all except you, Joe. That's because you need the time to study and bring up your grades."

What a crushing blow! I was sure my brothers Edward, Harrington, and Morris would be attending the wedding in Yonkers — a rare chance for me to see them and to feel once again like a member of a family. I hadn't felt that way since leaving Honolulu at the age of twelve.

Suddenly I had a compulsive need to assert myself — to do something dramatic, something that would keep me from simply becoming lost and forgotten forever by my family.

On the day of the wedding, after Aunt Mary had left her home for the ceremony, I took a bus to Wilmington, jimmied open her garage window, found the keys to her new Chevy, and, with heart pounding, hit the accelerator, backed out, sideswiped some lilac bushes, and sped on my way — I didn't know where. But I soon had an idea.

Several of my schoolmates had seen the burlesque show at the Trocadero Theatre in Philadelphia, known as "the Troc." I had never forgotten the wild tales they told me about that place. Itching to see for myself, I called Bill Ashton, a friend who had once lived in Honolulu, and asked him to come along. He leaped at the chance.

His alibi to his parents? "Joe and I are headed for the intercollegiate crew races on the Schuylkill."

What a ball we had, Bill and I, at the "burley-que," as many called it! When Sophisticated Sophie came onstage, wearing nothing but a G-string, and started doing rapid forward thrusts of her belly while lying on her back, the small elderly man on my left leaned over and spoke to us:

"Dis ya foist time at da boiley-que?" he asked.

"Yep," I answered.

"Yep," said Bill.

"Ya know what Sophie's doin'?" he said. "She's doin' grinds on da floor. I been comin' here for twenny years an' I never seen grinds on da floor. Ya know what grinds on da floor are?"

"No," I confessed.

"No," echoed Bill.

"To do grinds on da floor, she hasta do all da twists an' bumps an' grinds of da belly dance, an' do 'em all while she's layin' on her back. It's almost impossible to do — 'specially da bumps."

Bill and I were transfixed. We sat there motionless throughout the show. Periodically our faithful guide would bring us up to speed as to what was going on.

"Look," he said. "Here comes Virginia Dare. She's da *real* bump artist. She can shoot her pelvis all da way across da stage an' get it back in half a second."

"Wow!" I said.

"Wow!" said Bill.

A little later, when Morganna the Wild One (45-23-39) came on, our trusty guide said to us, "Watch her carefully. She'll flash her G-string. She lifts it just enough to spice up da act, an' everybody goes nuts! She can get fined fifty bucks for doin' dat if da manager catches her. He don't wanna get raided by da cops."

At the end of the show, we thanked our friend profusely for the bump-by-bump commentary. On the way out, to our surprise, he caught up with us again. "My name's Charley," he said. "Wanna see a pitcher of me and my ex — my oistwhile wife? She's a ecdysiast.

Dat's da fancy woid for a stripper — ecdysiast. I used to call her 'Dizzy-ass.' Her professional name is Lady Starbuck. We was married for three months. One night she took off all her clothes at da boiley-que an' den took off wid all my money. I didn't know she already had a husbin'."

Charley showed us a snapshot of himself with Lady Starbuck. She was a tall, supermammillary blonde standing there with nothing on but high heels. Charley, wearing a natty pin-striped suit and bow tie, was standing in front of her, close up, his small head nestled between two gigantic boobs.

"Dat's me in da middle!" he chuckled.

We said good-bye to Charley again, and at the entrance I bought a couple of postcards of a *maxi*-mammillary ecdysiast riding a camel. "One of these is for the boys at school to prove I was here," I told Bill. "And the other is to send to my uncle Elton so he can see what he missed by going to that dumb wedding."

That evening I returned Aunt Mary's car, took the bus back to school, and told my wide-eyed schoolmates all about the burlesque.

When Aunt Mary returned from the wedding, her neighbor told her she'd seen me take her car out of the garage. I was in big trouble. Not only had I taken her car without permission, but I had put a dent in a front fender. Ouch! When Uncle Elton heard about this, he told Aunt Mary that, being my guardian, he himself would set my punish-ment. He decreed that I should repay Aunt Mary for the damage done to her car — about sixty dollars — by giving up my thirty cents' weekly allowance for as many years as it took to repay her. Mercifully, Aunt Mary never pressed me for the payments. She seemed, in fact, quite happy to forget the whole idea. I apologized to Aunt Mary for taking her car and promised it would never happen again.

In spite of its aftermath, the Saturday that Bill and I spent in Philadelphia was a wonderful, memorable day. I never did tell Aunt Mary that I had parked her car for most of the day in front of a burlesque house; there were just some things that the president of the Women's Auxiliary of the Episcopal Diocese of Delaware didn't need to know. Nor did I ever tell Uncle Elton that at the same time the bridesmaids were at the church trying to catch Ashley's bouquet, I was at the burley-que trying to catch the kisses that Morganna the Wild One (45-23-39) was blowing to all of us in the audience. Whoopee!

It was thirty-five years later, in the 1970s, that I drove past the Troc while I was in Philadelphia for a sales meeting of my publishing company. Although the theater looked seedier than I had remembered it, otherwise it appeared much the same — except, of course, for a fresh set of names on the marquee: Ann Teaque, Luna Landing, and Polly Esther.

Plus ça change, plus c'est la même chose.

MY FIRST LOVE

Oh, that Patty Dupree — that tiny brunette with the flashing smile — she was my first girl. When I was sixteen, I met her at a party at Bill Ashton's house in Wilmington. Five feet tall, with curly brown hair, brown eyes, and a perky, turned-up nose, she was friendly, so easy to talk to — in fact, she absolutely wowed me!

Whatever gripes we had about boarding school, there were three events each year that excited and delighted us. Those were the house parties — weekends that aroused wild anticipation for weeks in advance. Yikes — the girls were coming! On those occasions, anywhere from seventy to a hundred girls descended on the school for a weekend of dances, interscholastic sports, and other activities. Mustering up my nerve, I invited Patty to be my date at the fall house party.

At the dance on Saturday night, Patty was a big hit with the boys — especially with Thomas Babington Hayes III, a suave, good-looking classmate who didn't have a date for the weekend. Once, after he had been dancing with Patty, she disappeared. Finally I found them out in the cloisters.

"Patty!" I complained, "I've been looking all over for you!"

"Oh," said Tom nonchalantly, "we were just getting a breath of fresh air. We're coming right in."

Later, Tom danced with Patty again. And again she disappeared. This time I found them down at Noxontown Pond.

"Patty," I said, a little more irritated this time, "I've been looking all over for you!"

"Oh," said Tom, "we were just getting another breath of fresh air. We'll be right in."

(If you have seen the 1989 movie *Dead Poets Society*, you will remember the cloisters and Noxontown Pond; St. Andrew's was the setting for that film.)

Toward the end of the evening Patty disappeared for a third time. I couldn't find her anywhere. Finally I asked Bill Sargent, another classmate, "Have you seen Patty? I haven't seen her for half an hour. I have a hunch she's with Tom Hayes."

"Haven't seen either of them," said Bill, "but if she's with Tom Hayes, you can be sure she's in good hands — and I mean *hands*."

"Humph!" I said. "Tom thinks he's God's gift to women. If he doesn't lay off her right away, I'm gonna go up to his room and swipe his Anti-Pimp." (Anti-Pimp was a popular skin-colored cream that boys used to cover up facial pimples.)

"Good idea," said Bill with a supportive laugh. "Does Tom still use Anti-Pimp?"

"Does he use it!" I laughed. "Haven't you noticed? He even puts it on before he goes to bed to impress the girls in his wet dreams."

"Well," said Bill, giving me further support, "maybe without his Anti-Pimp, he'll turn tail every time he sees Patty so she won't get a look at his pimples and blotches. You'd like that, wouldn't you?"

"You're darned right!" I grinned.

After a further search, I still couldn't find Patty. Finally I went upstairs to Tom's room to see if he had taken her there. I doubted it, because a boy could be expelled from school for being caught with a girl in his room. Nope, he wasn't there. But seeing his bed, I took a moment to pour half a jug of apple cider between his sheets so that when he crawled under the covers that night, he'd say to himself, "Oh, God, did I wet my bed last night?"

False alarm. Patty hadn't been with Tom at all. I found her chatting with another girl in the school kitchen. "Oh, well," I thought, "it still won't hurt if Tom panics, wondering if he's gone back to bed-wetting. He's given me a royal pain all weekend."

I invited Patty to the next weekend party in January. Just before it started, I confronted Tom. "Listen, Buddy, I don't mind if you dance with Patty this weekend, but don't pull any funny stuff like taking her out for fresh air all the time. Okay?"

"Who, *me?*" replied Tom in feigned shock. "Would I do a thing like that?"

My velvet-gloved approach to Tom worked, because this time I didn't have to keep solving the Mystery of the Missing Date.

Another big event loomed, scheduled for Saturday afternoon in the gym. It was the wrestling meet between St. Andrew's and Lawrenceville. I was on the school wrestling team, representing the 165-pound class, and had the formidable task of taking on the undefeated captain of the Lawrenceville team. The gym was jam-packed, with students and faculty hanging from the rafters, it seemed. On the mat, I was a raging bull — not so much because I wanted to win for the school, but because I sure didn't want to lose in front of Patty. It was an exciting, seesaw match, with several near falls registered by each wrestler. At the end, few among the hundreds of spectators could tell who had won, and when the referee held up my hand, the gym exploded.

After the meet, who should come up to me, of all people, but Thomas Babington Hayes III. Right in the presence of Patty he shook my hand and said, "Nice going, Joe — good match."

"Aha!" I thought. "A ritual admission of defeat on his part! Two stags have locked horns in a fierce struggle for possession of a mate, and one, bruised and weary of the battle, has withdrawn, giving the victor his sign of submission." Just call me a dreamer! The idea, at any rate, made me very happy.

During my senior year I wangled occasional Saturdays away from school just to see Patty. Whenever I held her hand or kissed her, I didn't care if I *never* saw my family again. "True love" it's called! And yet I wasn't sure if she liked me — I mean, *really* liked me. I did notice, though, that when we were together she laughed a lot. I figured that if a girl laughs a lot when neither of you is saying anything funny, that's a very good sign. It means she really likes you. I felt good about that.

Patty told me things no one else — not even family members — had ever told me: that I was smart, clever, interesting. For sure, my parents and others had hinted that I had "a lot of potential," but never once did they go so far as to suggest that I might be using any of it. With eyes afire, Patty talked of her aspirations — her wanting to do well in high school, her ambitions to enter the University of Chicago, to wind up as a history teacher. Strange — by contrast, I had hardly given thought to college or career. Without preaching, she kindled a fire in me, forced me to face my own future, to realize that *now* was the time to prepare for the next stage of life, whatever that might be. Nobody had ever before tried to engender in me any such interest in my future. It took a sixteen-year-old girl to do that! And yes, when she said, "Joe, you're smart — you have a lot going for you upstairs," this made a strong impact on me. Before I knew it, I began to believe it, then act it, then *be* it! *"Carpe diem!"* I said to myself. "Seize the day!"

Graduating from St. Andrew's in June 1942, I took a summer job as a camp counselor and in the fall entered Trinity College, the alma mater of my father, my brother Harrington, and my uncle Elton. Likewise, Patty graduated from high school in Wilmington and entered the University of Chicago. We vowed to write to each other and to meet again during the Christmas holidays. But of course we couldn't foresee what circumstances would dash those hopes.

CAGED LIKE A COUGAR!

It was a great day — that day in September 1942 when, as a freshman, I first set foot on the Trinity College campus. The freedom afforded me was intoxicating. I could come and go as I pleased, set up my own schedule, choose my own courses. Exhilarating, too, being a member of the Alpha Delta Phi fraternity, where an air of "eat, drink, and be merry" prevailed. Parties, girls, sprang up everywhere, and for me, with my family five thousand miles away, the company of a pert, vivacious girl (if it couldn't be Patty) was a comforting substitute.

However, there were uncertainties, scary ones. The ground was no longer solidly under my feet, for now, almost a year after the Japanese attack on Pearl Harbor, the vibrations of that horrific war were becoming increasingly felt here in the States. Already two of my brothers were in the South Pacific — Edward an army chaplain, Harrington a navy lieutenant. And here I was, expecting to be called up at any time.

By the end of the fall semester, I wasn't at all proud of my grades — an A, three Bs, and a C. Passing grades, yes, but nothing to crow about. Apparently this didn't bother my parents, but blast it! Why did my report card have to fall into the hands of my uncle Elton? Who decided? I had a hunch, when he and Aunt Nancy invited me to their home for the holidays, that he would show displeasure at my failure to apply myself. But in no way was I prepared for the reception that awaited me in Yonkers. No smile at the front door. In grim silence he escorted me upstairs, straight to my room. Then came his stern admonition: "Joe, I find your report card a distinct disappointment. For your entire vacation you are to remain in your room and do nothing but study. Here, take these history and literature books and study them from cover to cover. I will bring up your breakfasts and lunches on a tray. Only for dinner may you come downstairs to join Aunt Nancy and me."

Stunned, thoroughly intimidated, I asked, "May I telephone friends in Wilmington I'm expecting to see?" He said no. "May I call a local friend from summer camp who is expecting to see me?" Again, a flat no.

Badly demoralized, I quickly wrote to Patty to tell her of my disappointment. I also wrote to my parents in Honolulu, telling them, not about my uncle's tyrannical treatment of me, but about college life. When I asked Uncle Elton, "Please, will you mail these two letters?" his response was noncommittal, but he took them anyway. A funny feeling inside made me sense that those letters would never reach their destinations. As I later learned, my hunch was correct.

When the upstairs telephone rang, I frequently overheard my uncle's voice: "No, he's studying. . . . No, he can't be disturbed. . . . No, he's not taking any messages. . . . Good-bye."

To top off these indignities, my close friend Cliff Nordstrom, a student at Williams College, knocked at the front door but was abruptly turned away. In the past, Aunt Nancy had scanned him disapprovingly because he lived in the Park Hill section of town — not in prestigious North Yonkers.

These unceasing humiliations made me scalding mad. Yet, because I was a guest, and because I had been reared in the Chinese tradition of showing respect for my elders, I kept quiet. But, churning inside, I wondered, "How can this man, my father's brother, this physician, this avowed churchman — how can he treat me with such disdain?" In defiance, I didn't even open the textbooks he had commanded me to study. Instead, I browsed through a stack of Ashley's books that she had hidden in her closet. One book, *Sex Comes After Marriage*, brought a devilish gleam to my eye. I thought of wrapping it up and giving it to Uncle Elton as a reminder of his conjugal duties, but then I concluded, "What the heck. It won't do that ossified old Victorian goat any more good than if it just stays in the closet!"

What an awkward affair, our Christmas dinner! At my place setting, nicely gift-wrapped, was a handsome pen and pencil set. "Thank you both," I said, and then added somewhat pointedly, "I had planned to give you a present, but unfortunately I have been unable to get to a store."

"We understand perfectly," replied Uncle Elton with the soothing solemnity of a funeral director.

It wasn't until later that evening that my uncle brought to my room two letters from my parents, one bearing the welcome news that Father was retiring. He and Mother would soon be moving to New York City. Fuming inside, I thought, "Why did my uncle withhold these letters from me? He should be sent up the river to Sing Sing for tampering with the U.S. mails. What right does he have to control my life this way?" As I thought about it, I felt sure that my parents never did formally, actually, make him my guardian. It all just came about by default.

The day after Christmas, still agitated, still caged like a cougar, I began pacing my room. With his eagle eye on the lookout, Uncle Elton must have suspected I was planning a jailbreak. So what did he do? He locked my room at night.

Of course I was plotting my escape! I recalled that Ashley had laughingly told some of us younger Littells of her own escape from paternal dominion. How? She let herself out from the second-floor window with a bedsheet in order to keep a forbidden date. That memory gave me the inspiration, the impetus I needed. I, too, would fly the coop!

At nine P.M. on December 27, I tied two sheets together and the end of one to the radiator by the window. Then, dropping my suitcase out the window and starting to climb out, I was sitting astride the sill when *oops!* Suddenly I heard a sickening sound. Could that be a key turning in the lock? I scrambled back into the room just as the face of Uncle Elton emerged. Spying my stripped bed, hit by a cold draft, he marched straight to the window. By now that face was the color purple! Out there hung two sheets, flapping in the breeze — for sure not out there to be dried in the sun (or moon!).

"Joseph Fletcher Littell! WHAT, WHAT, WHAT do you think you are doing?" he roared.

Coming up with the best ad lib of my life, I replied, "I was just going out to mail a letter."

"Well, young man, you're not going to mail any letters, and you're not going to escape," he warned. "There's a perfectly good front door for you to use on January fifth when you're due back at college. Just try to leave here before that date and you'll be mighty sorry, I promise you."

Damn! I had been caught red-handed! Anyway, I was not about to abandon the idea of making a break. Then, just as I was plotting my strategy for a second try, something dawned on me. Holy mackerel! Did my uncle say I was due back on the *fifth?* The due date was the *eighth!* He had misread the calendar! If I could hang in there until January fifth, I'd still have three whole days to see Patty. What a break!

I was a model prisoner until January fifth, even when I had to celebrate New Year's Eve all alone in my room. On the fifth, I quickly said my good-byes to my aunt and uncle and hightailed it out of there — three days early! I made a beeline for Patty.

When I told her how I had spent my vacation, she hugged me and kissed me and ran her fingers through my hair and told me, "You're the most wonderful person I've ever met." While she was saying and doing those things, I kept thinking, "I might just be interested in going back into Uncle Elton's lockup for another three weeks if this is the result it produces!"

The following April it came — the notice for me to report for induction into the U.S. Army. I had fully expected that notice. But never in my wildest nightmares could I have imagined that within the next two years I would be in the thick of the greatest battle of the European war; that I would receive a battle wound in the leg; that I would be taken prisoner by the Germans; that I would escape from prison camp only to be recaptured by the enemy and threatened with death; and that I would finally — Well, hold on! The next chapters will tell the tale.

THE BATTLE
OF THE BULGE

ZIGGING AND ZAGGING ACROSS THE ATLANTIC

It was an ill-fated day, that October 1944, when a mammoth troopship pulled away from her New York pier and headed for the European battle zone. Aboard this former British luxury liner were crammed fourteen thousand soldiers, including me, of the 106th Infantry Division — the youngest, greenest bunch of peach-fuzzed draftees ever to set sail. Most of us, no more than eighteen or nineteen years old, had been taken almost in mid-milkshake from the corner drugstore — rank-and-filers who had acquired no more than five months of infantry training at Camp Atterbury, Indiana. It's a blessing we didn't realize the magnitude of the confrontation with the Germans that lay in wait!

The 106th Division was on its way to face the Wehrmacht on Germany's western border. In command was Major General Alan Jones, a stocky, fifty-two-year-old regular army man with no combat experience whatever. Under General Jones, in command of the 422nd Regiment (to which I belonged) was Colonel George Descheneaux, who, likewise, had never been tested in battle. With that manifest lack of experience, both in the ranks and at the command level, it was perhaps inevitable that we would be headed for a collision of disastrous proportions with the enemy.

To avoid the usual shipping lanes where German subs lay in wait, the *Aquitania* took seven days rather than the usual five to reach England. Steaming due east to the Azores, she then cut north toward England. To further distract the subs, she made sharp, irregularly timed zigzags, changing course slightly every thirty seconds or so to dodge whatever torpedoes might be scudding in her direction. All of these maneuvers resulted in sudden lurches to the left and right that had many of my fellow GIs holding their seasick bags at the ready. Add to that the pitching and rolling of the ship when the sea got rough. Sometimes the stern rose so high out of the water that the churning propellers sent the ship into convulsive shudders. Many GIs, never having been to sea, lay in their triple-decker bunks, puking and mewling. My particular quarters became a giant barfatorium. This I was happy to escape; having had sea legs ever since I could remember (on many a rough sea voyage to and from China), I simply took my sleeping bag topside and slept the sleep of kings under the stars.

Soon after the ship set sail, my company commander, Captain David Ormiston, called all of us in I Company to the smoking lounge. "Men," he said, "you will have two meals a day. You'll get your mess schedule shortly. If you're late, you miss your chow. Right now there are two important things to remember on this trip. First, water is extremely scarce — use only what you absolutely need. Second, fire and panic are more of a danger to us than German submarines. Smoke only in the designated areas, and I caution you — snuff out your cigarettes completely. And whatever happens, stay calm." What he didn't tell us was that if the ship were sunk, there would be lifeboats enough for only three thousand men.

Feeding fourteen thousand troops was a logistical nightmare. We often had to wait in line for half an hour in a narrow, hot, crowded corridor to get to where the food was served cafeteria-style. On our second day out, several of us in I Company complained among ourselves that the GIs who had already eaten had to scrape their trays into huge metal garbage cans not more than four feet from our chow line. The deafening clatter of all those trays slamming against metal cans was more than we could stand. Unaware of the possible consequences, I decided to assume the mantle of leadership and have the situation corrected myself. And so, as he walked by, I buttonholed the mess sergeant.

"Sergeant," I said politely, "would it be possible to have the garbage cans placed a little farther away from the chow line? The noise is intolerable, and the smell is enough to make us lose our appetites."

The sergeant looked me over thoughtfully. "Gee, fella," he responded with an outrageously exaggerated smile, "I really can't put those slop cans anywhere else because we're so tight on space. You see, the corridors in this old tub are much too narrow. But if it'll please Your Highness, I'll be happy to have nice white lace doilies placed under the garbage cans so you'll feel more comfortable dining here." Then, with a jerk, he moved right up close to me, thrust his chin in my face, and in a voice that spat venom between clenched teeth he sneered: "Listen, soldier. This is wartime. This is a troopship. Who the fuck told you you were being booked into the Waldorf-Astoria?" His face now beet red, he wheeled around and disappeared into the galley. My humiliation, my embarrassment, in front of my buddies was total.

The 106th Division passed the month of November near the village of Stow-on-the-Wold in Gloucestershire, awaiting combat orders. My regiment, the 422nd, was billeted on a seventeenth-century English manor lent to the U.S. military by the earl of Gloucester. The palatial manor house became Regimental HQ, while we men lived in Nissen huts set up around it. On the evening of November 30, we received our orders. "We move out at 0500 tomorrow," said Captain Ormiston. "Until then, you are restricted — and I mean restricted — to quarters."

"Restricted, hell!" said two GIs in my hut, knowing full well that within ten days we'd be in the front lines. Ignoring the order, they sneaked out to Stow, soon to return with four sudsy buckets of ale. Before any of us could whip out our canteen cups, however, the call came down from Regimental HQ to assemble in front of the manor house for final orders. This we did, on the double. While we were there, Eddie Callahan, a freckle-faced Irish kid from Pittsburgh, returned to our now-deserted hut from an AWOL walk in the woods. Spotting four buckets of what looked like excellent soapy water, he rinsed out all five pairs of his filthy, smelly GI socks and hung them up to dry. Shortly, the rest of us returned, and while Eddie sat on his bunk, staring in disbelief, we dispatched all four buckets of the lip-smacking brew, agreeing to a man with Sergeant Elmer White of Muncie, Indiana, who happily declared, "English beer is the best fuckin' beer in the whole fuckin' world!"

It wasn't until December 11 that Eddie Callahan came clean about how and where he had washed his socks — that was after we had moved into the line facing the Germans in the Ardennes. "I thought I'd better 'fess up in case I don't make it outa here," he told us. "But if I do make it back to the States, I'm gonna become a millionaire. I'm gonna head straight for the Anheuser-Busch Brewing Company and sell 'em my recipe for the best beer in the whole world. They won't even have to change their brewing process — just add one step!"

Eddie did make it back to the States. But he was one of the lucky ones. Five days later, endless, terrifying thunderbursts of German artillery fire crashed down on the 106th to signal the beginning of the greatest battle of the war in Europe, the Battle of the Bulge.

The 106th Division's lack of experienced leadership, the inexperience of almost all of the young soldiers, and some outrageous doses of bad luck that we were forced to swallow every day conspired to put us all into the history books. In four days the 106th suffered almost complete annihilation. Some nine thousand troops were killed, wounded, or captured. It was the greatest U.S. defeat in Europe in World War II. It was also the largest mass surrender of U.S. troops, with the exception of Bataan, since the Civil War.

Exactly what happened? Although history books record in detail the Battle of the Bulge — the thwarted efforts, the collapse of those valiant U.S. regiments — let me tell you my version — my personally experienced, on-the-scene version — of that last, pivotal engagement on the Western Front. Here is how it looked from the eyes of a survivor — an ordinary, rank-and-file GI infantryman.

THE GERMANS ATTACK!

On December 11, 1944, just two months after we left New York, the 106th Division went into the line. Our assignment was to defend a front twenty-seven miles long on the Schnee Eifel, a high ridge in the heavily wooded hills of the Ardennes. My regiment, the 422nd, took over the northern end of this front. The two other regiments, the 423rd and 424th, were strung out to the south of us. Our sleeping quarters were log-buttressed dugouts covered with earth.

Our regimental commander, Colonel Descheneaux — who had never fired a shot in anger — was now in command of three thousand troops in the U.S. Army's most advanced position in Germany.

It was the coldest winter in a quarter of a century. On the Schnee Eifel, face-freezing winds swept up the long slope to the ridge that I Company was to defend. We took comfort in the commander's words: "The Ardennes has been designated a 'quiet sector' — a training ground for you so that you can get toughened and get used to fire." Well, at least with Christmas coming, this would be a place free of fear and anxiety. Or so I thought.

No sooner had we moved into the line than Captain Ormiston, our company commander, announced that through an unfortunate oversight the 422nd Regiment's overshoes had been left behind in the move across the English Channel. It wasn't long before wet feet in freezing temperatures caused severe cases of trenchfoot, with about twenty percent of the regiment suffering swollen feet and painful circulatory problems. "Thank God for all my barefoot years in Honolulu!" I thought. With my soles and heels as tough as leather, I developed no trace of trenchfoot.

Five days later, on December 16 at 5:30 A.M., our world blew up on us. A hell-directed bombardment of rockets and artillery shells such as we had never heard, seen, or even imagined screamed over our heads and crashed into the night behind us. Red and yellow flashes lit up the sky. Deafening detonations shook our dugout. Amid the thunder we could make out the distinctive screeching sound of what we later learned was the *Nebelwerfer*, a multiple-barreled rocket called the "screaming meemie."

In I Company we were more stunned than afraid. "What the hell's going on?" we asked one another. No one knew. But soon appeared a breathless runner from Regimental HQ with instructions from the commander: "Go on combat alert for a German ground attack and await further orders."

For a full hour, the bombardment raged on. Then, just as suddenly as it had started, it stopped. Immediately the German ground attack started. All along the Ardennes it burst forth — all along an eighty-mile front. At this point no one on the American side had any idea of the scope of the enemy offensive. No idea that *three German armies — a force of 300,000 men in fifteen divisions, 1,000 tanks, and 2,100 artillery pieces — were moving west through the forests to attack a force of 83,000 unsuspecting Americans!*

This was Hitler's last chance. He was throwing all of his might into a desperate effort to destroy the Allied armies poised on Germany's western border. The battle that took place, in which the Germans punched out a salient sixty miles wide and fifty miles deep, came to be known worldwide as the Battle of the Bulge.

By late morning, as still no German activity was observed in my company's area, word came down from Regimental HQ that the thrust of the enemy assault was to the north of us, on the 422nd Regiment's northern flank, and to the south of us, on the 423rd's southern flank. The Germans, it seemed, were pushing west along the *outer* flanks of the two regiments and leaving most of us in the 422nd alone — at least for the time being. Our orders? "Dig in along the ridge and, in the event of an attack, hold the ridge at all costs."

For the rest of the day and throughout that night, all was quiet in my immediate area. When I went on patrol, no German activity was revealed at the bottom of the slope. All we could hear was a continuing distant rumble of artillery to the north and south of us, where battles were raging.

On the seventeenth, I had my first real taste of combat. This was without question the most upsetting experience of my entire life.

That morning, our company was still dug in along that ridge sloping down to the east. About five hundred feet down the slope was a stand of tall fir trees. Suddenly, from behind those trees emerged a dozen German soldiers. At top speed they started to run up the slope toward us.

"Here they come!" I called over to Art Kranz from the shallow foxhole I had dug out of the frozen ground. Art was dug in on my right.

"I see 'em!" called Art.

"Jesus Christ!" exclaimed Ben Kruger, dug in on my left. Several other GIs up and down the line tightened their grips on their M-1 rifles as the enemy soldiers charged up the hill toward us.

"Hold your fire," ordered Sergeant J. B. Parish, our platoon sergeant. "Wait till they get closer. I'll tell you when to fire."

Clutching my rifle, I aimed it at the Germans. I gulped several times. To me, each gulp sounded like a cannon shot.

The Germans continued up the slope. Whether they saw us or not, I don't know, but they were charging straight at us, rifles in hand, their green greatcoats flying. A squadron of butterflies did a power dive in my stomach.

Then something strange happened. When the Germans were about three hundred feet away, unaccountably they made a quick about-face, as if to obey a command from the rear, and ran back into the woods. "Why are they withdrawing so suddenly?" I puzzled. "Were they surprised to find Americans defending this ridge? Were they a reconnaissance patrol that had orders not to get into a firefight? Were they being told to wait for reinforcements?" I didn't know. The butterflies started to level off in my stomach.

But wait a minute! Not *all* of the Germans withdrew. Two of them still kept running toward us. Apparently they hadn't heard the order to withdraw. Perhaps the thunder of artillery fire in the distance had made it impossible for them to hear the order. By now, in their overeagerness or inexperience, they had simply gotten themselves too far forward.

The two Germans ran with that gangling, loping stride that you sometimes see in teenagers. They kept advancing, advancing, advancing. Now they were less than a hundred feet from us. The soldier in the lead could not have been more than a boy. As I squinted at him through my rifle sights, I had a strange hallucination: he was bathed in a silvery metallic glow and he kept running in stops and starts, as in a stop-action sequence — first in speeded-up motion, then in a freeze-frame, then in a speeded-up motion . . .

"FIRE!" ordered Sergeant Parish. Ben, on my left, fired. A split second later, so did I — at the German in the lead. Instantly he straightened up, lurched forward, and fell in the snow. His rifle fell on top of him and bounced off his helmet. He lay motionless, face down in the snow. I was the one who got him. It was my bullet that killed him.

With another crack of rifle fire from Art, on my right, and others down the line, the second German straightened up, threw out his arms, and collapsed in the snow. And now, except for the distant rumble of cannon fire to the north, all was still.

Two Germans had been our adversaries, and we had dealt with them. Was all of this somehow familiar? Of course. My mind reverted to those war games I had played, years before, when I had been an exchange student in Germany. "But oh, how different this time!" I thought. "These are no NPEA war games. This time we didn't just grab two boys, wrestle them to the ground, and take their wristbands. This time we killed them. KILLED THEM! And I myself had shot and killed one of them!" I was now in near shock — numbed by the enormity of what I had done. I had snuffed out the life of another human being! Hit by this realization, I felt my entire body go limp, my legs wobble under me. Leaving the ridge for a moment, in a trancelike state I paced the frozen, snow-packed ground, trying to pull myself together. Thinking some food might help, I dug out a cracker and an Army D ration (chocolate bar) from my pocket, but no sooner had I swallowed them than I threw up everything on the snow. Returning to my foxhole, I tried to keep my buddies from noticing how distraught I had become after that incident on the slope.

What a grim moment — what a twist of fate — that soon after, on patrol duty, I had to revisit the scene — had to pass very close by the corpse of the soldier I had slain. As he lay on his stomach I could see one side of his face. Surely he was no more than sixteen years old. (It was only after the war that I learned that the Germans were conscripting sixteen-year-olds into the Volksgrenadier or "People's Infantry" divisions. They had to make up for enormous losses on the Russian and Western fronts.) I now looked at the other dead German. He had been shot in the face. Everything from his neck up was a huge blob of bloody dough. A horrible sight!

SURROUNDED BY THE GERMANS!

Late in the afternoon, German tanks and infantry succeeded in slipping behind the 422nd and 423rd regiments, stuck on the forward slopes of the Schnee Eifel, and cut them off from the rest of the 106th Division. By midnight, eight thousand American troops were surrounded. Colonel Descheneaux called General Jones, back at Division HQ, with an urgent request for help. Jones, in turn, called the commander of VIII Corps, who promised to send the 7th Armored Division to relieve the two trapped regiments. VIII Corps also promised an air drop of much-needed ammunition, food, and water. The 7th Armored, delayed by clogged roads leading to the front, never arrived. For a number of other reasons, including bad weather, the air drop didn't materialize either.

Early on December 18, General Jones finally gave the order to the two regimental commanders to break out of the Schnee Eifel trap and attack the flank of one of the German spearheads speeding westward. That morning, with high hopes, the 422nd and 423rd started their breakout.

But what a cruel letdown awaited us! My regiment, the 422nd, got lost in the woods and took a snow-covered road that dissolved into half a dozen paths. We ended up a whole mile from the place planned for the breakout. The 423rd's breakout was then called off. Meanwhile, as the German noose drew tighter and tighter around us, the two regiments were contained within an area of less than two square miles. We knew the situation was desperate.

On December 19, the 422nd made another attempt to break out of the pocket. Heading down a road leading west, we suddenly bumped into the Führer Begleitbrigade (Hitler's Bodyguard Brigade) and came under heavy fire. Armed only with M-1s, light machine guns, and bazookas, we were in no position to attack German tanks and flak-wagons mounting 20mm guns. Plunging into the woods for cover, we fired at the German infantry behind the tanks. All I could do with my feelings of hopelessness and fear was fire away at everything that moved in a forest-green uniform. Even if I wasn't sure I had hit anything, I was able to soothe my nerves by taking up the GI war cry: "Take that, you Kraut sonofabitches!" Then, from out of nowhere, came a large force of Volksgrenadier troops, who proceeded to attack our right flank. Down went one GI. Then another. I was terror-stricken. From behind a tree, I didn't know where to fire next. To make matters even worse, I sensed that I was no longer with I Company. Had I become lost in the fog and confusion? Then, suddenly — from I don't know where — came the yell of an American officer: "Pull back! Let's get outa here!" Rapidly we withdrew toward our pocket on the Schnee Eifel. A good thing, too, because, attacked from two directions, we'd have been butchered, wholesale, into oblivion.

Then, good God! Just when I thought I was safe, something slammed me to the ground. I was hit! Instantly, I was out cold. Remembered nothing more. Absolutely nothing.

How long was I blacked out? God knows. When I awoke, I was lying on a blanket. A medic with a red cross pasted on his helmet was kneeling over me. Sharp pains shot up and down my left leg. Looking down, I saw it was covered below the knee with bandages.

When the medic saw my eyes open, he reassured me. "You're going to be fine, soldier," he said. "I pulled a pretty good shell fragment out of your leg at midcalf, cleaned the wound, and treated it with sulfa. You're going to be okay. What you need to do is lie here and rest for a while."

"I appreciate what you did," I told him, noting his expression of concern and sympathy. "Where am I?"

"You're at the Battalion Aid Station."

Looking around, I saw a number of other casualties, either on stretchers or wrapped in blankets. Among them I spotted a friendly face from I Company. It was Eddie Callahan, the kid who washes his socks in beer. His shoulder was crisscrossed with heavy bandages.

By now, the 422nd and 423rd Regiments were squeezed into an area of just over one square mile. From all directions, incoming shells were exploding, and we were taking bad casualties. We were nearly out of ammunition. We had no artillery. No antitank guns. By midafternoon, back at Regimental HQ, Colonel Descheneaux viewed the situation as hopeless, especially when patrols scouting the perimeters of the area could find no escape routes. At a later date, it was reported that when Descheneaux saw long lines of wounded being carried into the Regimental Aid Station, he was sick at heart. When finally he saw one of his company commanders being carried in on a stretcher with his leg blown off, he made up his mind about what he was going to do. At about the same time, the commander of the 423rd was ready to make a similar decision.

SURRENDER TO THE ENEMY!

At about four o'clock that afternoon, while I was dozing on my blanket, I found my platoon sergeant standing over me.

"Littell, how're you doing?"

"I'm okay," I said.

"Can you walk?"

"Yep, I think so."

"Well, you better get up then, 'cause the order came down for us to surrender."

Surrender? Being still only half awake, I hardly grasped the significance of what he had said, unable to react to it emotionally. I sat up. Where was my rifle? Nowhere in sight. Then I noticed about forty feet away a truck and a weapons carrier stacked to the railings with rifles, mortars, machine guns, and pistols. Those were *our* weapons!

I decided to walk over to Regimental HQ, nearby. A lot of activity was going on there — soldiers milling about, trucks backing and forthing noisily. I spotted several German officers talking with a group of American officers. In a few minutes, the Germans beckoned to their troops waiting at the bottom of the slope. They now ran triumphantly up the hill and, upon orders, searched the Americans for pistols, knives, and other weapons. A Volksgrenadier frisked me, snatching my watch and a pack of cigarettes. Flipping through my wallet, he stopped to glance at a snapshot I had of Father and Mother standing in front of their New York apartment and one of Patty holding up her Persian cat. "Is this bastard going to take my photos?" I thought, trying to control my anger. *"Darf ich bitte die Bilder behalten?"* ("May I please keep the photographs?") I asked. Apparently surprised to hear me address him in German, he glanced at me for a second, then handed back my wallet.

Before long, all of us in my company, along with hundreds of others in the 422nd, were trudging over the ridge, double file, guarded by German soldiers. We soon reached a road that would take us eastward into Germany. Only then did I come to the full realization that I was no longer a combat infantryman in the United States Army. I was a prisoner of war!

Thoroughly dejected, I turned to the prisoner walking beside me. "You know, Jim, I expected that one of these days I'd march into Germany, but never for a second did I expect it would be *this* way. If only it *hadn't* been this way! I'm much too proud an American for this to happen. What about you?"

Jim just nodded and said nothing. Bone-weary, he was too disheartened to talk. He just shuffled along. As with most of the other men, his head hung low.

No, I had never dreamed it would end this way. Nor had I imagined that for the rest of my days I would carry around on my left leg a piece of scar tissue four inches long and one inch wide. It clings to me constantly, wherever I go, whatever I do. Refusing to let me forget my four days on the Schnee Eifel, it is a leechlike legacy of the Battle of the Bulge.

9

Prisoner of War!

GERMANY ON 400 CALORIES A DAY

Under heavy guard, we began our trek eastward into Germany — a long column of tired, wet, hungry, unshaven GIs wearing expressions ranging from bewilderment to resignation. My own spirits, already depressed, sank even lower when a German guard strutted up and down the line of prisoners, giving us in his best textbook English the latest "news" from the front. "American prisoners!" he bellowed in an insufferably haughty tone, "the war now goes in Germany's favor! American and British forces are thrown back in a catastrophic defeat until they reach the North Sea! Germany will therefore win the war after all!" I found that news almost impossible to believe, but hearing it only added to my confusion and misery.

After nightfall we reached the village of Bleialf, which had been heavily damaged by American artillery. There, in a churchyard, we spent the night, many of us with only a single blanket to ward off the bitter wind. I shared my blanket with another prisoner, and together we were able to fend off the cold. At dawn I could see that the village was deserted. But in the early morning mist, my eyes caught sight of — God, what *was* that? A trio of clowns putting on an act for our entertainment? No, it wasn't! Straining my eyes to identify the ghostly formation, I shuddered, for now I could tell. It was the corpses of three German soldiers. Each one was frozen into a grotesque position. One sat on his motorcycle with an outstretched arm, his index finger pointing to the moon. Another was lying on the ground, the front of his torso raised as if he were doing pushups. The third was just sitting upright in the snow. All three, no doubt victims of the U.S. bombardment of Bleialf, still wore their helmets. The almost choreographed nature of that little tableau on a snow-covered road was an unnerving sight — one that never will be erased from my mind.

In the morning, still without food since our capture the previous afternoon, we continued our march. "Where are they taking us?" we asked one another. Our uncertainty placed added strain on nerves already drawn taut from tension and fatigue.

After an hour's march, the guards halted our column for some reason. It was during that period of waiting that a German noncom ordered one prisoner: "Take off your boots — I want to try them on for size." Then another German started walking down the line of prisoners to see whose boots might fit him. Each one of us became inwardly upset, then aghast, as we realized the dire consequence to any soldier forced to remove his boots. In that sub-zero temperature, in a matter of hours he would expire. In no way could he walk barefoot through the snow — he'd be left by the wayside, abandoned. In protest, many of us emitted long, loud groans and shouts of "Hey!" At the sight of a prisoner with one boot already off, we became frantic. "That Kraut bastard!" exclaimed one prisoner to me. "That murdering sonofabitch!" I echoed. Finally a German officer, investigating the commotion, instructed his guards to quit removing the boots. What a relief — especially since any one of us could have been next! I now shook the snow off my boots — I had packed the white stuff all over them and stood there rooted to one spot in hopes of making them look as unattractive to the Germans as possible — all the while praying, of course, that none of them wore a size 11D.

As we continued our march to Destination Unknown, sharp shafts of pain streaked up my leg where that enemy shell had slammed into me.

"How're you doing?" an American medic inquired after he saw me limping. "I'm afraid I have no medication to give you."

"It hurts," I told him. "But painful as it gets, I console myself thinking how lucky I am. That fragment could have fractured a bone in my leg and prevented me from walking at all. If I falter on this march, the German guards will leave me by the side of the road to die. I'll freeze to death. I'm not going to let that happen!"

Exhausted after four more hours of marching, we reached the town of Gerolstein, where our guards led us to the railroad station and herded us like cattle into boxcars, sixty of us in each car. There we endured the long, dark night.

And what a miserable night it was! In my car we were packed together so tightly we couldn't move. Everyone had to sit upright on sweepings of stale straw. Fresh air could enter only through small slits near the roof, so that soon the atmosphere became stuffy and unbearably smelly. The next morning the guards brought us the only food we would receive until Christmas, four days later. Each prisoner got two slices of dark bread, a tablespoon of molasses, and a slice of corned beef. When the guard slid open the door to bring us the food, I called out to him in German, "Where are we going?" To my surprise, he obliged me with an answer: "You are being taken to a POW camp near Frankfurt." That, I reckoned from my knowledge of German geography, would be about two hundred kilometers to the east. "Well," I said to a couple of other prisoners, "at least we now know where we're headed."

It took four days to cover those two hundred kilometers. The train constantly lurched forward and scraped to a halt, moving only when an engine was available. No rush. We were low-priority cargo. Much of the time our cars sat idle in a railroad yard.

After the first night, a prisoner called to a guard, "Will you let us out to go to the toilet? We have no place to go in here."

"Create your own sanitation facilities," the guard shouted back.

This situation, we saw, would require extraordinary creativity! But one GI rose to the occasion. Said he, "Why not designate several GI helmets as toilets? We can dump the contents through those slits up there onto the tracks. For toilet tissue, we've got straw," he added. "Not exactly smooth, quilted, scented, two-ply straw, but — well, this really isn't very funny!" So that's what we did. We used straw for toilet paper, and when we ran out of that we used — my God, I hate to tell you this — we used letters from home.

BOMBED IN OUR BOXCARS BY THE BRITISH!

The third night of this horror trip we spent in Limburg — in the railroad yards. It was there that the British taught us the meaning of "friendly fire." They almost bombed us into the next world! Mosquito bombers of the Royal Air Force dropped flares all around the station and then splattered bombs all over the tracks. High explosives landing close to my boxcar sent it rock-and-rolling. The sharp, piercing crack of exploding bombs nearly ruptured my eardrums, sent my brains flying through my ears. By the light of the flares, I could see my fellow prisoners. Some were praying the rosary. All were strangely quiet except for one who kept screaming, "What town is this? What town is this?" His fear was driving him mad! And his screaming was driving the rest of us mad, too! As for me, anything I might say aloud would merely trivialize my terror, so I sat there quietly shuddering, my blood running cold. Our German guards had long since fled into the woods and left five hundred of us exposed to our deaths. Why was my end of the train spared when, at the other end, two cars were blown up? I have no idea how many GIs back there were killed.

As our train inched along the track, I peered through a tiny crack in the wall to confront a grisly panorama: twisted boxcars, human bodies, scattered body parts. I wanted to throw up. With no food in my stomach, however, all I could do was retch. (After the war, I learned that, the skies having cleared over the Ardennes by now, Allied bombers were striking at German railroad stations through which supplies would have to come. The stations in Limburg and Gerolstein were ordered attacked until they were unusable.)

AT STALAG IX B (BAD ORB)

On Christmas Day we reached our destination. "This is Bad Orb," said a guard, "the location of Stalag IX B, the POW camp where you will be held."

Did he say "Bad Orb"? Hadn't I heard of that place before? This was the town where Fritz Esser, my sister Nancy's prewar fiancé, had been a physician at the sanatorium! As we trudged through the town on our way to the Stalag, we passed, of all places, Fritz's medical facility. "Whatever happened to Fritz?" I wondered. Very soon I was to find out.

Surrounded by a barbed-wire fence, Stalag IX B was a compound of thirty rundown wooden barracks. As many as eighty-five of us were crammed into one of them. There were no beds, no bedding. No soap, no water beyond a trickle from one faucet. As for the toilet — just a hole in the floor. When the five hundred of us arrived, there were already nine hundred Russians and five hundred Frenchmen in the camp, with more Americans due to arrive at any time.

This was Christmas Day. One GI tried to launch some carol-singing, but who had the energy, the motivation, to make music? All we had for dinner was three thimble-size potatoes, a cup of watery turnip soup, and a slice of black bread. That diet provided fewer than a thousand calories. Three thousand are necessary for an average active man of twenty. As our captors well knew, this was a starvation diet. Soon, as the lack of food and medical attention took their toll, most prisoners became weak, listless, unable to ward off pneumonia. Within four weeks, five Americans would be dead.

We noticed, by contrast, how healthy and well fed the German guards and administrative staff appeared. I was perpetually angry at the sight of all those jowly, florid-faced soldiers in our midst.

There was still one more intolerable cross we had to bear. Like many of the other prisoners, I became infested with lice. The nasty creatures attached themselves to the thick inner seams of my combat fatigues, especially under the arms, where they lived and reproduced.

I lay awake at night scratching myself raw. The Germans ignored our repeated requests to be deloused.

HANS KASTEN, "CHIEF MAN OF CONFIDENCE"

Soon after we arrived in camp, there rose to prominence a man by the name of Hans Kasten. What was special about him? Why was his name on everyone's lips, captives' and captors' alike? Who was this man, Hans Kasten?

No, Hans was not a German, although his name might lead you to think so. "Hans," in fact, was the German nickname for Johann, his real given name. Hans was an American prisoner of war, of German descent, from Milwaukee. He had been captured in the Battle of the Bulge along with many others from the 28th Infantry Division. He was a tall, spare man of twenty-seven with brown hair and a striking Van Dyke beard. An aura of self-confidence surrounded him. His blue eyes had the sharp, searching look of an eagle. Though he spoke German fluently, he was an American through and through. Make no mistake about it: every bone, every sinew in his body, was American. And soon enough — very soon, in fact — the Germans would find that out, and it would not be at all to their liking.

The American prisoners, who were living in fifteen barracks, chose a leader for each unit. In turn, the fifteen leaders chose an overall leader. It was Hans Kasten who was selected for this role as overall leader. Hans acquired the title "chief man of confidence," or *Hauptvertrauensmann*, following the European military tradition — a leader who speaks the language of his captors and interprets their instructions to his fellow prisoners while at the same time working on the prisoners' behalf. A man of confidence receives no additional food or special favors.

Hans designated two German-speaking assistants to help keep communications flowing between him and the rest of the prisoners. One of the persons he selected was me. The other was Ernst Sinner, a short, dark-haired man in his mid-twenties who, like Hans, was an

Hans Kasten, the leader of the American prisoners at Stalag IX B (Bad Orb) and later at Work Camp 650 (Berga). Though of German ancestry, he was an American through and through.

American of German descent. A native of New York City, Ernst had been a waiter at Elisabeth Flynn's Restaurant.

Once he became the leader of the American prisoners, Hans lost no time in tackling our two most urgent problems. He got permission to have the terrible Russian cooks replaced with Americans. Immediately the soup became a little more edible, especially with the addition of some barley. He also persuaded the Germans to have the prisoners deloused. Soon we were all taking showers in water containing a foul-smelling delousing agent. But do you think that any of us cared about the smell? Show me a man who has lice falling off him and I'll show you a happy man! With treated steam, our clothes, too, were thoroughly deloused.

By now, with lice no longer plaguing my body, my curiosity peaked. Where was Fritz Esser — what happened to him? Through a chance meeting with a civilian worker at the Stalag who had worked in the sanatorium, I got my answer. "Major Fritz Esser, commander of a German medical unit," he told me, "was killed at Stalingrad in November 1942." Ironic it is that in wartime, one can grieve over an enemy officer! I couldn't help but think:

Fritz, you were like a big brother to me. Back in 1939, during that summer in Heidelberg, you talked to me about American sports and movies and music. Although I was only fourteen, you made me feel like a grownup. And now you're dead. I'll cherish your memory, Fritz. You were a good friend. I'll miss you.

In mid-January came exciting news from an American fighter pilot who had been shot down and was being held at Bad Orb: "The Allied armies have taken back all of the territory lost in the Battle of the Bulge." He beamed. "They're pushing eastward across the German border." We were deliriously happy to hear that.

More and more frequently now, prisoners in the compound craned their necks heavenward to watch American P-51s tangle with Messerschmitt 110s. One day, when a Messerschmitt went down in flames almost directly over the Stalag, a soft cheer went up from the American prisoners. I say "soft" because no one wanted to anger the Germans to the point where they would withhold a meal from us, as they had several times threatened to do. Besides, they were probably still smarting from a graffito that someone had penciled on the wall of the German staff building:

> One, two! Eins, zwei!
> Soon you'll all eat pig shit pie!

An incident now occurred that was to have enormous repercussions throughout the camp. It would alter the lives of a great many of the prisoners.

The camp was to be inspected. Toward the end of January, a delegation from the International Red Cross was due to arrive to check out conditions in the camp. Guards hustled to patch windows, place buckets of coal briquettes next to each stove (with admonitions that the coal was not to be used), and worked feverishly to add other temporary niceties. Hans was then summoned to the Kommandant's office and advised exactly what he could and could not tell the expected visitors. When the delegates arrived, he spent two hours with them. Ignoring his orders, he divulged everything he was instructed not to tell, sure that whatever he said would be kept in strict confidence.

"Imagine my shock," he told me later, "when those Red Cross bastards took me down to the big boss — the Kommandant himself — where they opened their notebooks and started from the beginning of my thought-to-be-confidential condemnations of the camp and its administrators! By the dagger looks the Germans gave me during the exposé, I could foretell my future."

Two days later, Hans was again summoned to the second floor of an office building. In a meeting room that had one table with eight chairs around it, he was told to sit in the chair that had a loaf of bread in front of it. Obviously a bribe. When all were seated and after some small talk, a German officer opened the meeting:

"We want you to supply us with the names of all those of the Jewish faith in the American sector of the camp."

Hans pushed the loaf of bread to the center of the table and said scornfully, "We're all Americans. We don't differentiate between religions."

This brought an uncontrolled response, sudden and violent. Two officers picked him up and threw him bodily down the stairs to the first floor. Luckily for Hans, no bones were broken. I do believe that after the Red Cross affair, these officers were salivating for the slightest excuse to do him harm.

Returning to our camp, Hans called together all barracks leaders, along with Ernst and me, and described what had just happened. "I want you all to tell the men in your barracks what has occurred," he said with great feeling. "Tell them that in all probability there will soon be repercussions. And tell them to get this absolutely straight: *No one, under any circumstances, is to admit to being Jewish.*"

That afternoon, armed guards with fixed bayonets marched into the American camp and forced us all to line up — the troops in back, the fifteen barracks leaders in front of them, and Hans at the very front, with his two assistants, Ernst and me, beside him.

A German officer stood on a platform, with the guards all around us, their guns at the ready. I can still hear these words from that infuriated officer: *"Alle Juden, ein Schritt vorwärts!"* ("All Jews, one step forward!") In view of Hans's earlier instructions, nobody moved. Obviously, this was of his doing. So angered was the officer that he leaped off his platform, grabbed a gun from a guard, swung it like a baseball bat, and slammed Hans across the chest. Hans flew backward and hit the ground, gasping. For a moment he couldn't get back his breath. While he lay there, the guards marched down the lines, picked out for a "train ride of reprisal" everyone they thought looked Jewish. When they finished, the officer raged: *"Kasten, du auch, und deine Assistenten."* ("Kasten, you're going too, and your assistants.")

That's how we found ourselves in the boxcars to further hell.

AT WORK CAMP 650 (BERGA AN DER ELSTER)

It was February 8 when a trainload of American prisoners that included Hans, Ernst, and me pulled out of Bad Orb for an undisclosed destination farther east. Aboard were three hundred and fifty Americans, including those thought by the Germans to be Jewish, plus sixty "troublemakers" of various nationalities. Things didn't look good for any of us.

It took five days, with overnight stops in Fulda, Gotha, Erfurt, and Weimar, to lurch two hundred kilometers. Finally, on February 13, we saw our new quarters: Arbeitslager (Work Camp) 650, in the mining village of Berga an der Elster, in the heavily forested region of Thuringia. This was an old coal-mining camp called the Erzgebirgische Steinkohlenfabrik, A.G. Now it was clear to us what the Germans were up to. They had brought us here to be slave laborers. In our emaciated condition, they were going to force us to work in the mines. My God! Our lives were now gravely at risk. Each of us knew it.

Work Camp 650 consisted of an old mine, snug up against the edge of a hill, plus a dozen old wooden barracks where we were to live. The barracks were enclosed by a high barbed-wire fence.

The day after we arrived, Hans and I witnessed German guards herding about a dozen American prisoners into a mine tunnel. We saw other prisoners straining and groaning as they pushed mining cars filled with dynamited rock out of another tunnel. We were enraged. (We didn't find out until after the war that we had been brought here to dig tunnels for what was to be an underground weapons plant.) At once Hans beckoned Ernst and me to accompany him to the office of the camp administrator. He was S.S. First Lieutenant Hack, a dark-haired man of medium build, about forty. His lips twisted slightly when he spoke. "What do you want?" he asked gruffly, leaning forward in his leather chair.

"We've come to ask that you not put the prisoners to work," said Hans. "They are far too weak. They will not survive. I respectfully request that you comply with the provisions of the Geneva Convention that pertain to the treatment of prisoners of war."

The lieutenant gave Hans a disgusted look and sat back in his chair. "The prisoners have been brought here to work," he snapped, "and that's what they will do."

Hans's voice became more urgent. "Lieutenant Hack," he insisted, "I'm sure you are aware that forcing prisoners of war to perform hard labor is a direct violation of the Geneva Convention. I'm sure you also know that anyone who issues such an order will one day be held to account for his actions. I respectfully request, once again, that you not put prisoners to work in the mine."

The lieutenant drummed his fingers on his desk. Then, dropping his voice, he said, "Kasten, I already know something about you. May I see your identification tag?"

Reaching beneath the jacket of his fatigues, Hans pulled out the dogtag that hung on a chain around his neck. The lieutenant rose from his chair, walked over to Hans, and, taking the dogtag in his hand, slowly and deliberately and in a mocking voice read the name on it:

"JOHANN CARL FRIEDRICH KASTEN.

"You are a German who has come over here to destroy the German Reich," he sneered. "You are a traitor to your country. You know, Kasten, there is only one thing in the world that is more despicable than a Jew. Do you know what that is?"

Hans didn't answer.

"It's a German who betrays his country. I should have you working in those tunnels — not just like everyone else, but working a double shift. But I won't do that. You see, Kasten," he added facetiously, "I have something more interesting in mind for you. Something much more interesting."

Turning to me, the lieutenant asked, "Are you Jewish?"

"I'm a Christian," I answered. "I am a follower of Jesus Christ. And Jesus was a Jew."

"Don't talk to me about Jesus," he snapped. "I asked you only if you're Jewish."

Then he turned to Ernst. "Are you Jewish?"

"No," said Ernst. He was telling only half the truth; his mother was a Jewish immigrant from Germany who grew up on New York's Lower East Side.

Abruptly, the lieutenant stood up. "It's time to end this meeting," he said. "I'm very busy."

The next day he put a large detail of prisoners to work hauling carloads of rock out of the damp, dusty tunnels. Many of those unfortunate souls emerged from the tunnels coughing and choking. All were covered from head to foot with rock dust.

One of the first to die was Victor Franck, who had served with me in I Company. He had been enfeebled by starvation and pneumonia even before he was forced to work in the mine. As I looked at his corpse, now only a rag-clad skeleton, I remembered the day in England when he confided in me. "I've sent a V-mail letter to my girl-friend," he told me happily. "I've asked her to marry me as soon as I return from the war." Vic left for the battlefront before he could receive her reply. And now I wondered: was that reply still waiting for him somewhere? Was it a yes or a no? And how would his girlfriend react when her next news of him would be not from him but from the War Department?

Nothing in the war angered me quite so much as the sight of that skeletal figure, the shape of his skull chiseled out through drawn cheeks. All I could think was: "May God damn to eternal hell the bastards who did this to these men!"

Food rations at Berga were even more meager than those at Bad Orb. All we received daily was a small bowl of watery potato or turnip-green soup and one or two thin slices of bread. Each of us now resembled a bag of bones — our skin drawn tightly over our skulls. Most of us were wracked with dysentery and, once again, suffering that slow torture — we were crawling with lice.

One day Hans made a distressing discovery. A convoy of food and medical supplies that the Red Cross had earmarked for POW camps in central Germany had all been diverted by the lieuten-ant to a German field hospital in Breslau. With Americans dying daily in Berga, Hans and I were beside ourselves with rage and frus-tration.

"If only someone could get word to the Allied forces about the plight of the prisoners here," I said to Hans.

Hans clearly had something else in mind. Wearing a preoccupied look I had never seen on him before, he scanned the high, forbidding barbed-wire fences that surrounded the camp. Then, slowly and softly he said, "If only someone could find a way to get out of Berga."

ESCAPE!

One morning — it was March 2, to be exact — Lieutenant Hack came to Hans with a huge cat-that-swallowed-the-canary grin on his face.

"Kasten," he said, "I have news! The camp has just acquired two dogs. They are attack dogs, trained to hunt people down. Try to get a good night's sleep tonight because tomorrow we plan to turn you loose and see if the dogs can get you. They're already trained to kill, but such dogs should, by constant practice, be kept in top condition, don't you think?"

Well! Rather than be torn apart by ferocious dogs, Hans made a quick decision. He would try to escape. At noon, he informed Ernst and me of his plan.

"I'm making an escape try after dark tonight," he confided.

"Take me with you," I said.

"Me, too," said Ernst.

"Ab-so-lute-ly not," declared Hans in a tone of flat rejection.

"Please!" begged Ernst. "We can help you to escape."

"And the three of us can all work to get back to the American lines," I pleaded.

"Look," said Hans. "You're both staying here. In the first place, that SOB has nothing against the two of you. In the second place, the chances of success are about one percent. The answer is no."

Ernst and I kept pressing Hans to take us along. Finally, worn down by our persistence, he agreed. That afternoon we gathered the items we needed for our escape. We now had the following:

- 1/2 loaf of dry rye bread
- a few spoonfuls of margarine
- 2 boxes of matches
- a razor and 2 razor blades
- 5 sticks of TNT and blasting caps, used in the mines
- 60 Reichsmarks

Late that afternoon, a prisoner by the name of Goldstein got wind of Hans's plan and offered him $20,000 in New York if he would take him along. Hans refused.

That evening, after the guards had locked the doors to our barracks, the three of us were lying flat on our bellies underneath the building, as shown, with just enough room to squeeze out when the time came.

To our good fortune, perhaps due to a power failure, floodlights A and B were out that night. Lights C and D, however, were intact and threw a shadow of the building onto the slope ahead of us. When guard #1 reached his turning point, the three of us crawled up to the barbed wire fence.

Hans and I pulled the wire to the right and left while Ernst went through. Ernst then pulled from the outside where I had been pulling from the inside. Then I went through and pulled where Hans had been pulling. Hans, the last one, was halfway through the fence *when the guard started down the stretch toward us!* We all lay dead still, our hearts thumping wildly. Any second I expected his gun to go off several times, and I figured that if he hit the dynamite in Hans's pockets, there wouldn't be much of us to find.

Remember, it was winter. The guard looked cold — his collar went up to his eyebrows. Amazingly, he failed to spot us, turned, and started back. Hans crawled the rest of the way through the fence, and for a moment we lay there pondering our chances; the shadow extended only about five meters ahead of us, and beyond that the ground was brightly lighted. Suddenly a shrill siren — an air raid

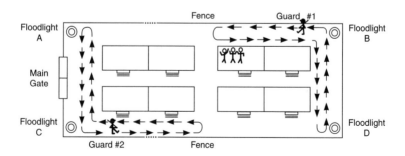

alarm — pierced the night. All the lights went out. This was our chance!

"Run! Run!" whispered Hans. We got up and ran like fury just as the guards poured out of their barracks. Would you believe that they, too, didn't see us? Perhaps, as they dashed out of their lighted rooms, their eyes had not adjusted to the sudden darkness. In any case, we flew right past them and kept right on running, spurred on by thoughts of those two vicious dogs.

All night long we hiked westward. With no compass, no stars to guide us, we had only Hans's intuition to point us toward freedom. With the dawn, we stopped and hid in the woods. We cut the shoulder straps off our overcoats and snipped off the brass buttons that displayed the telltale American eagle. Hans then shaved off his beard.

For two days, hiking westward through woods, across fields, and on side roads, we tried to avoid farmers and burghers. To augment our meager rations, we dug sugar beets out of the mounds made by farmers to feed their cattle in winter. In this fashion we weren't making more than twenty-five kilometers a day — a worry, because we knew that the U.S. lines were at least three hundred kilometers away. We needed to make better progress. We soon found a way. On the afternoon of March 4, a light snow began to fall, turning our olive drab overcoats into a wonderful, anonymous white. We were now emboldened to hike along the better, straighter roads in order to make faster time — even though doing so meant meeting an occasional passerby. When someone greeted us with an amiable *"Guten Tag"* or *"Heil Hitler"* along with a Nazi hand salute, we cheerfully returned the greeting and salute. After a while, to forestall any suspicions, we ourselves initiated the *"Heil Hitler"* and salute. (If only our draft boards could have seen us!)

At nine o'clock that evening, we came to the village of Göschwitz. Spotting an inn, we entered to see if we could get a room for the night. The innkeeper looked at us incredulously. *"Sind Sie wahnsinnig?"* he asked. "Are you crazy? Don't you know that since the bombings people have been sleeping in the hallways? Try the inn up the street."

We did but had no luck there either. So we peeked inside the

Bierstube, or tavern part of the inn. With all the drinking and noise-making going on in that crowded, dimly lit, smoke-filled room, we figured it would be safe to go inside, warm up, order some food, and be lost in the crowd. So into the *Bierstube* we went, seated ourselves at a corner table, and gave the waiter our order for bread, sausage, and dark beer. (We didn't plan to drink the beer, in our exhausted condition, but thought we could blend into the scene better with seidels of suds in front of us.) How good it felt to be warm again! We hadn't been that warm since the Germans captured us back in December.

It was then that we became careless and everything started to unravel.

OUR DOWNFALL: A TAVERN IN THE TOWN

Sitting near us in the tavern was a German air force officer. We took little notice of him, and he seemed not to pay much attention to us either. We went about our happy business of savoring the food and pretending to drink the beer.

I then made a terrible mistake. It was stupid, unforgivable. As the waiter brought our order, I complained, *"Ich habe ein furchtbares Durst."* ("I have a terrific thirst.") That was a grammatical error. I should have said, *"Ich habe einen furchtbaren Durst,"* to make the adjectives match the masculine noun *Durst.* It was an error that no German makes, but that of a foreign student who hasn't mastered the gender of German nouns. At once realizing my mistake, I became grievously upset. Why had I been so careless in the presence of the waiter? But when he returned to our table later — all smiles — and asked if there was anything more he could get for us, I began to relax.

But now the air force officer began to look at us suspiciously. He must have heard my remark. He made us so nervous, we decided to leave. He decided to also. Catching up with us at the door, he asked, "May I see your papers?"

Drawing himself up to his full height, Hans replied haughtily, "We don't have to show you anything."

The officer now took another tone. "You are trying to find a room?"

he asked. "The innkeeper down the street is a friend of mine. I think I can help you."

He escorted us to the inn we had previously left, and once we were in the common room, with many people around us, he again demanded, "May I see your papers?"

"We don't have to show you anything," repeated Hans, bluffing. "If you want to see our papers, why don't you call the police?"

Which is exactly what he did. Within minutes, two elderly policemen showed up in their green coats and shiny black helmets, carrying rifles. Politely they said, *"Bitte, meine Herren, Papiere zeigen."* ("Please, gentlemen, may we see your papers.")

Replied Hans: *"Leider haben wir keine Papiere."* ("Sorry, we have no papers.")

At this point the policemen got excited. Cried one: *"Was! Keine Papiere? Das geht ja aber nicht! Hände hoch!"* ("What! No papers? That just won't do. Hands up!")

Obediently we put up our hands, and one of the policemen started to search us for weapons. Sticking his hand into Hans's pocket, he pulled out a stick of TNT. Startled, he gaped at it, held it high in the air, and at the top of his lungs cried, *"SPRENGSTOFF!"* ("DYNAMITE!") Instantly, everyone ran for cover. (This would have been a riotous comedy if it hadn't had such serious implications for us three Americans.) With trembling hands, the policeman holding the TNT ran outside while the other, his hand shaking just as violently, pointed his rifle at us. In no time at all, the Gestapo were there with two cars. Hans was shoved into one of the cars, covered by three uniformed guards, while Ernst and I were pushed into the other. Two menacing policemen kept a keen eye on our every move. Then, *pfft!* Like felons, we were whisked, at full speed, to the headquarters of the almighty Gestapo, our ultimate fate in their hands.

GESTAPO HEADQUARTERS

At high speed we were driven to the regional Gestapo headquarters in Gera, a town forty kilometers to the east. My head was pounding.

"Is this real? Am I hallucinating? Is this some movie script with Hans, Ernst, and me the top stars in a horror scene? And now, for us three, what's next?"

When we arrived, we were made to sit on a bench outside the office of the Gestapo chief until, one by one, we were summoned inside. They called me first. Behind a long, ornately carved, dark wood table sat the Gestapo chief and an army colonel. On the wall behind them hung a large portrait of the *Führer,* whose beady eyes were already fastened on me. The Gestapo chief was a short, jowly man with a Hitler mustache. The colonel was a tall, slim, erect Prussian type with rimless glasses and pursed lips. It was clearly he who was in charge. His interrogation of me was fierce and direct.

"What were you three doing?" he demanded to know. "Are you spies? Are you commandos dropped behind the German lines to disrupt communications? You'd better tell me exactly what you were doing or the very worst will happen to you."

While waiting on the bench, Hans, Ernst, and I had decided that the least dangerous course to take was to tell the truth. So that's what I did. It somehow gave me a sense of confidence.

"We are American prisoners of war," I stated, looking the colonel straight in the eye. "Two days ago we escaped from Work Camp 650 in Berga an der Elster. Our one, our *only* objective was to find our way back to the American lines."

"Nonsense!" snorted the colonel. "If it was such a harmless little outing, as you assert, what was the dynamite for?"

That question upset me. I truly did not know why Hans had brought along dynamite sticks. I had no good answer. To add to my dismay, I was aware that dynamite is most often used to carry out specific plans to destroy something, and that having been caught with it would refute completely my story about our innocent purpose in escaping from Berga.

"We took a few sticks of dynamite along just in case of an emergency," I said lamely. "We never once discussed how or when we might use it."

The smirk on the colonel's face told me he didn't buy that answer either. A sense of panic now welled up in me. For the first time, I feared for my life.

Then came more questions: "How did you escape from Berga? What route did you take to get to Göschwitz?" And so on and on.

I answered them all truthfully. At the end of my ordeal, the colonel shook his finger at me. "Whatever the truth," he said ominously, "you three have created a very serious situation for yourselves." Then, turning to the Gestapo chief, he said, "Have him locked up for the night."

A guard took me to a cell in the basement. As he turned the key in the latch, he couldn't resist saying, *"Sie wissen natürlich, daß Sie erschossen werden."* ("You realize, of course, that you will be shot.")

I had been tucked into bed with happier thoughts.

After their interrogations, Hans and Ernst were locked up in nearby cells, but we were forbidden to talk to one another.

All night long I lay on my hard metal bunk, drenched in a cold sweat. I was certain the three of us would be shot in the morning. I lay there in dread of hearing the early morning footfalls of guards coming to take us out to the courtyard, where we would be lined up against a wall, blindfolded, and shot. During the night I had a thousand thoughts. I thought of Father and Mother in New York and wondered if the army had notified them that I was a POW. I thought of Patty, now a senior at the University of Chicago, and wondered if she had answered my two letters written from England. I thought of the final seven-course meal I would like to have served to me before I was executed. And, last, I thought of all the things I would have done with my life if it hadn't been so tragically cut short at twenty.

Came the dawn and those dreaded footfalls. "Good-bye world!" I said to myself. This was it. My heart pounded right out of my chest as the key turned in the lock. But who was that entering my cell? It wasn't the guards but the jailer! And what was that in his hands — a breakfast tray? "He's serving me breakfast!" I exulted. "The Germans wouldn't feed someone they're about to shoot — they're much too practical for that! They've given me a reprieve of execution!" I nearly exploded with relief.

I couldn't even eat the slice of bread or drink the sickening coffee substitute — I was much too nervous and excited.

At ten o'clock, guards hauled the three of us upstairs to a room where, to our shock, who should be there to confront us but S.S. Lieutenant Hack, from the camp at Berga!

"So!" he boomed. "You escaped! And Kasten, I see you have shaved off your beard! Come, come now, Kasten — you think you can deceive others by shaving it off? A traitor is still a traitor, beard or no beard. I have already given the order as to what shall be done with you. No one will much care whether you have a beard or not after you and your two friends have been shot."

With a look of flaming hatred in his eyes, he walked up to Hans and pushed him backward until, with a thud, his head hit the wall behind him. Then, taking the rifle from one of the guards, the lieutenant slammed Hans repeatedly across the neck and chest. Too wobbly to stand, Hans slid down the wall to the floor, where the two guards kicked him mercilessly. Only with the help of Ernst and me could Hans get back to his cell.

Around noon we were taken upstairs again, this time to the office of the Gestapo chief. It was to be another meeting with the colonel, who had with him two junior officers armed with pistols. For a moment, the colonel glared murderously at us. Then he asked, "Are you aware that on February 13 and 14, American and British fliers slaughtered over fifty thousand innocent women and children in day-and-night bombings of Dresden? Do you know that?" Again, "Do you know that?" he bellowed, raging with anger. Having heard nothing about the bombings, we shook our heads.

There was another moment of silence. Erect and motionless, the three of us stood in a row facing the Germans. The colonel now started pacing the floor — up and down, up and down, endlessly — his hands clasped behind his back. Abruptly he stopped in front of Hans and looked at him for a full minute, his head so close that only inches separated their faces. Hans, though obviously still in pain after his beating, stood erect, his chin up, looking the colonel straight in the eye. Suddenly the colonel raised his right hand and brought it crashing down on Hans's cheek. My God, that was a jaw-smasher! Hans remained motionless, his eyes still fixed on the colonel's, his jaw jutting out in proud defiance. Again the colonel struck, this time with the back of his hand on the other cheek. Another smasher! Again, Hans never moved a muscle, never twitched an eyelash — just kept his eyes fastened on the colonel's, sending the message: "You can get me, and you can get my two buddies, but you can't get the Americans. They're coming. They're on the way. And believe me, buster, whatever you do to us, somehow, somewhere, sometime soon, you'll pay for it. Trust me."

Once again the colonel paced the floor, immersed in thought. He was obviously deciding whether to have us shot right then and there. I kept the air locked up in my lungs until it hurt. Suddenly he turned to one of his aides and said, "Take these three to Stalag IX C at Bad Sulza. Solitary confinement."

I blew the air out of my lungs. That was a close call! I firmly believe that in the few minutes that had just transpired, Hans Kasten, without saying a word, without moving a muscle, without flicking an eyelash, had saved our lives. Never was I prouder of anyone! Never was I prouder to be a citizen of the United States of America!

THE TRIP TO "PUNISHMENT AND CONTROL"

Stalag IX C, to which the colonel had sentenced us, was actually Straf-und-Prüflager IX C (Punishment and Control Camp IX C) in the village of Bad Sulza, seventy kilometers to the west, near Weimar. To say that the trip to Bad Sulza was bizarre would be to beggar the experience. In preparation for the journey, our captors shackled us together with heavy chains round our wrists. A lieutenant and a sergeant then marched us through the streets of Gera toward the railroad station, from which, the lieutenant told us, we would take a train to Weimar and then an automobile to Bad Sulza. As we marched down the cobblestoned main street of the quaint medieval town of Gera, a bystander, pointing at us, shouted to the noontime

crowd: "*Sie sind amerikanische Flieger!*" ("They're American airmen!")
— whereupon a near riot ensued. People shook their fists at us. An
older woman spat on the cobblestones in front of us. Shouting "Dresden, Dresden," a man screwed up his face in hateful contortions.
Another yelled, "*Amerikanische Unmenschen!* [American beasts!] Did
you cause that firestorm in Dresden? Did you drop all that death on a
nonmilitary city? Shame! Perpetual shame on you!" As things heated
up, the lieutenant had to restrain the crowd from attacking us by
explaining, "No, these aren't airmen — they're ground troops."

For the train ride, only the sergeant accompanied us. Still shackled
together, we sat on a bench in a first-class compartment. We were
soon confronted by an unexpected problem. Ernst declared that he
had to go to the bathroom and asked the guard's permission to use the
toilet. The guard gave his permission but refused to remove Ernst's
shackles. He said we would all have to go into the toilet together or
we couldn't go at all. So we all had to squeeze ourselves into that tiny,
three-foot-square cubbyhole — and with Ernst's left hand shackled to
Hans's right hand, and his right hand shackled to my left hand, he
heeded both calls of nature! (Picture that scene if you can!)

At eight P.M. we arrived in Weimar, where German staff cars were
waiting to take us to the Stalag at Bad Sulza. Without delay, we were
taken to the *Haftbaracke* (solitary confinement barracks) and turned
over to the jailer.

The *Haftbaracke* was a long, one-story fieldstone building. The
jailer and a guard marched us down a long corridor where we passed
about forty dungeons, each about six by ten feet, with thick stone
walls. They were dark except for a faint glimmer of light coming from
a weak ceiling bulb in the corridor. In many of these tiny "castle
keeps," I could discern, just barely, the still forms of prisoners stretched
out on their crude, makeshift wooden slats.

"In here!" said the jailer as he shoved Hans into one of the cells
and turned the key. "In here!" he said to Ernst as he pushed him into
another cell. Then he turned to me. When I got a look at his face, I
shrank back in horror! It was my uncle Elton! Yes, my uncle Elton of
Yonkers, who, just two years earlier, had locked me up for three

weeks of solitary confinement. And now he was here to lock me up again!

Of course it was not my uncle Elton. It was, on my part, pure hallucination. Exhausted, I was certain I had seen my uncle's face on the jailer, who had a similar round red face, brown mustache, and tortoiseshell spectacles and who, like my autocratic uncle, was incarcerating me, wielding his power over me. Strange, the workings of a stressed-out mind!

Before the jailer could slam shut the dungeon door, I asked the crucial question: "How long will we be kept in solitary?"

"Your sentence is for six months."

Six months! After contemplating that ghastly news, I decided to change it, at least in my own mind. "Six months, hell! It will be only until I am rescued by a U.S. armored division — that's how long!" Now I felt better.

So now, after three torturous days and nights that had brought not even a moment's rest or respite, I stretched out on my hard, splintery, wooden slats and had the sleep of my life.

SOLITARY CONFINEMENT

When I awoke, the room was drenched in sunshine. Through a small window near the ceiling, the sun was sending in long, misty shafts of light — eerie as they hit the rugged walls. Soon the jailer brought me my breakfast — two slices of hard bread and a cup of bitter ersatz coffee. Except for a grunted *"Guten Morgen,"* he said no more. Then, at sundown, he brought my supper: a bowl of watery soup with two tiny potatoes. That was it.

During the first week, I saw no one but the jailer, who came only to bring my two meals. With nothing to do but think, I became paranoid — increasingly ridden with guilt and self-loathing for having made that stupid grammatical error in the *Bierstube*. This recapture by the Germans — why did I cause it? I deserved whatever punishment was to plague my days, and I alone — not Hans, not Ernst.

After a week, the jailer became friendlier, introducing himself as Gefreiter (Corporal) Werner Quint. A short, fat, fortyish man, he seemed all right — not a bit threatening.

"Tell me something about this Stalag," I asked him. "I can't see out through the little window up there."

"Of course," he replied amiably. "The Stalag is part of a vast complex of buildings known as Buchenwald. It's scattered over many kilometers. This part of Buchenwald is reserved for foreign political agitators, prisoners of war, and 'troublemakers.' Right now, in addition to you three Americans, we're holding two thousand French, five hundred Russian, and three hundred and fifty British prisoners. Here in the Haftbaracke, along with you three, we're holding six Frenchmen and eight Russians — all prisoners who have assaulted guards or tried to escape." And *each*, I thought to myself, with stories as hair-raising, as terrifying, as ours!

One morning a pleasant surprise awaited me. Beaming all over, Werner Quint showed up at my dungeon door with an armful of books. "I have good news," he said. "The British Man of Confidence heard that you Yanks were in camp and sent these books with his compliments." What a stroke of good fortune! Ravenously, I delved into *Moll Flanders* and *Roxana* by Daniel Defoe, *Young Man of Caracas* by T. R. Ybarra, *Wild Geese Calling* by Stewart Edward White, and *A Tree Grows in Brooklyn* by Betty Smith. There, in solitary, I read them all. These books helped, if only slightly, to keep my mind off my gnawing, aching hunger.

One day I heard shouts of jubilation outside my window. A convoy of trucks from the Croix Rouge Française had just roared in with a glorious windfall: four thousand French food parcels and two thousand American parcels filled with canned corned beef and chicken, an assortment of cheeses, crackers, jams, dried fruits, Swiss chocolates, and other barely remembered delicacies. Such whooping, such hollering with joy, at the very sight of these goodies — so craved by all!

That same day the British Man of Confidence was allowed to visit the *Haftbaracke* to make sure that Hans, Ernst, and I had duly received parcels. He reminded me of David Niven — cool, suave, always in control of himself and everyone else. Hans leaped at the chance to inform him of the plight of the three hundred and fifty sick and starved Americans at Berga. "Could you use your influence to see that they get some of these parcels?"

Promising to do his best, the Briton went to see the camp *Kommandant*. The following conversation, as I later learned, took place between the two:

"I'd like a truckload of those Red Cross parcels sent over to the American prisoners at Berga, if you don't mind," said the Briton.

"Fine," responded the *Kommandant*. "I'll see to it that a truck is loaded up and sent to Berga promptly."

"I'm afraid that won't do, old boy," replied the Briton. "I'd like to accompany the parcels myself. I want to be certain that the prisoners get their parcels."

"What?" exclaimed the *Kommandant*. "You want to go with the truck to Berga? That's impossible! You're a prisoner. Nothing like that has ever been done before."

"Well," said the Briton, "there are lots of things in this bloody war that have never been done before. So if you don't mind, I'll be going along with the parcels. I'll be back — you needn't worry. I'll be back to take care of my men."

The next morning, a truck loaded with Red Cross emergency food and medical supplies left for Berga. In the cab of the truck sat a strange trio: a German driver at the wheel, the British Man of Confidence squeezed into the middle, and, on his right, a German guard holding a pistol to his ribs!

As soon as the Briton returned to Bad Sulza, he gave Hans his report and paid a brief visit to my cell. "The Berga prisoners were elated to see the parcels," he told me, "and I personally observed some of them being distributed. Let's hope the additional food will tide them over until this bloody war ends." And then, becoming subdued, he added, "I'm afraid the rest of the news from Berga is rather grim. Of the three hundred and fifty Americans shipped there on February eighth, at least forty have died of malnutrition, pneumonia, exhaustion, or a combination of the three. Many more are in bad shape.

"There's something else you should know," he continued. "The prisoners at Berga were told that Kasten, Littell, and Sinner had tried to escape but had got no farther than thirty meters beyond the fence and had been shot. Another prisoner by the name of Goldstein tried to escape but was shot and his body brought back to the camp and left on the ground for a week as an example to the other prisoners."

After the parcels arrived, Quint allowed the three of us to get together in Hans's cell to heat up our corned beef and chicken on a portable stove. I quickly took advantage of my captive audience and poured out my guilt to them: "Listen, you two — I want to apologize to both of you for being responsible for our recapture. It was all my fault, it was inexcusable, and I feel absolutely rotten about the whole thing." They were both nice about it — much too nice, in my opinion.

"Don't get all worked up over it," said Hans. "There are any number of reasons for us to have been recognized — not the least of which was our clothing. So come on, Joe, quit talking about it."

I remained inconsolable.

We now noticed that Quint was becoming increasingly nervous as reports came in that the Allied forces were getting closer and closer. He began to confide his fears to us. "I'm afraid," he lamented, "that when the American troops arrive and see that I've kept you in solitary, and in such a dismal place, they will take their revenge. I did plead with the *Kommandant* to transfer you to the *Revierbaracke* [sick bay] or to the British compound, but he refused. I'm scared. Don't breathe a word of it, but I'm thinking seriously of deserting — heading for home."

"Look," said Hans. "You were only carrying out orders. You'd be far wiser to remain here."

"I agree," I told Quint. "And as for us," I added, looking pointedly at his fat belly, "we'd be happier if we got even one third of the rations you obviously receive."

Well, Quint decided to stay. He also served us extra slices of bread and much thicker soup every day. I felt guilty some time later when it occurred to me that he must have been shortchanging the French and the Russians — giving us their portion of the solids at the bottom of the soup pot. Throughout the agony of slow starvation, seen all around us, Quint remained fat as a barrel.

After I had read the books given to me, I hit upon the idea of copying over my diary. That flimsy little booklet had fought beside me in the Battle of the Bulge. From various pockets in my overcoat and combat fatigues it had waged a valiant battle against the ravages of cold, dampness, and mud. It had been sat on, lain on, bent, soaked, and in countless ways brutalized. The binding was falling apart, and many of the pages — torn, smudged, and stained — would soon be completely illegible. I needed to copy out the entries into a fresh, clean book. Luckily, I was able to prevail upon Quint to locate a replacement for me. The one he brought was a large school notebook with lined pages and a tan linen cover — just what I needed. He also lent me a pen.

That diary, copied out in the Bad Sulza dungeon, is the very one I have spread out before me as I write this chapter. Although the cover is the worse for wear and the whole thing has a faint smell of mildew, it is intact and the entries are legible.

One day when we three were again allowed to be together in Hans's dungeon, I once more unloaded my guilt on them. "You know," I sighed, "we wouldn't be here if it weren't for my stupid carelessness. If I hadn't screwed up my German grammar in the *Bierstube* and made people suspicious, we never would have been recaptured — or living in this hellpit."

Abruptly, Hans turned on me. "Dammit, Joe," he said, scowling. "I'm tired of hearing you bitch about how it was all your fault. Did it ever occur to you that our being recaptured was probably the best thing that could have happened?"

I was dumbfounded. "You kidding?" I said.

"No, I'm *not* kidding," said Hans. "If we hadn't been caught, it would have taken us a week, at least, to get to the American lines — assuming we got there at all. Then, Joe, think how many weeks it would have taken for word to go through army and Red Cross channels to get a truckload of food and medical supplies over to the Berga prisoners. At least one month. As things worked out, we went to Bad Sulza, met the British Man of Confidence when the parcels arrived, and *bingo!* Thanks to him, stacks of food and supplies went straight to

Berga. Just like that. Who knows how many American lives he may
have saved. Had you thought of that?"

"No, I hadn't," I confessed.

"Well, then, quit your bellyaching and shut up!"

"Okay," I said. I never ever again brought up the matter.

LIBERATED BY PATTON'S 6TH
ARMORED DIVISION

By now, the Allied Armies had crossed the Rhine and were racing
toward central Germany. The lightning speed of their advance had
an enormous impact even within the walls of our Stalag. I'll let the
entries in my diary tell the story of that last hectic week in prison
camp as the Allies approached.

APRIL 5. Quint is going to pieces as U.S. armor reaches his home
town, Eisenach, 100 km. to west. He's still fearful the Americans
will punish him, even kill him, for keeping the three of us in
solitary.

Germans close *Haftbaracke* in P.M., move 14 Frenchmen and
Russians to their national compounds. Hans, Ernst, and I move
into *Revierbaracke* [sick bay], along with 350 British prisoners just
arrived after 320 km. death march from Upper Silesia — captives
since Dunkerque (1940), El Alamein, and Messina.

APRIL 6. Truckload of American Red Cross parcels arrives. The
three of us get preference: one whole Christmas parcel apiece.
Contents: one plum pudding, cherries, dates, mixed nuts, mixed
candies, cheese, pineapple jam, Vienna sausage, boned turkey,
chopped ham, honey, preserved butter, briar pipe, cribbage set, 3
packs of Luckies.

APRIL 7. Dogfights increase over Stalag. A plane shot down in flames.
Couldn't tell whether it was German or American.

German transport column with 150 men flees to Bavaria, leaving skeleton guard of about 50 men to surrender camp to U.S.
troops. Quint goes, Gefreiter Columbus takes his place as jailer.

APRIL 8. P-47s and P-51s raise hell with railroad station, sidings, and locomotives near camp.

German army communiqué reports U.S. tanks repulsed west of Schweinfurt. They're getting closer, and the Supermen are dazed, scared, shamelessly subservient, and usually stinking drunk, even on guard duty.

Bad Sulza civilian population seeks refuge from our planes by clinging to Stalag boundaries.

APRIL 9. Battery of horse-drawn 88s rolls into position in hills commanding *Landstrasse* [highway]. If Leipzig is U.S. objective, Bad Sulza will be directly in path of advance.

APRIL 10. German staff cars, bicycles, oxcarts, etc., flee east as Weimar, 20 km. to S.W. of us, is reported in U.S. hands.

Serb short-wave radio reports U.S. troops have been in Philippines two months, have taken Manila.

APRIL 11, 0900 HOURS. *Kommandant* tells British Man of Confidence that Americans are 14 km. away on Weimar-Naumburg road.

1200 HOURS. Only small arms fire heard as Bad Sulza, 4 km. away, is captured. British and French Men of Confidence stand outside gate to warn Americans of Stalag's position.

1412 HOURS. The first U.S. tank rolls past Stalag. Pandemonium in camp! Shouts and cheers for Americans from French and Russians. British, more reserved, prefer to clap. Other M-4 tanks appear, pull to side of road, as 6th Armored Division spearhead halts while engineers move up to repair demolished bridge 6 km. ahead. Tank battalion commander enters camp. Delirium everywhere!

An hour after the U.S. Army had liberated Stalag IX C, a medical unit arrived on the scene. Finding three Americans in the camp, the medics arranged to have us evacuated without delay. They told us that a driver would take us in a Jeep to Weimar and from there an army transport plane would fly us to a U.S. Army hospital in France. Freedom! Liberation! No longer prisoners of war! Our joy was boundless — except for one unsolvable mystery.

While Ernst and I were waiting for the Jeep to arrive, I noticed that Hans had disappeared. "Where's Hans?" I asked. Ernst didn't know.

We cast our eyes around the Stalag compound, but in the milling crowd of excited ex-POWs we couldn't spot him anywhere. Increasingly concerned, we searched the entire Stalag. Hans was nowhere to be found. Finally, in exasperation, Ernst and I got into the Jeep and headed for Weimar. The two of us flew off to France wondering and worrying about Hans.

Within three hours, Ernst and I were propped up in adjoining beds at the 50th General Hospital in the town of Commercy, two-hundred kilometers east of Paris. Army doctors told us we would stay there for about three weeks for observation and treatment and should then be ready for shipment back to the States. The scales showed that I had lost forty-eight pounds since December. Ernst had lost thirty-four pounds.

But Hans Kasten — our friend, our leader, our savior — where was he? Was he safe? Had he become a last-minute casualty of the war? Had he been mugged or stabbed in some alley? It would be two months before I knew the answers. I would not know what had happened to Hans until I returned to the States and dialed his telephone number in Wisconsin.

"FOREST OF BEECH TREES"

Soon after our liberation from Stalag IX C, Ernst and I were in that Jeep speeding toward the Weimar air strip. On the way we passed the turnoff to a place called Buchenwald — the vast complex of buildings that included the Stalag. I hadn't thought much about the name "Buchenwald," which meant "forest of beech trees." Such a name sounded too innocent to deserve a second thought; it fitted perfectly the pastoral landscape that surrounded us — the lush green valleys, the forested hillsides, and now the yellow spring wildflowers dotting the meadows as far as the eye could see. No ogres or monsters or agents of evil could ever inhabit a place called Buchenwald.

The ugly truth hit me all too soon — a couple of days later, when it hit the rest of the world as well. The long-guarded secret was out.

Buchenwald was no idyllic "forest of beech trees" but a place where depraved people, working for the Nazi state, gave the world a new, sickening twist to the meaning of evil. It was a vast concentration camp from which eighty-one thousand sick, starved inmates found their freedom — thanks to General Patton's U.S. Third Army — on the same day as those of us at Bad Sulza.

Throughout the war, the Nazis operated more than twenty of these concentration camps in which they systematically exterminated more than six million Jews, Poles, and elderly and handicapped prisoners. But the Buchenwald camp was the scene of tortures and murders that were the most monstrous of all. The world was now hearing of those thousands of starved prisoners, put to work in quarries until they died of exhaustion, and of those thousands of others forced to become guinea pigs for often fatal experiments performed by Nazi physicians. Crematoria were discovered where bodies were burned but their tattooed skins saved for ornamental lampshades and other mementos. The nations of the world were finding out that, in all, more than a hundred thousand people died barbaric deaths at this place with the lovely name Buchenwald.

One cannot help but ponder: How could a countryside that looked so much like a fairyland be the setting for such unspeakable violence, cruelty, and murder? How could a sizable number of Germans in a nation devoted to literature, music, art, good manners, and fastidious behavior become the architects of such beastliness? How could those trim little houses with their quaint, overhanging eaves and their window boxes filled with bright, cheery flowers be the homes of human beings who gave the world such grisly new perspectives on the outer limits of malignity? The paradox of the Germans has yet to be fully understood. It ultimately poses an even greater mystery about the nature of all humankind.

The English mystery writer Julian Symons says, "What absorbs me most in our age is the violence behind respectable faces: the civil servant planning how to kill Jews more efficiently; the judge speaking with passion about the need for capital punishment; the quiet, obedient boy who kills for fun."

We still have so much to learn about ourselves.

10

READJUSTING TO CIVILIAN LIFE

"I'LL HAVE THE PRIME RIB, BUT HOLD THE O JOOSE"

It is late June of 1945. Our shipload of ex-POWs has just docked in New York. It's discharge time — then head for home.

Oops! Not quite. The redeployment officer at Fort Dix has bad news for me: "Soldier, we have your medical file from the 50th General Hospital in France. You dropped from 180 pounds to 132 during your months in prison camp. You need to get more meat on your bones before you go home for good. Also, army doctors will need to monitor your physical and mental condition. For these reasons, you're being assigned to two months of R&R in Asheville, North Carolina."

Two months?

Then the news got better. A pleasant surprise awaited me. I reported for duty at the magnificent Asheville-Biltmore Hotel, which the army had leased as a rehabilitation center for ex-POWs. It had luxurious bedrooms, plush lounges with "Off to the Hunt" paintings on the walls, and a stately dining room glowing in the soft light of a dozen chandeliers. It was here that five hundred of us, still gaunt and hollow-eyed, would live in royal splendor, happy to obey the one set of orders the army gave us: "Eat, exercise, and enjoy yourselves." We had passes to movie houses, public golf courses, and bus tours of the surrounding Great Smoky Mountains.

For its new army clientele, the hotel kept its regular menu and its Blue Ribbon chef. When we entered the dining room, the maître d' snapped his fingers at the headwaiter, who promptly ushered us to a table. Favorite orders? The prime rib au jus ("Make mine medium, but hold the o joose"); filet of sole poached in white wine; the dessert tray ("I'll have the EE-claire and the chocolate mouse") — all topped off with a demitasse ("I'll have a small demmy tassy coffee cup"). As we dined, a string quartet serenaded us with "Tales from the Vienna Woods," "Voices of Spring," and other Strauss waltzes. So this is life in the U.S. Army? I think I'll do another hitch!

It wasn't until we arrived in Asheville that we heard the nasty things that the commentator Drew Pearson had said on the home radio about our 106th Division and its performance in the Battle of the Bulge. From top to bottom he ripped us apart for allowing the Germans to break through and make deep penetrations into Allied territory. Pearson came in for bitter comment at the dinner table one evening.

"You know," I said to the others around the table, "it's too bad Drew Pearson couldn't have been right there alongside us while we were trying to fend off two panzer divisions. He would have instantly lost control over his bodily functions."

"Whaddaya mean?" piped up another GI. "He would've shit in his pants!"

The string quartet kept on playing waltzes. "*Strauss waltzes,*" I mused. "This takes me back to Heidelberg, to those afternoons at the restaurant Zum Ritter with my sister Nancy and Fritz . . . to that string quartet playing those same waltzes for a world that was at peace. And now I'm hearing that music again! Is it possible that in the brief interim the world has obliterated *fifty million* of its inhabitants? Just between waltzes?"

Fritz, you were one of those fifty million. You were my special friend. You told me that someday you hoped to see the Statue of Liberty, the

Empire State Building, a baseball game, and the Grand Canyon. I'm
sorry, Fritz. I'm so sorry.

While in Asheville, those of us who had fought with the 106th Division received some much-needed salve for the wounds inflicted on us
by Drew Pearson. Journalists and generals alike — men who had
been at the scene — declared that the troops of the 106th had fought
with tenacity and valor, had slowed the Germans' westward push and
seriously upset their timetable. Hitler had boasted that he would
capture Antwerp in a week and split the British and American armies.
It took him six days to capture Saint-Vith, a key road junction just ten
miles from where he had started. It was here, in the first few days, that
the Germans actually lost the Battle of the Bulge. This is where the
106th Division — along with the 28th and 99th — held its ground,
giving the 101st Airborne Division precious time to move up for its
epic defense of Bastogne and giving the Allied armies time to mount
counterattacks against the German spearheads.

Probably the truest account of what happened to the 106th came
from Ivan H. ("Cy") Peterman, war correspondent for the *Philadel-*
phia Inquirer, who was with the division throughout the battle.

GREEN DIVISION IS MAULED
AS HUNS HIT 'QUIET FRONT'

WITH THE 106TH INFANTRY DIVISION ON THE WESTERN FRONT — The
worst-smacked and heaviest loser of all American units in front of
Field Marshal von Rundstedt's counter-offensive in Belgium was
the 106th Infantry Division. What happened to it may produce a
late but needed lesson for our Army.

The doughboys were as green as the average rookie division and
had just moved freshly into line. They had had comparatively short
maneuvers and preparation at home — six months is one report —
and they had inexperienced officers in command of many elements. If they were to become a tragic unit when the score was
known, do not, like Drew Pearson on the home radio, stigmatize
the whole outfit — a great many fought like veterans, many died
and at least one regiment remains to redeem its missing companions.

This story will relate the facts and circumstances — you must be the judge, and after you have learned about the Ardennes your verdict is not to be feared.

On the morning of December 16 it was cold, with snow on the ground. The 422d, 423d and 424th Regiments were strung out from north to south along twenty-seven miles of mountainous area overlooking the Siegfried Line east of Saint-Vith. Their mission was to hold and protect roads from this pleasant little town in the Belgian uplands. Through this town in 1940, Nazi panzers had rolled to Sedan; through it in war after war the Germans had attacked France and Belgium. It would be a big order if anything were to happen . . . and it happened.

Like the men of the 28th and 99th Divisions, the 106th freshman class got its salutation at 5:40 A.M. that fateful morning, and if they were scared by Field Marshal von Rundstedt's artillery barrage and his medium and heavy guns plus railway howitzers shoved secretly into position the previous night, they were certainly startled by their first introduction to the *Nebelwerfer* or "screaming meemie" mortar multiples. Rockets also landed with flashes and deafening detonations as the massed spearhead of the Wehrmacht came through. It was the thundering prelude to a gigantic Hun offensive and it was nothing like the 106th had ever heard.

The Germans knew this, too. They knew that both the 99th and the 106th lay side by side, with the 28th just to the south. It was the longed-for "soft spot" the panzers craved and they figured to go through in a couple of hours. In that they failed to compute American guts. The 106th wasn't immediately brushed aside.

Its men were stunned at first and some gave ground but then returned and dug in. Once accustomed to the battle, they fought with everything at hand. German bodies piled up as wave after wave advanced.

The timetable of the enemy was already slowing when the 106th remained intact by nightfall of the first day of battle. Men like Sergeant Leland Lynch, of Indianapolis, stood ankle deep in freezing water, firing machine guns while under constant fire, to stop the Germans at key points. Liaison officers repeatedly drove through fire to keep orders flowing, and one driver, Private Bob Rupe, of Logansport, Ind., drove a loaded ammunition truck through a townful of Huns, holding the vehicle with one hand and a rifle with the other, prepared to fire through the windshield.

Perhaps they saw what he hauled, for the Germans didn't shoot.

On December 17 the lines held firm, but that afternoon two Nazi spearheads succeeded in cutting off the 422d and 423d Regiments, and closed in behind them.

The two surrounded regiments fought on, their ammunition low and their ranks depleted by shells. They stood against a growing horde of panzers, fighting with bazookas, rifles and machine guns. . . . Their last message was, "Can you get some ammunition through?"

After reading accounts of the battle, I became more and more at ease with myself for having been in combat for so brief a time and for having been taken prisoner. I began to take pride, in fact, in the part the men of the 106th had played in helping to win the war on the Western front.

In Asheville, I received a letter from the U.S. Army Chief of Staff informing me that I had been awarded the Purple Heart. The army awards this medal "for wounds or death in combat." To this day I treasure my Purple Heart and keep it in its little blue case in my study.

On September 1, the army gave me my discharge. The next day, at the front door of my parents' New York apartment, stood a slim, trim ex-soldier beside a big, fat duffel bag. It was me! We had a joyous, tearful reunion.

WHAT HAPPENED TO HANS KASTEN?

When I called Hans's telephone number in Milwaukee, his family said that he was on his way to New York. The next day he called me at my parents' apartment and we met for lunch. He had just spent a month at the Shorecrest Hotel in Miami Beach, another one of those posh places leased by the army for recovering POWs.

The minute I saw Hans, I lit into him. "Dammit, Hans," I beefed, "why did you pull that disappearing act on us the minute we were freed? I almost got ulcers worrying about you. Why the hell did you do that? And for Christ's sake, where have you been?"

"Well, Joe," said Hans in a conciliatory tone, "here's what happened. After writing my family, I hitched a ride to Weimar and liberated a Mercedes-Benz, which the GIs filled with gas. Upon learning of my mission, they gave me some extra jerrycans of gas and some C rations [stew, beans, and hash] and I started out on the search of my life for — you know who."

"It had to be S.S. Lieutenant Hack."

"You bet! I stopped at every collection camp for German prisoners, looking for that SOB. I must have scanned a hundred thousand German faces. Finally, down thirty-five pounds or more from all those bumholes that begin with *B* — Bad Orb, Berga, Buchenwald, Bad Sulza — I collapsed and was flown to the U.S. Army hospital in Camp Lucky Strike, near Le Havre."

My imagination can give me only the faintest clue as to what Hans would have done to Lieutenant Hack if he had found him. Hans still has five vertebrae in his back, just below his neck, that are badly damaged as a result of his brutal treatment at the lieutenant's hands.

Even though the Germans had put Hans through countless strip searches, they always missed the Big Item. Sewn into the lining of his fur vest was a list of German officers and noncoms who had brutalized prisoners at Bad Orb and Berga. Who do you suppose was at the top of that list? Right. S.S. Lieutenant Hack, "the Beast of Berga," the man who had kept weak, starved American prisoners digging tunnels in the mountain.

Arriving in the United States, Hans turned the list over to Army Intelligence and later to the War Crimes Commission. Hans and I were sure the day would come when Hack's body, hanging from a rope, would be swinging in the wind. (That day never came. In the postwar trial of the administrators of Berga, Hack somehow evaded prosecution. Two underlings, Ludwig Merz and Erwin Metz, who had held supervisory positions in the camp, were tried and sentenced to be hanged. Their sentences were later reduced to a few years in prison.)

Also included on Hans's list were the names I had given him of two Germans whom I myself had observed mistreating American prisoners: Unteroffizier Ernst Ellenwein, who repeatedly slammed a rifle butt across the back of a GI who had dropped from exhaustion in the Berga mine, and Gefreiter Wolfgang Moltke, whom I witnessed knocking a prisoner down and kicking him in the head and chest because he was too weak to pick up a load of wood on a work detail.

Hans had a long and painful readjustment to civilian life. He had already endured months of tough combat with the 28th Infantry Division before he was captured in the Battle of the Bulge. Then came the beatings that he took as a POW. As the memories gradually receded into the background, Hans settled down to a happy and productive life. He took a job with an import-export company in Manila, and in a few years became president of the largest general merchandise distributing company in the Philippines. Now in his seventies, he lives in Manila with his wife, Florinda — who is forty-five years his junior — and his six-year-old twin daughters. His latest communiqué: "I'm trying for triplets."

THE TRUTH ABOUT FRITZ ESSER

Fritz Esser . . . that wonderful young German doctor whom my sister Nancy was about to marry in Heidelberg that summer of '39 . . . that great pal of mine who took me on as a younger brother. What a tragedy that a grand romance such as theirs had to be blown to bits by World War II! Yet I had understood Nancy's need to break off the engagement and return to Honolulu. Clearly, she couldn't face the life of a *Hausfrau* in a country that might soon become the deadly enemy of the United States. Nor, I concluded, could she bear to be cut off from her home, her family, her country, her roots. And that was all there was to it.

Not quite! Soon after receiving my discharge, I visited Nancy at Camp Lejeune, North Carolina, where she was living with her husband, a lieutenant colonel in the U.S. Marine Corps. Inevitably, the subject of Fritz came up. As we reminisced about him, I detected a strange look on her face — a look I had never seen before. Could there be more to their story than she had let on?

"Out with it, Nancy," I blurted. "What's still troubling you about Fritz? Come on — you can tell your kid brother."

After a long hesitation, she let go. "All right," she said, "I'll tell you the story. I've never told it to anyone before.

"At the time Fritz and I were engaged," she began, "he vehemently denied the existence of any German concentration camps. 'All that nonsense is American propaganda!' he insisted. Naive as I was, I believed him. But one day when his sister Else and I were lunching together, she shattered my illusions. What she said nearly flattened me. I'll quote: 'Fritz and I rejoice that Hitler is doing such a great job of wiping out those ugly subhumans, the Jews.'

"I couldn't respond. Stunned, I didn't know how. Later, when I confronted Fritz with this — although he laughed aloud, his laughter sounded forced. 'Yes,' he admitted, 'there are a few camps, but not as many as the Americans claim. Besides, the Jews are being exterminated in a kind and humane way.'

"Gradually," continued my sister, "Fritz's devotion to the Nazi cause rose to a crescendo. He became fanatical. I was torn, confused, wanting to stay in love with him, deluding myself that this Jewish situation was merely a figment of the imagination of misguided American journalists. And there was Mother, in Honolulu, writing about financing our trip to Honolulu, where Father could marry us. And there was Fritz saying, 'I'm not sure I want to go to the United States — it has the reputation of being decadent, a country that does not understand us Germans.'

"And so, as Hitler overpowered one country after another, Fritz became wildly excited over Germany's successes. All this began to supersede his love for me, his *'kleine Schatzli'* [little treasure], as he called me.

"'I need to explain something to you,' he said one day, not taking me totally by surprise. 'Instead of marriage, let's have an affair. There's a chance you may have some Jewish blood in you. I fear this because your fingers are not long and tapered. You are a brunette — you haven't the fair, slender look of a pure Aryan. I really should marry a blond Nordic type. My superiors would not approve of you as my wife.'

"'I can't agree to that,' I said, deeply hurt and angry. 'A secret affair?'

"'Come on, Nancy,' he replied. 'If you're worried about getting pregnant, you needn't. The Third Reich needs to double its population so that we can rule the world for a thousand years. [Here he ignored his thought that I might not be a pure Aryan!] And, *Schatzli*, you will be honored and held in high esteem by our leaders if we make lots of babies. We must cooperate with the goals of our beloved *Vaterland*. You will be given a place to live, along with other unselfish women doing their duty, and you will be financed by our political establishment.'

"I felt giddy. No one to turn to — didn't know my own mind. I loved him. I hated him. Fritz was all I had — my only security — being half a world away from my family. Why didn't I have the gumption to slap him across the face and just say no? We sneaked through the window into his bedroom, became lovers — but only that one time. Finally, overcome with guilt and self-loathing, I took a stand. 'Fritz, I'm leaving!'

"When he seemed unmoved by that decision, my inner hurt seemed unbearable. He saw me off the next day at the train depot — my tears of agony bemoaning his rejection of me and my stupidity in loving such a man. Love, hate — both, I guess — and now, I'd never see him again.

"So now, Joe, you know the real story. And you thought it was the coming war — my common sense — that blew to bits this great romance!"

I was dumbfounded. Everything Nancy said ran counter to the fond memories of Fritz that I had cherished over the years. How was

I to know that the man she nearly married was a genocidal Nazi freak . . . someone who might have become my brother-in-law . . . someone Father would have joined in holy matrimony in the cathedral in Honolulu . . . someone for whom Mother would have hosted a gala reception in the Bishop's House. Close call!

After this revelation, never again did Nancy and I speak of Fritz.

You'll never know, Fritz, how crushed I was when I learned that you'd been killed in Stalingrad. How I grieved for you! Believe me, I'll grieve no more.

STOP THE WORLD, I WANT TO GET ON!

After my army discharge in September 1945, I enrolled at Trinity College for the second semester of my freshman year, to start the following January. Meanwhile, I had four months to adjust to civilian life. Most of that time, in my parents' New York apartment, I spent reading, writing letters, taking walks up and down Riverside Drive, and swimming with Father in a public indoor pool. But, like many veterans, I was terribly restless and had difficulty concentrating on anything for more than an hour at a time.

One day, on my return from a walk, Mother greeted me at the door, bubbling with excitement. "Joe," she said, beaming, "I have a surprise! Tomorrow we're going to the Metropolitan Opera House to see *Die Meistersinger*. Look, I have tickets!" Now I had become something of a Wagner buff, and she knew that. But right now I was much too restless to sit through what I knew to be the world's longest regularly performed opera — around five hours! Nevertheless, how could I disappoint Mother, excited as she was? And so, together, we took our seats at the opera.

Why did I agree to subject myself to such torture? Thirty minutes after the opera was in progress I could sit still no longer. "Mother," I leaned over and whispered, "I'm going to stand at the rear for a while to listen. Be back soon."

When I got to the rear of the hall, my legs wouldn't stop. I soon found myself out on the street, walking briskly down Broadway. Before long I was standing in front of a theater where the movie showing was *Casablanca*. *Casablanca!* That was the romantic thriller I had heard so much about while I was overseas and was dying to see. Here was my chance. I walked into the theater, saw the movie from beginning to end (or rather from middle to middle), and returned to my seat next to Mother just in time to catch the final act of *Die Meistersinger*.

As we left the Met, Mother asked, "Well, Joe, how did you enjoy the evening?"

"It was fabulous!" I raved. "I loved it!"

I was thinking, of course, of that heart-stopping scene in Rick's Café when the French patriots drown out those insufferable German soldiers with a thunderous, passionate singing of "La Marseillaise." Thinking, too, of that great love affair in Paris between Bogart and Bergman — cut short by the German capture of the city. Thinking also of that tense, final showdown at the airport when Conrad Veidt, reaching for his pistol, is beaten to the draw by Bogart and, dying, slumps to the ground, still clutching the telephone.

"Yes," I told Mother, "I had an absolutely wonderful evening!"

"I'm so pleased — I knew you would," she said. "So did I!"

On my twenty-first birthday, September 19, my parents threw a party for me at the Mandarin Chinese restaurant near Carnegie Hall. As the headwaiter seated us, Father addressed him in Chinese. Soon, other waiters gathered around as Father recounted a side-splitting story in Chinese, complete with wheezing and whirring sounds and wild gesticulations. The waiters doubled up with laughter. If the other patrons were bothered by the abrupt halt in their service, they didn't show it — their eyes were fixed on that white-haired man wearing a black suit, a clerical collar, a purple dickey, and a pectoral cross around his neck — and spouting Chinese at a furious rate!

Mother had ordered Peking duck in advance, and we all enjoyed a superb feast. Afterward, a waiter set before me a bowl containing three scoops of ice cream and a side of fortune cookies. The other waiters then gathered behind my chair and, clapping their hands, cried, "*Kung hsi! Kung hsi!*" ("Congratulations! Congratulations!") To top off the evening, Father sang the Happy Birthday song in Chinese, to the delight and applause of the eighty-some patrons of the restaurant.

"What a twenty-first birthday!" I mused. "Today I became of age. Today I am an adult, old enough to vote, drink beer, wine, even liquor. (Ha!) It's amazing, thinking back to all that has happened to me in the past year, that only now am I no longer legally a child! Maybe someday the laws will change — at least the laws that say at what age a person can vote. If you're old enough to fight for your fellow citizens' democratic right to vote, shouldn't you be allowed to cast your own ballot?"

The week before Christmas, I went to Wilmington to see Patty, who was home from the University of Chicago. Even though I hadn't seen her for almost three years, over the past few months I had persuaded myself that Patty was my love, my true love, my only love, the love of my life, the one I would love forever. But as the hour for our date drew nearer, I began to worry: "How does she feel about *me?*" Soon I had a first-class case of jitters about how the evening would go.

When I picked Patty up at her house, she told me she had arranged for dinner at Piggy's, a favorite barbecue hangout, and had invited another couple to join us. "Fine," I said. But the moment we all sat down to dinner, I knew I was in trouble. I couldn't begin to keep up with the fast, brassy badinage being tossed around the table. The jousting and joking swirled around me with dizzying speed until suddenly a great blanket of heaviness descended on me and clamped itself around me like a vise.

My brain shut down and I couldn't think. Excusing myself, I went to the men's room, where I retched and threw up for about five minutes. When I returned to the table, feeling better and ready to try again, someone asked me, in a lighthearted way, something frivolous about my army life. Those experiences having been too profoundly disturbing for me to trivialize in idle conversation, I made a lame comment that turned out to stop the conversation, and the strained silence that followed told the group that it was time to switch to another subject. For me, more and more, the evening became a nightmare. Though I struggled to shake my discomfort and the resulting embarrassment, they were twin enemies that kept me in a continual cold sweat.

Obviously not wanting to see me suffer any longer, Patty cut the evening short. I knew I had lost her forever, but at that moment I didn't care. I was just relieved to be out of my misery.

Back in New York, I knew I'd never see Patty again.

So long, Patty. Wherever you go, whatever you do, have a wonderful life. You deserve it. I won't forget the way you helped me in boarding school — how you built up my self-esteem, how you got me to apply myself when I was so lonely and homesick. I owe you more than I can ever tell you, Patty.

And now it was January. Time to go back to college. The war was over, and it was up to me to make a new beginning. Though I was still restless and rudderless, though I felt ill equipped to return to college, I went anyway. I hoped that just being there would help me crank up my energies and formulate some goals.

What a pipe dream that turned out to be!

11

TRINITY, COLUMBIA, AND BREAD LOAF U.

TWO UNEXPECTED SETBACKS

Indeed, just *being* in college did help me to formulate goals, stabilize my life. Good decisions resulted. I'd take a major in English, a minor in history — two sure bets for getting a good general education. There was, however, one slight complication. I was still trying to cope with a postwar syndrome — occasional, sudden collapses of body energy and bouts of mental fatigue. Each lasting an hour or two, those episodes put me under strain. Fortunately, they were becoming less and less frequent with each passing month.

Then, just as I was getting settled into the rhythm of classes and study — slam! I was flattened by two new setbacks. The first had to do with Patty. The second, with my parents.

Patty again? Still haunted by her, I was never able to expunge her from my mind. During the six years I had known her, we had laughed too much, enjoyed too many good times together, for the memories to be blotted out. But one day the mailman brought an unwelcome, jolting piece of news — a formal invitation to Patty's forthcoming marriage. Between the folds of the engraved card, she had enclosed a brief note: "Joe, my fiancé is a University of Chicago graduate student. I've known him for three years. Hope you're fine."

"Well! That explains a lot of things," I said to myself. *"That's* why she never answered my letters from England. *That's* why she had another couple join us at Piggy's Barbecue when I so desperately wanted, after three years' absence, to see her alone. *That's* why she appeared so poised, so self-assured, so much the woman who had replaced the girl. She was in love with someone else the whole time! Yep. Not only that but in love with some creep who had hung around — hadn't even taken part in the war! While I was freezing my tail off in a foxhole and eating watery soup in a dungeon, this 4-F with bifocals and flat feet was making time with my girl! Why do I have this wild desire to take the next available transportation to Chicago and punch his lights out?" That urge lasted only an hour or so. The maturity that had been forced on me during the past year took hold, and I dismissed such unproductive thoughts.

Now, finally, I could close the book on Patty. It was just as well, too, for doing so freed my mind to deal with the second shocker — another letter in the mail. This one was from my mother.

"Exciting news!" she wrote. Already I was groaning. "What now?" I thought. "I don't *need* excitement — exams are coming up — long, three-hour finals in just two weeks, and I've got to cram, cram, cram — got to study furiously just to get by." "Guess what, Joe," continued Mother. "In two weeks Father and I are throwing an 'Extravaganza' in your honor. It's a weekend party — a grand celebration of your return home from the war. A dozen of our friends have been invited from all over the U.S. We're throwing a gala Chinese dinner — octopus, birds' nest soup, egg rolls — the works — on Saturday night. Then, on Sunday, we'll have a Hawaiian luau, with a guitarist, leis, poi, even a hula dancer! Get yourself over here — remember, two weeks from today — *all in your honor!"*

I went limp. Head to toe. Now I know how a car feels when it's been totaled! I should attend this bash when — starting the very next day — I'd be facing a week of crucial exams? With my powers of retention not yet back to normal, surely I needed to devise every strategy at my command in order to pass those grueling tests.

I telephoned Mother and explained all this to her, concluding with, "Thanks so much, but there's no way I can make it."

Unaccustomed to taking no for an answer, Mother turned up the heat. "Listen, dear," she pounded, "Uncle Albert is coming all the way from Kansas to see 'good old Joe.'"

"But Uncle Albert hasn't seen me since I was twelve," I protested. "He can't be coming solely on my account."

"Oh, yes he is," insisted Mother. "He and a dozen others from Maryland, California, Massachusetts — from all over. They *can't wait* to see you, Joe. You just *cannot* let them down. They've all been in touch with us ever since the army declared you missing in action, then a prisoner of war. They all feel as if they've shared your ordeal. Just be here, Joe — just come. It's all decided — all planned."

Now it became clear. I got it. My fur began to rise. My blood began to boil in my veins. "This gala bash — it's not for me," I told myself angrily. "It's being staged by and for my parents. Not even one of *my* friends has been invited — George Thornburg, Bill Ashton, Cliff Nordstrom, or Hans Kasten. I'm being exploited. My parents are basking in the reflected glow of a son they've built up to be a super-hero." (Father, in fact, had even compared me with Richard, Coeur de Lion, who embarked on a Great Crusade to free Jerusalem from the Turks, only to be captured and imprisoned in Austria on his way home.) Yes, it was now quite clear to me as memories flashed through my mind. I recalled how my parents so often plucked me out of one school and dropped me into another. How they took me on endless travels at the expense of my emotional and educational needs. And now my father and mother were stepping in once again to upset my schooling! All that mattered to them was this — this damn-blasted "Extravaganza"!

Never before had I refused my parents anything. But this time, with a burst of resolve, I phoned them back. "Thanks again, but I'm skipping the weekend party to study for my finals. I'm afraid that has to be the end of the discussion."

Having been certain that I would eventually bow to their wishes, they were stunned and deeply hurt when they realized that my decision was final.

It was after that episode that I decided I *must* take complete control of my life. My salvation demanded it. Having taken this stand, I knew that now I could handle four years of college and that afterward I could make it on my own. Such thoughts gave me a wondrous sense of release, a welcome shot of adrenaline to boost my sense of self.

Gradually I drifted away from my parents, becoming absorbed with my studies and, later, with my job, wife, and children. But because this episode happened at an especially fragile time of my life, the emotional strain took a heavy toll on our relationship. It would be twenty years before I felt ready to close my eyes on the past and, once again, be a son to my father and mother.

THE HIDDEN WORLD OF MR. WILBUR

During my junior year at college, I took a part-time job at the Institute of Living, a pricey, very private retreat for people with mental disorders. There was an assurance of absolute confidentiality about the people who were "guests" there. Many New York and Hollywood notables or their relatives were reported to have been guests. The best accommodations at the institute were private cottages.

Mr. Wilbur lived in a luxurious private cottage. He was obviously getting the best abandonment that money could buy. A tall, spare man, probably about forty, he had a gentle manner and a soft, cultured voice that had just a trace of a southern accent.

My assignment seemed easy. I was to be a companion to Mr. Wilbur. During my orientation, the supervisor advised me: "Mr. Wilbur likes to be read to. He also enjoys walks on the grounds. But remember," she continued, "under no circumstances is he to be left alone, as he could conceivably do himself some bodily harm. At all times keep him close to you. On occasion he becomes agitated and exclaims, 'It's time to catch the four fifty-five.' When that occurs, just divert him to another subject."

Using little clues that Mr. Wilbur dropped, I learned that many years earlier, while a student at Duke University in Durham, he was in the habit of taking the 4:55 train to Chapel Hill to see his fiancée, a student with whom he was very much in love. I also gathered that just a few days before they were to be married she broke off their engagement and walked out of his life.

Mr. Wilbur liked to have me read the *New York Times* to him. I would read the headlines, and he would choose the articles he wanted to hear. During these sessions he would rock in his chair and smile at me appreciatively. The only subject he hated was sports. He had a particular aversion to baseball, a subject in which I had a fanatical interest, especially at this time of year, when the pennant races were heating up.

Occasionally, as I read to him, his eyes would glaze over and he would sink into a trance. When that happened, I would quickly switch to the sports page and the topic dearest to my heart: the league-leading St. Louis Cardinals. I would read him the box scores and the feature articles on Stan Musial, Marty Marion, Enos Slaughter, Harry "the Cat" Brecheen, and all the rest of my Cardinal heroes. He would just keep on smiling and rocking.

Once, when Mr. Wilbur's shirtsleeve was pulled up, I observed a half-dozen slash marks on his wrist. How dismaying! Why would there be marks of violence on so sweet, so gentle a person?

One day, while I was reading to him, he suddenly jumped up, announced, "It's time to catch the four fifty-five," and dashed out the door. I ran out after him. He did a fast lap around the cottage with me in full pursuit, then led me on a merry chase around the maintenance building. On his second lap around, I caught up, grabbed him around the waist, and escorted him back to the cottage.

A week later it happened again. "It's time to catch the four fifty-five," he declared, sprinting out the door. This time a delivery truck was approaching. Mr. Wilbur was running directly toward it. "My God!" I gasped aloud. "He's going to throw himself in front of that vehicle!" Charging after him, I grabbed his legs and toppled him to the ground. Without protest, he returned to the cottage and sat down. Seeing his eyes begin to glaze over, I read him the latest on the hot pennant race between the Cardinals and the Dodgers.

Three months later, I began to feel the growing pressures of my academic work and quit my job at the institute, at least for the time being. I said good-bye to Mr. Wilbur, with whom I felt a close kinship, and expressed the hope that we would meet again.

The next spring I returned to the institute for some more part-time work. This time I was assigned to a different guest. I looked for Mr. Wilbur, but someone else was occupying his cottage. No one seemed to know where he was. Finally I went to see the supervisor.

"Apparently someone else is living in Mr. Wilbur's cottage," I said to her. "What's happened to him?"

In view of her awareness that I had enjoyed a close relationship with Mr. Wilbur, her cold-as-steel reply sent me rocking on my heels: "Sorry, but I can't reveal any information about any guest other than the one to whom you are assigned." The evasive look in her eyes told me that she knew exactly what had happened to Mr. Wilbur. It was something that would be forever hidden from the outside world and from me.

That evening, instead of taking the bus back to college, I decided to walk the two miles. I was feeling very sad and walked very, very slowly.

THE ADVANTAGES OF MOZART OVER SEX

One of the most delightful and rewarding courses at Trinity was one in music appreciation called Music 1. It was taught by Professor Clarence Watters, a puckish little man who was the college organist and head of the Music Department. He opened every class with a long, folksy warmup on one of his two favorite topics, airplane design and gourmet food preparation, so his course became affectionately known around campus as Aerodynamics and French Cooking.

Inevitably, in every class, he brought the subject around to music. When he did, he got straight down to business. He taught us a simple concept about classical music that became the key to my lifelong enjoyment of it: "Most movements, or sections, of a symphony or concerto have a structure called *sonata form*. If you are aware of sonata form, you have the key to lasting rewards in listening."

With infectious enthusiasm, Professor Watters explained how sonata form in a movement of a symphony takes the following pattern:

1. *The Exposition:* a section that presents the two themes, or melodies, that are basic to the movement.
2. *The Development:* a section that presents variations on the two themes — embellishing, expanding, inverting, and moving them around in various ways.
3. *The Recapitulation:* a return to the themes as originally presented, with some nuances or further variations.
4. *The Coda:* a short section that ends the movement with a flourish.

Sometimes, when I talk to people about the importance of understanding sonata form, their eyes glaze over and they say, "Who needs to know about that? The music is there and if you like it, you like it. If you don't, you don't." 'Taint so, folks. Not in my experience, at least, or in the experience of my classmates in Music 1. Most of us had revelations. Learning the structure of a symphonic movement helped me to follow the work and to become more aware of the musical elements. It was the beginning of understanding, and it made my listening a much richer experience. Professor Watters converted thousands of musical ignoramuses like me — people who said, "I like classical music," but really liked only a handful of often-heard works with themes they could whistle.

Since taking Music 1, I have been listening to a much wider range of classical works and listening more attentively. That the world's most glorious music comes from Mozart I now have no doubt — except every time I listen to Beethoven. If Mozart is my faithful wife, Beethoven is my seductive mistress. If Mozart wrote hundreds of works that are inexpressibly sublime, the two greatest of all musical compositions, in my opinion, are by Beethoven.

Professor Watters was less equivocal. He went straight down the line for Mozart. "Listening to Mozart," he told us, "is an experience rivaled by nothing else in the world except sex. In fact, Mozart has a couple of distinct advantages over sex. For one thing, you can enjoy Mozart while doing chores. For another, Mozart can provide you with hours and hours of unending pleasure, whereas after half an hour of sex you want to do something else."

It was in Professor Watters's class that I first learned that fun was not the natural enemy of learning. His classes were such a pleasure that the following year I signed up for his other course, Aerodynamics and French Cooking 2. That was a course in Harmony.

ROBERT FROST LOOKS AT MY POETRY

One August day I made a delightful discovery. It came after I had graduated from Trinity and just before I was to enter Columbia University. A college friend approached me and, with great animation in his eyes, admonished me: "Joe — this is for you. Get yourself right up to the rolling hills of western Vermont. You simply must not miss the tremendous Bread Loaf Writers' Conference. It starts next week — workshops led by Robert Frost and other literary luminaries. You're an aspiring writer — just your cup of tea, Joe!" How perfect! I myself had written some poetry in recent years and fancied myself a talented, if as yet undiscovered, poet.

I was an ardent admirer of Robert Frost, whom I considered the World's Greatest Living Poet. The conference seemed an ideal opportunity for me to get his opinion of my poems. As soon as I arrived at Bread Loaf, I placed an envelope containing three of my poems in his mailbox, along with a note entreating him to evaluate them. Because he was to be at the conference for only one day, I felt some urgency and was emboldened to approach him in that manner.

The next day was one I will never forget. Mr. Frost, running his fingers through his tousled white hair, addressed a hushed audience on the nature of poetry. Toward the end of his talk came the surprise, as he said to the group, "Now let me read a poem submitted by one of you. Let's see how it conveys the feeling of despair. This one is called 'It Is Cold Somewhere.'" My mind flipped. That was *my* poem! It was one I had written in POW camp to ward off the pain of hunger, cold, and fatigue. Robert Lee Frost, the World's Greatest Living Poet, was about to read and discuss *my* poem! That was the break I needed. He would be my discoverer, and I would be on my way! Just as he started to read the poem, however, someone in the audience asked him a question. Then another asked one. Then another. By now Mr. Frost had become so thoroughly distracted that he never got back to my poem. I was crestfallen. But I really couldn't blame Mr. Frost — he couldn't help it if he was constantly being interrupted.

More determined than ever, I now firmly resolved to get his verdict before he left the conference. That afternoon, following his custom, he invited all of the participants to visit his farm. He loved to play softball, and as soon as he got up a game, I made sure I was on his team. Toward the end of the game, while he was waiting his turn at bat, I saw my chance. "Mr. Frost," I asked, "did you have time to look at the three poems I left in your mailbox?"

"Oh, yes," he replied amiably, "I read them all. There was one called 'It Is Cold Somewhere.' That one —"

"Mr. Frost!" yelled a member of the team. "You're up! It's your turn to bat!"

Without finishing his sentence, Mr. Frost hurried over to face the pitcher. Unfortunately, he popped up for the fourth time that day. Even more unfortunately for me, he forgot to come back and finish his sentence. What a huge disappointment! Perhaps he was disturbed by his performance at bat. And if he was, who could blame him? The World's Greatest Living Poet had popped up four times. The poet who depicted our human tragedies and fears, who wrote of our reactions to the complexities of life and our ultimate acceptance of its burdens — the internationally acclaimed four-time Pulitzer Prize–winning poet — just couldn't get good wood on the ball. When he left the conference that evening, I still didn't know what he thought of my poems.

A few years later — on January 20, 1961, to be exact — John F. Kennedy was about to be inaugurated in Washington. I flipped on the TV and there, standing on the podium before a huge crowd assembled in front of the Capitol — his tousled white hair blowing in a stiff wind — was Robert Frost, the World's Greatest Living Poet. He was about to read a poem. Now here was a perfect chance, if ever there was one, for him to read my poem — and without any interruptions. But he didn't. He read one of his own. I really can't blame him for that either. I'd have read my own stuff, too, if it had been me up there.

MIRACLE OF MIRACLES!

After the Bread Loaf Writers' Conference, I moved to New York City to do graduate work at Columbia. But first, where should I live? Not near my parents — of that I was sure. Since they lived on the Upper West Side, I chose the Lower East Side, to put as much of Manhattan between us as possible. Still hurting, still smarting, I had not yet forgiven them for the trauma of those lonely, homeless teenage years, nor for dumping me on reluctant relatives during holidays. However, I was now grateful for one benefit — the heaven-sent GI Bill of Rights, which gave me the financial independence to continue with my education. No more humiliating "Need Money — Urgent" pleas to my parents.

For a year I shared an apartment with Howard Rosenberg, a Princeton graduate and trainee in one of the big New York City banks. We got along fine except for the times he devilishly introduced me to his Princeton friends as a graduate of Bread Loaf U.

Of all the courses I took at Columbia, the most stimulating was one on American history taught by the noted historian Henry Steele Commager. What a seditious gift he had for keeping his students awake! Using the English language as his co-conspirator, he could distill an entire series of events into one quick metaphor. For example, after discussing the sale of U.S. scrap iron to Japan prior to World War II, he introduced America's entry into the war simply by saying: "And when the Japanese dropped the Second Avenue El on Pearl Harbor . . ."

It was during that course that I made my big decision. It may take a miracle, I decided, but I must find a career that centers around the use of language — a job such as writing or publishing.

After a year at Columbia, I ran out of GI credits. At this point I wasn't about to ask my parents for tuition money. Nor did I feel up to tackling anything as arduous as part-time work while attending college. But wasn't it high time I started to work? Here I was, twenty-five years old, and I had never held a job — unless you count the camp counseling I did for a pittance, and unless you count my three-year hitch in the U.S. Army, when I was paid $60 a month, even for the days I hiked along a road in central Germany, right in the middle of the war, saying *"Heil Hitler"* to every passerby.

"Get a job!" I said to myself. And — miracle of miracles — I did.

THE WORLD OF
TEXTBOOK
PUBLISHING

MY FIRST JOB: ALMOST GETTING THE AX

"Get a job!" I had told myself. But wait! What kind of job? It had to be connected with writing or publishing — that much I knew.

In the fall of 1950, I applied to the textbook division of several New York publishers for an entry-level job in the editorial department. Why the textbook division? I reasoned that such a line of work involved three areas in which I had a consuming interest: producing books, which held for me a romantic allure; working with the English language, which had already become an abiding passion; and constructing materials designed to help young people learn, which struck me as a Lofty Endeavor. It seemed an eminently worthy and purposeful kind of vocation — especially to someone who didn't know diddly about it.

In response to my inquiries, the Macmillan Company and Harcourt, Brace & Company said they had no editorial openings. But at World Book Company the door swung open. To my boundless delight, I was offered a trainee position at the munificent salary of $2,000 a year. My horizon looked clear. But into each job, apparently, some rain must fall. Not just rain, I later learned — sometimes a deluge!

World Book Company was a medium-sized publisher in Yonkers. It had its modest beginnings in the home of Caspar Hodgson, who founded the company in 1905. His remodeled home, now the company headquarters, was on Park Hill, a residential outcropping which by some geological gerrymandering rose high above the dreary row houses of South Yonkers.

Ross Marvin, the editor-in-chief, hired me as understudy to Edward Bryant, the company's copy editor. It was Mr. Bryant's job to read every textbook in progress to make sure that it conformed to established rules of grammar, usage, capitalization, punctuation, and spelling. Little did I know that a gigantic generation gap was soon to open up between us, to the detriment of him, of me, and of the company.

Mr. Bryant, aged eighty-three, had been with World Book Company since its founding in "aught-five," as he referred to it. A Harvard graduate, he was a soft-voiced gentleman who always dropped his pencil and rose from his leather chair when a woman entered his office. He bore a fine shock of white hair, a ready smile, and pince-nez that sat low on his nose. He was always nattily dressed in a gray or black suit, but his trademark was a starched white Hoover collar and dark knit tie. With his wife he lived in a cozy neo-Colonial home, surrounded by old-fashioned roses, at the bottom of Park Hill.

When I arrived on the job, it was evident that Mr. Ferguson, the new company president, was impatient with the slow, dragging, behind-schedule pace of Mr. Bryant. Not just impatient, but often peevish and irritable. For Mr. Ferguson was an aggressive, market-oriented executive who had just set the company on an ambitious expansion program that meant producing, not just the accustomed handful of math books a year, but a hundred textbooks yearly in math, reading, English, spelling, and other subjects. Mr. Bryant, increasingly unable to keep up with the pace, was buried under an avalanche of manuscripts being dumped on his desk. He was the company bottleneck — a serious threat to Mr. Ferguson's plan to expand the company's offerings dramatically and become a publisher to be reckoned with on a national scale.

Mr. Ferguson was desperate for Mr. Bryant to retire and for a younger, more productive person like me to take his place. Frantic as he was, however, he could never quite muster up the moxie to tell Mr. Bryant that since he was eighty-three he should go fishing. The only time he made a suggestion to that effect, Mr. Bryant took it more in sorrow than in anger. Said he: "I can't believe that you could even think of suddenly abandoning the high standards of quality for which the company has come to be known since aught-five." Mr. Ferguson also knew that it was often whispered around that if Mr. Bryant ever stopped working, he'd be dead within a month. Mr. Ferguson had no wish to have the weight of Mr. Bryant's demise placed squarely on his shoulders.

After I had received six months' training from Mr. Bryant, Mr. Ferguson made his move. He directed Mr. Marvin, the editor-in-chief, to take half of the books in progress away from Mr. Bryant and turn them over to me. That decision made Mr. Bryant livid. It also thrust our amicable relationship into a bitterly adversarial one.

Swift and brutal was the counterattack from Mr. Bryant. He beckoned Mr. Ferguson and Mr. Marvin into his office and in my presence told them: "Gentlemen, I'm afraid I must report to you that young Littell here is far too inexperienced to copy-edit manuscripts at a professional level. He fails to catch hundreds of errors at the manuscript stage, necessitating expensive corrections after the manuscript has been set in type. I regret to say that he is costing you thousands of dollars per month. Here are just two examples of grammatical errors that Littell failed to catch. [He showed them the errors.] If you wish to protect the company's good name, for Heaven's sake, direct the editors to route all manuscripts through me as they have done in the past. I suggest, too, that it would be wise if you informed Littell that he should seek other employment."

Obviously finding that whole scene embarrassing, Messrs. Ferguson and Marvin backpedaled out of Mr. Bryant's office — Mr. Ferguson promising that "we'll give the matter some thought and get back to you."

So shaken was I after that ordeal that when the day's work was done, I sat dejectedly in my rented room, wondering what was to become of me. I figured the chances were better than fifty-fifty that soon I would be clearing out my desk.

At about this time the company was looking for a new advertising copywriter to replace a fired employee. Taking a chance, Mr. Ferguson directed that I be tried out for the job, green as I was. "Littell, I'd like you to write the copy for an advertising brochure which announces the forthcoming publication of a major new program — a series of beginning readers authored by two world-renowned reading specialists, Drs. Donald Durrell and Helen Sullivan of Boston University. Think you can do it?" Well, I hoped I could, but that idea soon fizzled: I bungled the attempt, and an outside writer was hired. However, shorthanded as he was in the advertising department, Mr. Ferguson again ventured to try me out — this time in handling the production, layout, and proofreading of this important brochure. Inspired by his perpetual faith in me, I set to work. This time I would prove to him that Littell was indispensable to World Book Company!

After completing the layout, I concluded that the whole thing looked dull as dust. "I've got to pep it up!" I told myself. "I know — I'll sprinkle around the margins a few of the small illustrations (children, animals, etc.) contained within the pages of the readers we are advertising. Great idea!"

Unfortunately, right next to the heading "DISTINGUISHED AUTHORS," I placed a pair of chimpanzees swinging with wild abandon on jungle vines. One chimp, wearing a giddy expression, flashed a mouthful of teeth at least three octaves wide. The other looked as if he were propelling himself happily through the trees on a bellyful of fermented jungle juice. As soon as the brochure was printed and copies distributed around the office, I got a ring-off-the-hook call from Mr. Ferguson. He was furious. "Littell," he sputtered, "what the hell have you done? Do you know that I'm going to have to reprint that whole goddamn brochure and throw out every one of the ten thousand copies that have just been printed?"

Even worse, some wag at the office posted the chimp page on the bulletin board, adding the caption "Our Swinging Authors." Other editors came along and added their own captions: "Our High Mon-key-Monks," "Our Top Bananas Have a Peel," and so on. The bulletin board was not twenty feet from the president's office — he had to pass it every time he went to the washroom.

Back I went to editorial! Management had apparently decided it was better to have me be a thorn in Mr. Bryant's side once again than a perpetual reminder to them of their folly in letting me have anything to do with advertising.

Mr. Bryant, of course, had no intention of letting up on me. Anything and everything I did aroused his ire to the point that I decided it was time for me to act. I would fight for my job.

"Mr. Bryant," I asked him, "will you kindly show me the 'hundreds of errors' I failed to catch?" Taken aback, he thumbed through my work and sheepishly came up with only two minor errors. That was my opening.

When I knocked on Mr. Marvin's door, there was Mr. Ferguson, chatting with him. I asked if I could see them both. They obliged.

"Gentlemen," I said in my most respectful manner, "I'd like to speak with you about my job. I don't believe my work has been represented to you fairly. I would like to take a few minutes of your time to discuss it.

"Mr. Bryant referred to my 'hundreds of errors.' However, after a two-hour search, he has found and shown me only two. I have been studying every manual I can lay my hands on and want to assure you that I am mastering the nuances of grammar, usage, capitalization, punctuation, and spelling. Phyllis Mertz and the other editors whose books I am copy-editing have complimented me on my thorough and meticulous work. You may wish to talk with those editors about the quality of my efforts.

"My purpose in coming to you is not just to defend my work. I'm asking your help and support in making my job a viable one. Mainly, I'm asking you for complete independence of Mr. Bryant. By independence I mean that he should not be allowed to spend most of his time double-checking my work when so much of his own is piling up on his desk.

"I have great respect for this company and enjoy working here. I simply want an opportunity to show you what I can do under more favorable circumstances. Will you give me a chance?"

Mr. Ferguson and Mr. Marvin looked at each other, totally speechless. They had apparently been taken aback by an aggressive side of me they had never seen before. Finally, Mr. Marvin found words. "Well, Joe," he said, "I already know the editors' opinion of your work. They speak very highly of you. I'm sympathetic to everything you've said, and I'll make certain that you're able to work without interference. I'll speak to Mr. Bryant about this."

"Go to it, Joe," added Mr. Ferguson with a reassuring nod and a smile. "You have our full support."

In that five-minute meeting, I may have saved my job!

After a year of working independently of Mr. Bryant, I received permission to hire an assistant. I brought in Margaret Halasz, a glamorous Hungarian blonde, about fifty, who was usually decked out in a black dress and pearl necklace and looked like a countess. Not only did she perform her office duties commendably, but her irrepressibly upbeat attitude delighted the entire staff. Every morning at eight-thirty she would appear at my office door, levitate on the toes of her high-heeled pumps, and say, "Joe! Eet ees going to be a *vonderful* day!" And, thanks to her, it *vas* a vonderful day.

One Sunday, Mr. Bryant failed to return home for dinner. His wife went to the office to look for him and found him at his desk, slumped over his galley proofs. He was dead.

Many times I thought of Mr. Bryant after his death. Sadly, he had been a man caught between the old, steady ways of doing things and the new age of change, upheaval, increasing competition, and dynamic corporate expansion.

Perhaps my bitter experience with Mr. Bryant made a difference in my life. I believe it may have contributed to my becoming a workaholic and to the marital problems I would later face. For more than thirty years in publishing, six days and nights a week, I drove myself mercilessly — drove myself not so much because of a desire to succeed but because of an overwhelming fear of failure. For many years it lurked around the corner, stalked me, haunted me — failure! Not being a psychologist, I can't presume to analyze all of my fears and motivations, but I do have the pleasure (and the pain) of knowing myself better than anyone else!

When Mr. Ferguson was ready to retire in 1962, he could find no executive in the company equipped to take over the presidency. Accordingly, he sold the company to Harcourt, Brace. The new, combined entity became Harcourt, Brace and World.

Greater challenge and change entered my life in the year 1956. At $7,000 a year, I was offered a bona fide editorial position at the Macmillan Company, headquartered in Manhattan. As an assistant editor, I would be fulfilling a long-term wish to be involved in the creation of textbooks — a field crucial to the young people of America. Now I would be in charge of a series of English textbooks for junior high schools. Now I would be able to work with the series' authors in shaping the content and organization of the books. That suited me just fine.

The ten years I spent at Macmillan were to be eventful times.

PAUL BUNYAN, KING GEORGE THE THIRD, AND MR. RATS

With its impressive list of school and college textbooks, the Macmillan Company was one of the top educational publishers in the nation.

As soon as I went to work there, I became acutely aware that the public perception of how elementary and secondary textbooks are created is pure myth. Most people think that the author writes the book, then passes the typewritten pages on to the publisher, who then turns it into a book. Not so! The publisher is a creative partner with the author and, more often than not, initiates the project. The publisher keeps tabs on what books the schools are using in all subjects, studies the market, determines teacher satisfaction with the books, and predicts educational trends. On seeing the need for a new textbook, the publisher will gather a team of experienced teachers who can write a text that fills the need. The publisher will also make sure that special features are included to give the text competitive appeal — a superior teaching format, improved study aids, a more useful teachers' manual, multimedia learning enhancers, and so on. A publisher-directed enterprise such as this demands that the editor in charge of a book or series of books have a thorough knowledge of the subject as well as the curriculum. For that reason, an editor benefits from having had some prior experience either in teaching school or in selling textbooks to schools. (Although I had never taught school, I had observed many classrooms and had sold books briefly in Pennsylvania.)

The person who hired me at Macmillan was Lee Deighton, head of the schoolbook department and one of the legendary figures in publishing. His creative imagination and instinct for the textbook market had made their mark during his fourteen years at Harcourt, Brace, where he became a major force in establishing that company as the leading publisher in the field of English. At Macmillan he took a revolutionary step, conceiving the idea of publishing texts for junior and senior high schools in a form never before used — the paperback textbook. Instead of having to tote around a huge hardback anthology more suitable as a doorstop, the students could now read from four attractive paperbacks that contained forty percent more reading selections. The paperback revolution had come to U.S. schools! When Deighton became president of Macmillan in 1960, I was promoted to senior editor and put in charge of producing that paperback program. Called Literary Heritage, it was successful from the start and forced Harcourt, Brace to drop everything and put out a paperback program of its own in order to stay competitive.

Deighton was a tall, full-chested man with a sharp, angular face and a large, jutting chin. Overall, he was ruggedly handsome. When near him, I felt I was in the presence of Paul Bunyan, the legendary giant lumberjack. To me, Deighton was easily the equal of that greatest of boss loggers who created the Grand Canyon and the Black Hills, who invented the gigantic hotcake griddle, greased by stooges who skated on it with sides of bacon strapped to their shoes. Lee Deighton could do anything Paul Bunyan could do. He was not just my mentor, not just my hero — he was my god.

Another notably gutsy decision that Deighton made was to publish the Bank Street Readers, the first integrated reading program, a significant step forward for inner-city students. What a welcome relief they were from Dick and Jane — the only alternative at that time! The books featured black and Hispanic children — some with only one parent — facing the challenges and opportunities unique to the inner city. When Macmillan salesmen balked at calling on inner-city schools that had small budgets for textbooks, Deighton became apoplectic. Angrily, he lashed out at them. "Listen," he stormed, "schools can always find money for truly promising projects. Besides, these books are just too important to be sabotaged by a bunch of money-grubbing salesmen who let them languish in the warehouse. Get out there — go to the inner cities and sell these books!" In no time at all, Macmillan had go-getters in the ghettos.

It was Lee Deighton who taught me virtually everything I ever learned about How to Publish Good Books That Are Right for the Market. In the planning stage of every textbook, he drummed into me these three basic principles:

- Know the competition.
- In some important way, make the book more useful than the competition.
- Pretend you are the salesman presenting the book to the adoption committee. What will you say to them?

The president of Macmillan was George P. Brett, the third generation of Bretts — all named George — to run the company. We called him King George the Third because, like his predecessors, he ruled with a monarchical hand. The company was located on Fifth Avenue and Twelfth Street. Brett lived around the corner in the "Executive Mansion," from which he had access to his office through a private passageway. His board of directors, by tradition, consisted of the nine department heads — a rather myopic setup, since he had no outside directors and little or no input from the business or financial commu-

nity. Even as I watched him show visitors around and proudly announce, "This is my education department," "This is my children's
book department," "This is my trade [general books] department,"
and so on, I sensed that there was something grandly obsolete about
this commanding figure.

Then Brett made a fatal blunder. In 1953, he needed capital and
took the company public. However, he neglected to retain for himself and his family enough shares of company stock to prevent a
takeover. The firm was now ripe for plucking.

The assault on Macmillan came in 1960. The Crowell-Collier
Publishing Company, famous for its *Collier's Encyclopedia*, bought
some initial shares from Macmillan in a low-key posture, then bought
up more on the open market, and finally pried loose the additional
shares it needed from Macmillan shareholders at a price they couldn't
resist. In no time, King George had been dethroned and his nine
liege lords banished from the kingdom. Macmillan now became a
wholly owned subsidiary of Crowell-Collier.

Where did this leave Macmillan's employees? In fear and trembling. Crowell-Collier had little experience in educational and trade
publishing and was known to be run by business interests rather than
"book people." Rumors were rife that seasoned editors who lavished
love and care on the making of books would be cast out and replaced
by production-minded technicians. In spite of Crowell-Collier's assurances that the integrity of the editorial departments would be
retained, fears persisted. Even when Deighton was made president of
Macmillan, it was small consolation; he would still be accountable to
the new directors, most of whom, coming either from Wall Street or
nonbook corporations, were nabobs of the bottom line.

To make things worse, it became known in the schoolbook department that Crowell-Collier was sending in a new editor-in-chief by the
name of Mr. Rats. There was panic at the editorial water cooler.
Rumors circulated that Mr. Rats was a monstrous, rodent-faced ogre
who ate slow or dawdling editors for lunch. As it turned out, Bob
Rahtz was the kindest, gentlest man ever to get a bad rap. And it was
Deighton, not Crowell-Collier, who had hired him. Rahtz was a slim,
baldish fellow who wore the scholarly mien of a person who had

spent a lifetime with books. Casual and courtly, he seemed most comfortable in an English tweed jacket with leather elbow pads. Strongly committed to making the best possible textbooks, Rahtz was also the person who kept the rest of us aware that we were human beings. If things got dicey between editors and authors, or between editors and editors, he was there to see to it that we all put forth our best selves.

True to their word, the Crowell-Collier people did not interfere with the editorial processes at Macmillan. They did, however, bring with them the new language of business. Macmillan folks soon learned that "marketing" was no longer just something a housewife did and that "fulfillment" was no longer just the realization of an individual's fondest dreams.

It was in 1964 — a big year for me — that I was made executive editor, the number-two spot next to Bob Rahtz, editor-in-chief. In addition to my responsibilities as director of Literary Heritage and other programs in the field of English, I was given charge of the elementary reading and adult education programs. Then, a year later, I was elected a vice-president of the Macmillan Company. "This just doesn't seem real!" I thought to myself, considering those days, years earlier, when I nearly got the ax; when I illustrated that brochure with chimps too close to the VIPs; when I started out in publishing so wet behind the ears! At any rate, it was a gratifying promotion, filled with exciting challenges.

Though Lee Deighton was now president of Macmillan, with responsibility for eight other departments besides education, he continued to take a personal interest in me. He invited me to write with him a book that would provide a clearer, more logical codification of English grammar and usage than had been available to schools up to that time. Titled *The Macmillan English Handbook*, it became a standard for its time. Lee and I had frequent contacts in book-planning meetings and on special projects. Without that experience at his side, I would have been pitifully unprepared, three years later, to co-found the publishing firm that became known as McDougal, Littell & Company.

13

THE BOILING FAMILY CAULDRON

HOW TO LIKE YOUR DETESTED UNCLE

I'm not a hating person. But in all my life, *he* was the one person I loathed — that sanctimonious, self-righteous tyrant of a man who, acting in loco parentis, became my unofficial guardian. It was during those years when I was tucked away in boarding school — homesick, rootless, vulnerable — that Father's brother, my uncle Elton Littell, grabbed the reins and cracked his whip over my young life. And it was during those same years that my parents, five thousand miles away in Honolulu, assumed the best. "Our Joe? Oh, he's doing just fine, thank you!"

This was the same uncle, you recall, who forbade me to attend his daughter's wedding at a time when I desperately needed to participate in the gathering of the clan. It was he who, during my Christmas visit to Yonkers, trotted out his jailer's keys and kept me incarcerated for three weeks. It was my uncle Elton who punished me for my report card Bs and Cs, never once praising me for my As. And I despised him, too, for not balancing the humiliations he inflicted on me with a single word of encouragement or an avuncular chat. Mine was a pure, blinding hatred, undiluted by any feelings of family loyalty, respect for age, or human compassion.

One February day — it was 1962 — I received a telegram that this detested uncle, aged eighty-five, had suddenly dropped dead. Can't say I was exactly stunned! Nevertheless, I couldn't refuse the request of his widow, Aunt Nancy, to attend his funeral at St. John's Episcopal Church in Yonkers. During the rose-colored eulogy, I hardly recognized the deceased — he had acquired a shining-bright halo! Then, at the cemetery, as his casket was being lowered into the grave, how Aunt Nancy's inner thoughts must have clashed with mine! She's murmuring, "God bless you and keep you, dear Elty," while I, holding her arm steady, am silently sputtering, "There goes the bastard at last!"

For years after my uncle's death, I was still carrying that heavy baggage of hatred. Wasn't time supposed to heal the wounds, dilute my devastating rancor toward him? Why was it that, on the contrary, the passage of time only served to increase my misery? Surely, for my own emotional health, this was something I should face and deal with directly. This was something I should get rid of, once and for all. But how?

Knowing that there are always reasons for a person's behavior, I plunged into some analysis. What motivated that man? Why had he felt the need to treat me with such cruelty? Perhaps if I gained some insights, if I knew him better, I might be able to reduce, if not eliminate entirely, these lingering, corrosive feelings of hostility.

I devised something I call "the Two-List System." I made two lists. One was headed "My Uncle's Possible Explanations for His Behavior"; here I would try to put myself in his shoes. The second was headed "My Own Attempts to Explain His Behavior"; here I was careful to exclude specific gripes and defensive statements that could block discovery of his underlying reasons for behavior. Here are the two lists:

THE TWO-LIST SYSTEM
The Question:
Why did my uncle, in my opinion, treat me so cruelly?

LIST 1:
MY UNCLE'S POSSIBLE EXPLANATIONS FOR HIS BEHAVIOR
    1. He thought my parents might consider any scholastic failure on

my part, while he was acting on their behalf, as a reflection on him.

2. He was simply motivating me in the same way that his own father had motivated him.

3. A surrogate parent who is not stern and demanding is derelict in his duty and can hardly command respect.

4. It is difficult to make decisions that normally belong in the domain of the parents. He did the best he knew how.

LIST 2:
MY OWN ATTEMPTS TO EXPLAIN HIS BEHAVIOR

1. He feared losing control over me as my guardian or appearing weak. He kept this control through acts of dominance: locking me up, keeping me from seeing my friends, forbidding me to attend family reunions.

2. His few interests were confined to medicine and health. Unlike the rest of the Littells, he traveled seldom and showed little interest in literature, music, theater, or sports. Feeling inadequate to provide personal guidance or intellectual leadership, he used his authority as a substitute.

3. He may not have liked me for some reason. I thought I had been a responsive and considerate guest in his home, but maybe not, in his view.

4. As he became older, he may have harbored an increasing resentment toward my parents for sending their children off to schools and colleges in his neighborhood, then expecting him to take charge of them. Aunt Nancy was found of observing, "The bishop begets 'em, then forgets 'em."

5. He may have been so frustrated about his failure to sire a son himself that he took it out on me.

My system worked! My anger started to level off. From the boiling point it eased to a gentle simmer and finally was replaced by empathy. Instead of hating my uncle, I began to understand why he acted as he did, to realize that the motives for some of his actions were the same ones that drive the rest of us, in varying degrees. We, too, are at times defensive or insecure, willful or capricious, intolerant or overreactive. The human frailties that we all share simply take different forms and disguises.

Something else I discovered. By the very act of writing about a relationship — by simply transferring my heart and head feelings onto a piece of paper — I was achieving a catharsis I had never thought possible. In acknowledging the anger and trying to understand it, I was succeeding in diminishing it. One day, I figured, it would disappear altogether.

The process I have just described would also help in later years to reduce the anger that I felt toward my parents, toward another relative, and toward a business associate. What an achievement — being able to cleanse my mind of all the emotional clutter that found its way into my life!

MORRIS BECOMES THE TOAST OF THE COCKTAIL CROWD

My lovable teddy bear of a brother! Do you recall briefly meeting that rare soul? Morris, that self-publishing teenager in Honolulu, with his infamous *ROTTEN EGG BEHIND EAR* and *BISHOP FIRES THE CANON* headlines in "The Littell Family Chronicle"? Well, there's more to tell — a story that becomes ever more poignant as the years roll on (it brings a lump to my throat), yet one that ends on a positive, unexpectedly joyous note.

Morris was a dreamer, an idealist. The older he grew, the more he became out of sync with the world about him. He couldn't possibly march in step. And when it came to shop class, he was hopeless. One day his shop teacher complained, "Morris, I can't tell whether you've made an airplane or a battleship!"

My brother's strengths lay elsewhere, his passions focusing on the beautiful things of this world, like music and poetry. At Iolani School he won the coveted poetry prize. That was his forte, where he shone. Morris couldn't get enough of poetry — he devoured it, hour after hour. He used to memorize long passages from Shakespeare, Tennyson, and Longfellow. Once he recited to me — in installments, of course — all ninety-seven stanzas of Tennyson's "Locksley Hall." "It excites me," said he, "to think that in a poem written in 1842, Tennyson foretold the coming of the airplane. Not only that but commercial aviation, military aviation, and aerial warfare. And, Joe, do you know that he also predicted the eventual end of all wars with the formation of a single world government, what he called the 'Parliament of man'? It takes a poet to have that kind of vision."

"Will it be all right if I memorize some of that poem, too?" I asked Morris, somehow feeling the need to obtain his permission, as if he were proprietor of the poem. He nodded. And so, committing to memory the prophetic part of the poem, I recited that portion to everyone in sight. Doing so gave me a sense of power over the ideas, as if I had originated them. And now I'll even recite it to you:

> For I dipped into the future, far as human eye could see,
> Saw the Vision of the world, and all the wonder that would be;
>
> Saw the heavens fill with commerce, argosies of purple sails,
> Pilots of the purple twilight, dropping down with costly bales;
>
> Heard the heavens fill with shouting, and there rained a
>   ghastly dew
> From the nations' airy navies grappling in the central blue;
>
> Far along the world-wide whisper of the south-wind rushing
>   warm,
> With the standards of the peoples plunging through the
>   thunder-storm;
>
> Till the war-drum throbbed no longer, and the battle flags
>   were furled
> In the Parliament of man, the Federation of the world.

When Morris was fourteen, Father made him go to confession once a month. Why Morris, when the rest of us were spared? I think he suspected that Morris had secret habits and was hoping that a full confession, followed by a fresh resolve, would do wonders for his soul and body. Father Bray, the priest who took Morris's confession, was a feisty, pipe-smoking Britisher with no understanding of my brother's character or inner needs. His misguided recommendation to my parents? "Morris should join the Junior ROTC at the Honolulu Armory. That will make a man out of him."

So now, two afternoons a month, Morris found himself doing close-order drill and trying to learn the care and cleaning of an army rifle — tasks hardly suited to his ethereal nature and talents. After two drill sessions, Morris spilled his frustrations out to me. "It's awful! When I march I'm always out of step and my rifle is always slipping off my shoulder. My fellow cadets become so amused by this that they pay no attention to the drill instructor's commands and they all march off in different directions! One of the cadets thought I was imitating Charlie Chaplin. Now they all call me 'Charlie.' I'll *never* make a soldier!" he groaned.

After a month of Junior ROTC, Morris dropped out.

What next? Again leaning on Father Bray for advice, my parents were delighted when he advised, "Have him go out for varsity football at Iolani. Surely that will make a man out of him."

After weeks of getting beat up in scrimmage by the first string, Morris quit showing up for practice. (That was the year the school fired the football coach. He made the mistake of calling his team "yellow," and all the Orientals quit. He ended the season with only ten players.)

Next, in desperation, my parents packed Morris off to Connecticut. At Kent School, he again revolted — hated the rigorous routine of a prep school. He daydreamed and paid little attention to his studies. The next step was Trinity College, where I suspect he was accepted out of deference to Father, an illustrious alumnus. Morris flunked out after a year.

Next? To Berea College in Kentucky, a Christian work-study college where the students, in addition to their academic pursuits, performed daily jobs and presumably learned the meaning of work, discipline, and personal responsibility. Surely this was the right answer for my brother! Morris lasted a year at Berea.

My brother Morris. For most of his short life, he drifted aimlessly. And then, toward the end, came the big break.

He now went to New York, where for three years, living in a rented room, he took on odd jobs. He ran errands for a bank, ushered in a theater, waited on tables. After the Japanese attack on Pearl Harbor he was drafted, but after a year the army discharged him.

Some of my impressions of Morris are embedded in my mind through family hearsay. Mother told me that as a child in China, Morris was frail, tubercular, and anemic. In his teenage years, his diagnosis was dementia praecox, or, to use today's catchall term, schizophrenia. No doubt, of all of us kids, he must have been the most difficult to rear, always, even in adulthood, behaving and speaking in unpredictable, unconventional ways, happy only when immersed in his own world of poetry and music. If only, from the beginning, somebody could have picked up on that clue, directing him along those lines of endeavor for which he was so ideally suited! What heartaches could have been spared him and all the family! I look at a photo of Morris in an army uniform and grieve to see his eyes, so sad, so lost — a man of promise so maladjusted to his environment!

Morris stood five feet eleven inches tall, with light brown hair, a well-chiseled nose, kindly eyes, a ready smile, and a pleasingly modulated voice. Over the years, many women gravitated to him. They were educated as well as uneducated, beautiful as well as plain, wealthy as well as poor. Some mothered him, some felt a romantic attachment to him, and some just felt sorry for him. He married three times, his first wife, Anna May, bearing him a daughter, Nancy, his only offspring. This very young wife had none of the intellectual interests he sought. "I left her," he told me, "because she bored me to death. Besides, it was just too hard for me to support a family."

Untrue to his gentle nature, Morris committed an act of vandalism for which my parents never forgave him. Puzzled by what he called their "bottomless pit of wealth" and mindful that when Father was bishop of Honolulu his adversaries circulated rumors that he had embezzled church funds, he broke into their New York apartment one day when they were out of town. He ransacked every drawer, every closet, dumping the contents helter-skelter in every direction, looking for evidence that they were embezzlers. Horror-struck, my parents again attached to him the label "schizo," a ready explanation for his occasional bizarre behavior. As to that "bottomless pit," I was not to find out for twenty years the source of their vast fortune.

One day Morris decided he had tackled enough odd jobs to last him a lifetime. But what else would he do? What else *could* he do? Thinking back to his teenage years, he recalled how, in Honolulu, he had relished his piano lessons, how he had sat at the Baldwin piano in the Bishop's House for hours, improvising, surprising the family with his creativity. Well, maybe he was all thumbs with a rifle, but on the keyboard he was a natural. His fingers seemed to know how to sprint from high to low octaves and back again, filling the air with ever-so-joyous sounds.

"Of course! I'll become a professional pianist!" he declared. "I'll play for pay and I'll have one heckuva time doing it!"

Practicing on an upright piano in a Brooklyn YMCA, he delighted large groups of Y residents with his clean, light, sparkling renditions of popular favorites from Broadway musicals. "I can do it! And all by ear — no score!" he cheered as he rediscovered this dormant talent. Learning to compose, he built up a good repertoire of songs and soon was ready to perform in cocktail lounges and piano bars. He had little trouble finding work. To delighted audiences in New York and Long Island, he played Cole Porter, George Gershwin, ragtime. He lent a touch of sophistication to otherwise ordinary surroundings.

One afternoon I visited Morris at Freddie's Bar and Cocktail Lounge in Mineola, Long Island. Sitting at the baby grand piano, playing a medley of Cole Porter songs, he was creating pure magic. As his fingers swept over the keys, he held his head high and, with a rhapsodic look on his face, slowly turned his head from side to side. At the end of a set, he acknowledged the applause with an engaging smile.

Morris must have told the boss that I was there. Before long, Freddie came over to my table and asked, "You Morris's brother?"

"That's right," I acknowledged.

"He's got real talent," he said. "You're very lucky to have a brother like Morris, you know."

"I know," I heartily agreed.

"Your drinks are on the house," he said. "For Morris's brother, drinks are on the house."

How proud I was of Morris! How happy I was for him! I was so happy I could hardly stand it.

For his finale every night he played "The Last Time I Saw Paris." That was his signature song and his favorite. Never had I heard it played so hauntingly.

Morris didn't play in one spot very long. Even though the owner often tried to persuade him to stay, he had a compulsive need to move on. Although he had not quite settled down, he was enjoying his work, supporting himself, and slowly finding his way. It may well be that for the very first time in his life he was in possession of some personal dignity.

NANCY GETS CAUGHT IN A
RELIGIOUS CROSSFIRE

Do you recall how my sister Nancy was on the verge of marrying that Nazi doctor, Fritz Esser, when World War II broke out? And how he suddenly broke off the engagement for fear she might be part Jewish? And how she returned to Honolulu, where she met and married a captain in the U.S. Marine Corps? From here we'll pick up the story — her tale of tangled, cross-cultural, cross-religious relationships — a four-sided power play in which nobody — certainly not Nancy — was a winner.

After the war, when her husband resumed his habits of heavy drinking and womanizing, my sister divorced him and took their two boys to a small town in western Pennsylvania to find peace and rest. There, when she met Don Riles, the drama began to unfold.

Don, a thirty-year-old Roman Catholic, was a gentle, soft-spoken schoolteacher who lived with his possessive mother, a massive Brunhilde-type woman who was a graduate of third grade. "Don, you is my blue-eyed favorite boy," she often told him. "Ooooh, how it hurt when you was born — my breeches baby. You cain't ever leave your old Mom!" She had successfully warded off all of his former girl-friends.

A recipe for disaster: Don and Nancy fell in love. His mother's reaction? Picking up a stack of dishes, she hurled them clear across the kitchen!

To entangle the plot further, enter my father, the retired bishop. Still full of missionary zeal, he persuaded Don to be received, via a short ceremony, into the Episcopal Church. Next (and in the absence of Don's irate parents and priest), he officiated at Don and Nancy's marriage in the living room of our parents' home. Further, he got Don a teaching job at a prestigious Episcopal high school.

And so, did the couple live happily ever after? Not a chance. Don's parents and their priest rushed to the battlements and vowed a war to the finish against this meddling Episcopal bishop. The priest announced that "in the sight of God, Nancy — who is a Protestant and a divorcée — does not exist and this marriage will be annulled." He further declared that "Don is living in sin, and if he continues to do so he will suffer the unendurable pain of everlasting damnation."

Two years and two children later, after relentless long-distance pressure from his mother and his priest, Don capitulated. "Nancy," he said, his voice trembling, "I love you, but it is God's will that I divorce you. I must go home. But hold on — we will be remarried once my mother has passed away and the priest has been relocated." Nancy was speechless.

But their two small sons — what about *them*, so innocently caught in this ugly crossfire? Who would get custody? At the hearing, Don's mother testified, "Naincy, she ain't fit to be a mother — she's a drunk and a prostitute — has no home. Them is *our* boys. She don't want to ever see them!" Here little Christopher, aged four, popped up in court and yelled, "Yes, she *wants* to see us, but you won't let her!" Pulling his collar, the grandmother said, "Sit down and shut up."

Don got custody. The boys would live with him in his parents' home. As the judge rose to leave, he did something rare in the annals of legal history: he summoned the weeping Nancy to his private chambers. "Nancy," he said apologetically, "I was not taken in by that family. It is *you* who should rear those boys. But you live in a small city apartment, whereas they have the rural home — lots of playing room for kids. This order can be temporary if you get yourself a suitable environment for them. Try again in a year or so to regain custody. You'll be sure to get them back."

Whenever my sister wrote to Don, inquiring about her boys, he always responded, "They lead an ideal life! They adore their grandmother and love their school. They're healthy and happy."

Nancy believed every word he wrote. Her dilemma? Should she now seek custody, uproot them, thrust them into a strange new environment when they were doing so well? Should she separate them from all their friends? Thinking back to her own unstable, rootless childhood, she made the most heart-rending decision of her life. She decided not to try to regain her boys.

Years later, Nancy learned that her twice-a-week letters to her boys had been, for the most part, withheld from them by their grandmother. They had been led to believe that their mother had abandoned them. But even worse, she learned that, in the name of discipline, her boys had endured much physical and psychological abuse. To this very day, in middle age, they retain many of the emotional scars that would naturally result from such an upbringing.

Years after the divorce, my sister and I had a heart-to-heart chat about this upheaval in her life.

"You know, Nancy," I said, "I'm curious about something. When Father converted Don, was he aware that doing so might be at the cost of your marriage?"

"No," said Nancy, "I don't think he really thought about the matter from that angle."

"For Heaven's sake," I said. "Don was already a devout Christian — not one of those millions of Chinese who had never heard of Jesus Christ. Did Father need the personal satisfaction of making Don the 'right kind' of Christian?"

"I think so," replied Nancy. "He was bound and determined to do it. You know how it is with Father and his indomitable will — just try to oppose him!"

"Listen," I said. "It was once said of Father: 'Put Bishop Littell in a roomful of Barbary apes and in two hours he will have made Episco-palians out of all of them. Not only that, but the apes will have put all their bananas in the collection plate.'"

And so — was this the grand finale to a no-win, never-ending family tragedy of errors? Convinced that their marriage was invalid and he was living in sin, Don initiated a divorce he never wanted, a divorce that Nancy never wanted. Would these lovers someday reunite? Espe-cially since, through the children, their paths would sometimes cross?
    We'll see.
    In a later chapter.

MOTHER'S SEVENTH-INNING STRETCH

For Father, the retirement years in New York were "most gratifying," as he liked to exclaim. Assisting the bishop of New York, he carried out duties that only a bishop can perform — confirmations, ordina-tions — keeping busy, useful, healthy, and cheerful. Not so my mother. Unaccustomed to a cramped apartment following that sprawling, seven-bedroom Honolulu household, she became bored with the lot of housewife, lonely in that vast metropolis where, mingling at the market with those faceless throngs, she was no longer a celebrated "somebody."
    "Oh, how I miss Honolulu!" she lamented. "How I miss the recep-tions, conventions, parties, the East-West visitors who adorned our dinner table, the speaking, the teaching I did! How I miss those dances we gave, before and after Pearl Harbor, for lonely servicemen! And the Bach Choir, which met at our house!" Separated from friends, her mind unchallenged, Mother began to show signs of forgetfulness. In time, Father's contentment was eroded by her painted-into-a-corner predicament.
    Then came the day of Mother's bizarre accident. The scene: Yan-kee Stadium. Along with Morris, Nancy, and me, she was sitting high in the bleachers watching a Yankees–Red Sox game. Suddenly, dur-ing the seventh-inning stretch, some crackpot hurled a beer bottle

What joy Mother derived from inviting hundreds of sailors and soldiers to our home for parties after the shock of Pearl Harbor had calmed down somewhat. Her doing so was truly radical, for in those days "nice" families would never allow their daughters to associate with sailors. However, Mother broached her idea to the army and navy commanders in the area, explaining that these servicemen were lonely, homesick, and had nowhere to go but the bars. Her project caught on, and many of the finest homes in Honolulu were opened to these young men. Army and navy dance bands, group singing, fruit punch — it was a unique idea in the annals of military history.

high into the air which landed smack on Mother's skull. Reeling, screaming, she was instantly surrounded by ballpark officials. "No, I don't want an ambulance!" she shouted hysterically. "Get me and my family back to my apartment. I'll sue you all, along with the whole Yankee baseball club, within an inch of your lives!"

Fearing just that, the officials apologized profusely, fawned all over her, and tried to quiet her down. Finally, they drove us home in a Yankee front-office limousine. Mother never did sue, but for months afterward she endured headaches and dizzy spells. The bottle had caused a small skull fracture.

New York City, then, was not exactly Mother's retirement Mecca. Feeling like a caged tiger, she would pace the floor, unable to make sense out of her new life. To complicate matters further, another critical event occurred that was to take her mind off her useless existence. It placed her attention elsewhere — squarely on the plight of her husband, who had just left town for a weekend of speaking engagements.

FATHER IS FELLED

During his trip to Pennsylvania in 1957, Father paused for a visit at Nancy's home in Ardmore. One afternoon, heading upstairs for his nap, he called to her, "Dear, I'll be down for tea at three. Hope you still have some of those marvelous scones!"

Water was still steaming from the kettle at four P.M. Father had not shown up. When the hands of the clock showed five, Nancy had a scary hunch. Bounding upstairs, she tore open his door to find — good God! There was Father, head rolled over the side of the mattress, arm paralyzed, mouth drooling and emitting guttural sounds. He had suffered a massive stroke.

Mother was summoned from New York City as Nancy, holding his limp arm, accompanied Father in the shrieking ambulance to Episcopal Hospital, ten miles away in Philadelphia. In a state of shock, she winced at the ghastly sight he presented.

Months later, when Father was released from the hospital, he and Mother returned to New York, where, with the help of a therapist, she devoted days and nights to his care. A hospital bed, a walker, and other medical aids were purchased as the long haul back to health was initiated.

To my discomfort, Father would telephone me at my office, his words garbled as if he were "speaking in tongues." My "Yes, Father" responses infuriated him, heightening his frustration as, raising his voice to a pitch, he would bawl me out for inappropriate answers to what he was asking. (Nancy told me later, when she had become a nurse, that this was not unusual in stroke patients. One of her own patients, frustrated by her inability to speak, threw a glass of orange juice in Nancy's face.)

Gradually, although Father improved in speech and strength, his left arm and leg remained permanently paralyzed.

After a month, instead of telephoning me, Father sent occasional short notes — always cheerful, always upbeat. They were painstakingly written. A typical note said: "Son, keep your faith in God and wear your glasses at night so you can see your dreams better."

MOTHER RECEIVES A DISASTROUS LETTER

One can date the beginning of the end for Mother from the very day that Father had his stroke. Now no longer free to travel or seek diversion, she had few outlets. What with Mother's skull fracture and Father's stroke, her troubles were unbearable. But still a third calamity was waiting to cloud her mind and break her spirit. When I visited their New York apartment, I saw that the stress, loneliness, and physical work were far too much for her to handle.

Taking Father aside, I asked him, "Is Mother all right? I'm shocked at her appearance — her hair hanging untidily down the sides of her face. She's so pale. She looks terrible."

"Son," he answered, "late every night, for the past few weeks, she's been pacing the living room floor. I just don't know what to make of it. I've tried often to get her to open up, to tell me what's troubling her, but with no luck. Will you see if you can draw her out?"

After spending a few minutes alone with her, making small talk, I asked, "Is everything all right, Mother? I have the feeling that something is bothering you."

Mother burst into tears and, without saying a word, took a letter from her pocket for me to read.

The letter was from Morris. It was a long, angry letter, a stinging rebuke, a bitter condemnation of what he regarded as her lifelong failure as a mother — a letter that placed the blame for all his problems squarely on her shoulders.

Normally a mild-mannered man, too insecure to be confrontational, Morris began his letter as follows:

"I've had a couple of decades to mull over what has gone wrong with my life, and why. I now know the reasons. From as early as I can remember, you placed me in one impossible situation after another — situations that left deep scars and made a successful adjustment to life in this world impossible.

"You destroyed my chances for a stable life and an effective education," he continued, "by constantly switching me from one school to another. You yanked me away from wherever I was, when it suited your purposes, on an average of once a year, hauling me around Europe, leaving me in hotel rooms at night while you went to plays and concerts. You dumped me with a family in Switzerland for months at a time even though I spoke no French and the family no English. Never did you or Father discuss my schoolwork with me, or my problems of continual adjustment to new curricula.

"Further," he raged, "you failed to buy clothes for me that fitted in with those of my peers. In Honolulu, where all the boys were wearing long pants, you made me wear the short pants I had worn at the Hankow British School. The boys teased me mercilessly, calling me a sissy and a pantywaist. When you finally bought me long pants, you spoiled it by saying, 'It's such a shame to waste all those nice clothes I bought you in China.'

"When I was a freshman in high school, you and Father made me

enroll in Junior ROTC, where I had to drill and mess with rifles —
activities for which I was temperamentally unsuited and which only
engendered further ridicule. All of those decisions, plus many others,
deprived me of a normal childhood and kept me from achieving
stability in my adult years.

"In sum, you failed to prepare me for the world. Instead, you made
your own reckless, relentless journey through life — actually more of
a rampage than a journey — dragging me and your other children
around with you, disrupting our home lives, our education and our
adjustment to society, and all in order to satisfy your own ravenous
appetite for travel — and doing all of the foregoing under the guise of
enriching our cultural lives. Those so-called cultural experiences,
random and disconnected, served only to displace the solid education we all so sorely needed. It's high time someone in the family
brought these matters to your attention so that you can reflect on
what you have done to the children you have brought into the world."

As I silently read Morris's letter, Mother was sobbing and dabbing her eyes with a handkerchief. After I had finished, I rose from
the couch, walked over to her, and put my arms around her to
comfort her.

But those gestures of comfort were a fake and a fraud! They gave
no clue to what I was really thinking. That letter had aroused in me
deep-seated feelings of anger toward my mother — not because of
what Morris claimed she had done to him, but for what she had done
to me. During those ten minutes I had my arms around her, my mind
swirled with thoughts that for decades I had suppressed.

*I remember, when our family arrived in Honolulu, you and Father
sent me for first and second grades to a private school for girls! Just
because it was closest to home — a school for GIRLS! Since it was an
Episcopal school, you had the clout, Father being bishop, to enroll me
despite my gender. In all its seventy years of existence, I was the only
boy ever to attend that school! In my scrapbook I have a formal photograph of myself, looking thoroughly disgusted, with two hundred girls,
all of us sitting on the front steps of the school, all with our legs crossed.*

In successive years you sent me to Hanahauoli School, to Iolani

School, to Punahou School, and then back to Iolani, yanking me out of fifth and sixth grades for half a year to accompany you to Europe. During that time my arithmetic education suffered seriously. I remember often crying myself to sleep because I couldn't do multiplication and division — couldn't keep up with my classmates.

You sent me away to boarding school in Delaware for five wretched years. How many times did you visit me? Once! Sure, you wrote me faithfully, but, to my mind, what it all boiled down to was that writing to me was preferable to seeing me.

While at St. Andrew's, I wrote to you in Honolulu with an important request. "Please send me my stamp collection so I can work on it some more." Imagine my dismay when I received a postcard from you informing me that you had given my collection to a "nice Chinese boy" because there was no room in the house for it! No room in the Bishop's House — that huge, rambling mansion with unused closets and a full-size attic? Impossible! That stamp collection had been a link to my past, to home, to family and security. It was proof that I had accomplished something, proof of my steadfastness, of my efforts to organize my activities, to create, to please myself and others. . . . Could I ever forget the sense of loss, the sense of betrayal that I felt when I received that postcard from you?

The more I thought about those things and the more tightly I held my mother in my arms, the angrier I became with her. I believed that Morris's letter had spelled out some truths that I, myself, had vaguely formulated in my adult years but had suppressed. Morris was right. *Morris was right!* And now, the angrier I became with my mother, the more tightly I hugged her and held her and the more I wiped her tears off her cheeks. At no time during that consolatory session with my mother did she suspect what I was really thinking. What good would it have done for me to add to her distress?

How one's attitude toward one's parents can change in the course of a lifetime! I recalled the words of Oscar Wilde: "Children begin by loving their parents; as they grow older they judge them; sometimes they forgive them." Would I find a way to resolve my mixed feelings about my parents while they were still alive? Only time would provide the answer — and neither my father nor my mother could have many years left.

FATHER GOES TO THE MEN'S WARD, MOTHER TO THE PSYCHIATRIC WARD

By now exhausted, Mother kept up her round-the-clock task of caring for her disabled husband. Sometimes he would fall on the floor and, with no help, she summoned titanic strength — she was sixty-seven at the time — to lift this 185-pound deadweight back onto the bed. Beset with fatigue, insomnia, muscle strain, pernicious anemia (twice she fainted dead away), she was drained. The toll on her health had reached the point of no return.

It was at this time that Father's substantial fortune finally gave out. Throughout his life, he had given princely sums to China missions, to the far-flung education of many children, and had made it possible for the whole family to travel the world on a lifelong spree equivalent in distance to one person's circling the globe thirty times. As a result of all that high living and giving, Father was now virtually penniless.

Because he was revered for his years of outstanding service, he was able to make arrangements with Episcopal Church headquarters for them to underwrite the services of a therapist. And it was Father David Bannion, chaplain of St. Alban's Hospital in New York City, who rescued Father and Mother and arranged their admission to that geriatric institution. All future bills were to be paid by the Church Missions Fund.

Once Father was admitted, the doctor decreed that Mother, too, should be institutionalized, but in the psychiatric ward. She had been confused, mislaying her purse, crossing streets without looking both ways. Her memory was failing, in large part, we believed, because of the horrendous strain of the past year.

I accompanied Mother as she was wheeled to her room on the third floor. I then escorted Father to his fancy first-floor private room. When Father saw his accommodations, he nearly plunged headlong out of his wheelchair. I was taken aback when he burst out with: "Get me the hospital administrator! These living quarters won't do! They just won't do at all!"

I fetched the administrator.

"I'm sorry," Father told him, "but I simply cannot be placed in a private room. I need to be in a ward with other people, to listen to their troubles, to counsel and comfort them."

"Our concern is only for you, Bishop," said the administrator. "We think you should have a private room, as befits a bishop of the Church. We also want to give you nothing less than the very best of care."

Father held fast. "I must be placed in a ward," he sputtered. "I am a Bishop, a Priest, a Shepherd — and those men are my flock!"

"As you wish, then, Bishop," consented the official. "We're most happy to have you here and will make your stay as comfortable as possible."

Father was wheeled into a cubicle in Ward A7, where he would live with fifteen other men, all between the ages of sixty-five and one hundred, all infirm, and most of them lonely.

And so it was that for ten years Mother lived, mostly bedridden, in the psychiatric ward while Father remained active, motivated, cheerful, assisting Father Bannion with chapel duties and giving counsel and comfort to his fellow patients. He was beloved by all, including the aides and orderlies, to whom he slipped forbidden tips in return for special favors, particularly pastry handouts. Not what he needed — those chocolate eclairs and blueberry tarts — in fact they were taboo on his diet, for, along with his other ailments, he was a borderline diabetic. In any case, he was most content with life on Ward A7 and with the care he received.

HOW TO LOVE YOUR PARENTS AGAIN

Throughout the 1950s I seldom saw my father and mother. As you know, I was struggling with the feelings of anger and resentment triggered by that college experience when they held me hostage to their "Extravaganza" weekend. That incident brought to the surface bitter memories of how they had managed my life as I was growing up: switching schools, interrupting semesters to take trips, abandoning me during my five years of boarding school, leaving me in the bumbling clutches of a blunt-witted uncle.

Around 1965, with two aging parents now permanently hospitalized, I began to feel guilty about my continued feelings of hostility toward them. Surely a son wasn't supposed to be angry with his father — ever. Nor with his mother — ever.

Once again, in an effort to repair relationships, I resorted to my Two-List System — used so successfully on Uncle Elton. All I had to do this time was to spotlight my parents in the lists. To my surprise, here is what resulted:

THE TWO-LIST SYSTEM
The Question:
Why did my parents make life so difficult for me as I grew up?

LIST 1:
MY PARENTS' POSSIBLE EXPLANATIONS FOR THEIR BEHAVIOR
1. Mother took me out of schools to go traveling because she thought the educational advantages of travel far outweighed those derived from the classroom. Despite a haphazard public school education and no college, she had managed through extensive travel and reading to acquire an education at least the equal of that of any college graduate in the family.
2. My parents sent me away to boarding school because that was the family tradition. Lacking suitable schools in China and Hawaii, they sent us to topnotch eastern schools. They didn't bring us home to China during the summers because the month-long trip by train, ship, and Yangtze riverboat was complicated and dangerous. Even a trip to Honolulu, though shorter, seemed too long for a teenager to make alone. Anyway, they felt that summer camp in the East would be more enjoyable for me, especially since I never told them anything to the contrary.

3. They loved me always, wherever I was. When I was home, they showed it clearly. When I was away at school, Mother wrote long, affectionate letters proclaiming her constant love for me. And although Father sent his love only in Mother's handwriting, it was still his love he was sending.

4. Mother was unaware that her letters only made me more homesick and miserable. If my parents had known how unhappy I was during those years, they would have promptly brought me home to Hawaii.

5. If, in retrospect, they made mistakes, they regretted them deeply. They tried to act in all of our best interests — to broaden our minds with travel experiences and to give us every advantage.

LIST 2:
MY OWN ATTEMPTS TO EXPLAIN THEIR BEHAVIOR

1. Mother took us out of school to go traveling because she had different personal needs, a different agenda from Father's. Not as zealous a Christian as he, she became fatigued by his missionary fervor. (She might have been better suited to be the wife of a diplomat.) She knew when she had reached her limit, and, being as impulsive as she was, she had to get away "this instant." She needed frequent drinks from the world's cultural wells: London, Paris, Rome, and Florence. Because going alone would look like running away, she took one or two of us along each time, to "educate" us. She had light regard for the consequences to our education of taking us out of school; having been mainly self-taught, she may have underestimated the value of a formal education.

2. Like many missionaries, my parents believed that close ties with kith and kin were as easily maintained at a great distance as in person. When they chose to live six hundred miles up the Yangtze, returning to the States only once every seven years, they counted on frequent letters to keep close ties. In one letter to his father, *whom he hadn't seen for six years*, Father wrote,

"Papa, I love you more and more every day." *Every day?* That's what I call closely calipered, incremental love! Mother wrote to all of us children, wherever we were, once every two weeks or so — letters that were newsy, affectionate, and written with loving care. Despite her faithfulness, most of her letters to me went unanswered.

3. Yes, my parents must have cared much for me and would not have kept me at school five thousand miles away at all costs. When Nancy was sent away to a girls' boarding school in Maryland, she told our parents after two years that she was unhappy and wished to come home. They honored her request immediately. I wish I had been as smart as Nancy.

4. "The barb in the arrow of childhood suffering," wrote Olive Schreiner, "is its intense loneliness, its intense ignorance." Many parents never learn this at all; many others, only after it's too late.

In my Two-List System, I now had one list in which I tried to put myself in my parents' shoes and a second list in which I tried to come up with my own reasons for their behavior. The procedure forced me to think of their underlying motives and, going from there, to turn aside some of my anger. A great start!

Later in life, I used the system to repair relationships with a neighbor, with a close business associate, and with one of my children. It works for me, and it has worked for others. Please don't misunderstand, however. I am not suggesting that if you use it you will instantly start loving or liking or appreciating someone you don't feel that way about. I'm suggesting merely that the system will help you to think about someone in a new way, a fresh way — and that's the key.

Not long after applying the system to my parents, I went to see them in the hospital, determined to do something I had never done before. I pulled a chair up to Father in his wheelchair and — hard as it was for me, speaking as one man to another — I told my father I loved him. "I love you, Father," I said to him. "I love you very much." With a happy look on his face and without a second's hesitation, he said, "I love you too, son." After leaving him that afternoon, I felt a happiness I had seldom known.

Next I went to see Mother in the psychiatric ward. She was sitting in a chair and looking straight ahead with a fixed stare. She showed no recognition of me. I sat beside her quietly for some time and held her hand. Then, for the first time in my life, I looked at her and told her I loved her. "I love you, Mother," I said softly. Then, after a pause: "I'm so sorry I didn't tell you this while you could still understand what I'm saying. I love you very much and I always will."

My mother didn't have to answer. She didn't have to tell me she loved me. I knew she did. I thought of a letter she had written to me while I was overseas during the war. It was returned to her unopened, the envelope stamped MISSING — RETURN TO SENDER. I had found that letter thirteen years later, still unopened, when asked to go through family papers. One part of her letter would remain with me always, the part where she wrote, "I fervently hope and pray that God will protect you and keep you safe and bring you home to us soon. Dear, dear boy. I love you very much."

For some time I lingered at my mother's side. When I left her, my eyes were flooded with tears.

Now, at long last, in the twilight of their lives, I had made my peace with my parents. More than that, I had experienced the profound joy that comes with understanding, with forgiveness, and with affirmation of mutual love.

THE WHEELCHAIR BRIGADE

It didn't take long for Father to get into the swing of things at the hospital. Less than a year after his arrival, the hospital newsletter carried this account of him:

> Bishop S. Harrington Littell starts the New Year off in great spirits, and on New Year's Eve, as he was singing "Auld Lang Syne" to us in Chinese, we thought of all the good times we have had with him at

St. Alban's. While he has been a patient here for quite some time, he continually adds joy and stimulation to all who know him. His keen mind and sharp wit enliven all our educational therapy classes, and his contributions in the current events classes sometimes set us to thinking for several days. He is loved by all who know him, and radiates a beautiful spiritual quality that has added much to the ministry at St. Alban's. To the Bishop's own words, "I love it here — it is just right for me," we want to add, "We love you too, Bishop Littell, and St. Alban's has become a finer place because you are here."

Father's stories about the Boxer Rebellion and his early China days kept me spellbound for hours. I kept asking him for more details — so important for me to be able to convey this heritage to my own children. Then, shortly before his ninety-fourth birthday, I asked him questions about several matters that had long bothered me. To understand him, I felt it urgent that I know the answers.

"Father," I began, "I don't see how you can maintain your cheerful outlook when you consider what has happened in China — your life's work of thirty-one years down the drain since the communist takeover. Look at the way you brought the Gospel to tens of thousands of Chinese. Look at the part you played in raising funds for churches, schools, and hospitals. Aren't you devastated by what has happened?" Leaning forward anxiously in my chair, I awaited his answer to this question, one that had also bothered many of my friends. People everywhere were wondering how he felt about the ultimate value of his lifelong missionary effort.

As though expecting this question, Father had a ready answer: "Well, son, contrary to popular belief, the Communists did not undo what the missionaries had accomplished, though they tried. Far from it. We brought lasting changes to China. History will attest to the quiet, effective work of a religion that introduced to that country modern medicine, built some of their best hospitals — most still in use today. History will also attest to the work of a religion that introduced modern schools, focusing on the education of girls and women for the first time in China's long history. And to a religion that made 'social service' and community spirit vital parts of its programs.

"For their part, the Chinese accepted, adapted, and improved upon many of the ideas of the missionaries. They also taught us much about their culture and values. Do you realize that this tremendous missionary movement, from the 1830s to 1949, was one of the greatest cross-cultural experiences the world has ever seen? Joe, I do believe that when communism collapses, as it inevitably must because of its Godlessness and anti-individualistic philosophy, Christianity will pick up and take off with ever-accelerating force in that country. No, Joe, a thousand times no. I am anything but disappointed. Nothing that we did was in vain. God's work may now be underground, but it waits for its chance to bubble up, to burst forth in a glorious renewal!"

"Father, I hope you won't mind my asking you this second question. No one in the family has ever known the answer. I hesitate to ask, but tell me, please: Where did your incredible fortune come from? Since your early days in China, you had the wherewithal to send your children to eastern prep schools and Ivy League colleges; to send the family on frequent, extended tours of Europe; to give millions of dollars to Chinese missions and Oriental parishes in Hawaii; to sponsor a seemingly endless number of projects. We know that the source of all that money was your father — but how? He was only a simple parish priest, and his father before him was a writer and lawyer whose work could not possibly have yielded such a fortune. Do clarify the matter for me, Father — what was really the source of our family's income?"

"Son, I'll be happy to give you a direct answer. Sorry it's been such a mystery. You see, back in the 1870s, my grandfather John Stockton Littell, the Philadelphia writer and lawyer, made shrewd investments. With our nation on the verge of an explosive expansion, John saw his chance. Believing that the railroads would play a leading role in opening up the West and in transforming the United States from an agrarian to an industrial nation, he put every dollar he could spare into railroad stocks — particularly Pennsylvania Railroad and Union Pacific. Besides that, his wife, Susan Sophia Morris, of a wealthy

Quaker family, was a source of funds for investment. When he died in 1875, my grandfather was a millionaire — one of the wealthiest men in Philadelphia. John left his stocks to his son, Thomas Gardiner Littell — my father.

"As you know, my father spent his pastoral life as rector of St. John's in Wilmington. His interests lay in tending to his flocks rather than tending to his stocks. During his lifetime, those stocks soared in value until they were worth many millions of dollars. When he died, his five children, including me, inherited the holdings about which, all his life, he had cared nothing. Joe, here's what you wanted to know: the share I received was worth eight million dollars."

For a moment I could hardly digest this revelation. But then, continuing, I asked, "Why didn't you mention this to anybody, especially since there were malcontents in the Honolulu diocese who spread the rumor that you were embezzling church funds? They simply could not understand the discrepancy between your expenditures and your modest salary as a bishop. It wasn't surprising, then, that vicious rumors began to circulate."

"I did tell some close friends, but rumors kept flying, originated by bitter people who had been given reduced responsibilities in the church. They knew my father to have been a simple man of God who had forsworn the trappings of this earthly life and could not possibly have been the source of such wealth. The only explanation left for them was that I was an embezzler."

"Well, Father, I mustered up the courage to ask you that question about your finances because when you entered this hospital nine years ago, you told me you were here on a full scholarship. Are you saying that you started out with eight million dollars and that you're now down to a goose egg — down to nothing? Are you saying that you're flat broke?"

With a twinkle in his eye, Father replied, "Well, son, I'm not certain that bishops go 'flat broke.' They may more appropriately become 'impecunious.'"

"Okay," I said with a laugh. "Are you impecunious?"

"Yep. *Flat* impecunious."

"Well, Father, one could say that you blew a fortune. Or, on the other hand, one could say that you timed everything perfectly."

"It all depends on your point of view, doesn't it, son?" he said softly.

Father and I spoke of many other things that day: of Evelyn, his beloved wife upstairs; of his children — particularly me.

"Joe," he said as his eyes welled up with tears, "how proud I've always been — so very proud of you!" I was profoundly moved. That meant a lot. We had a wonderful talk — a heart-to-heart such as I'd never known before. As the psalm says: "My cup runneth over."

After our two-hour visit, we parted with a long, warm hug. That was the last time I saw Father.

One week after Father celebrated his ninety-fourth birthday, he caught a cold that turned into pneumonia. This time he couldn't fight. The "strife was over." Two days later he drew his last breath.

As prescribed by the Book of Common Prayer, Father's funeral was the same as those at which he had officiated thousands of times. The chapel was filled to overflowing with mourners of four generations. Drawn up into two long rows of wheelchairs at the sanctuary sat the men of Ward A7, paying their final tribute to a man they loved.

Fervently, and in a tremulous voice, Father Bannion delivered the eulogy. It was his personal tribute to a man whose long life had blessed the lives of many. This is what he said:

> After a long journey of ninety-four years, one week and two days, the Right Reverend Samuel Harrington Littell, D.D., completed his earthly pilgrimage on Wednesday morning, November 15th, in this hospital where he had first been admitted in October 1958. . . .
>
> If the story of his life were ever to be written, what a biography that would make! It might be titled: *From Boxer Rebellion to Pearl Harbor.* He went to China in 1898, and the Boxer Rebellion was in 1900. He retired in 1942, and Pearl Harbor was in 1941. . . .
>
> For thirty-one years in China, he helped build churches, hospitals, and schools. As Chairman of the China-International Famine Relief Commission, he worked with selfless dedication to help thousands stricken by famine, floods and disease. . . . In regard to

the Bishop's ministry in Hawaii, the work that he and Mrs. Littell did for our service personnel after Pearl Harbor is a brave, noble story yet to be written. . . .

The Bishop's humor is well known to all. He was a jolly man, very human, with a cheery word for everybody and a helping hand for all. Typical of the Bishop is that upon entering the hospital, he asked to be placed in a ward rather than a private room. The men on A7 all held him in the highest esteem and affection, as evidenced by the number from that ward here present. . . .

It is said that God buries his workmen but carries on His work. May the Bishop's long life of selflessness and service be an inspiration to all of us to pick up the load of the world's sin, sickness, sorrow and sadness, and do our part in our day as he so fully did his part in his day.

To those left behind, to his children, to his widow, and to all other members of the family, we extend our sincerest condolences. He loved you all in life, and is now waiting to welcome you into that realm of endless day where there shall be no more partings. Don't disappoint him; he'll be looking for you.

Samuel Harrington Littell, Doctor of Divinity, Priest, Bishop in the Church of God. Rest eternal grant unto him, O Lord. May light perpetual shine upon him.

Elizabeth Barrett Browning wrote some lines that might well have applied to my father: "Thy love shall chant its own beatitudes. . . . A poor man served by thee shall make thee rich; a sick man helped by thee shall make thee strong. Thou shalt be served thyself by every sense of service which thou renderest."

And so, Father, farewell. For you, the evening has come, and your work is done. May you rest in peace.

A NOBLE HEART

With Father gone, I now began to focus my thoughts on Mother. Whatever my past disenchantment with her, increasingly I thought of her not as the invalid felled by the ravages of time and stress, but as a vital, colorful, prime-of-life personality, ever alive to the fullness and fragrance of the world about her. Increasingly I came to admire the person that she was. More and more I came to value the legacy she imparted to me.

Mother's global interests simply had to rub off on her family. What genuine concern she had for public affairs, civil rights, and (I suspect it was she who invented the word) ecumenism! For look how she opened up our Honolulu home to people of all walks of life! Tossed together like a salad, the guests might include a Buddhist student, a lonesome sailor, a senator, a Catholic monsignor, a nursing home invalid, a recovering alcoholic, an ambassador, or a down-and-out playwright. Mother didn't care who — her gatherings could be hilarious, full of swapped yarns, or serious, with discussions of world affairs. Everyone took part. All had a "stupendous time," as one guest commented, while she and Father had as good a time as any.

Another area in which Mother had a lasting influence on me was her ability to keep a promise. You recall when her aunt Henrietta cruelly rejected her, reneging on her promise to take her on a Grand Tour of Europe. Through her tears, Mother vowed that if ever she had children, she would "open up the world" to them. That was precisely what she did. Even though we were "dragged" out of school, how could we help but benefit by her enthusiasm, her excitement, when she had us bumping along on camels to the Pyramids, elephants in Saigon, skis in the Alps, gondolas in Venice, bikes in Belgium, rickshaws in Japan — even a plane ride over Stonehenge!

Again, how could we not be affected as we watched her, awestruck, almost bowled over by the majesty of European cathedrals, palaces, castles, museums, national parks? And, to our delight, she "made" us enjoy sunsets over Scotland, the Sistine Chapel, Oberammergau, the Alhambra, the Ponte Vecchio, and even Le Casino de Paris (where — oh — that Maurice Chevalier was a riot!).

We can't complain — Mother even bought us tickets to hear a Bach organ recital by Dr. Albert Schweitzer, a lecture by T. S. Eliot, a Don Cossacks Choir concert, opera at La Scala. She even went so far as to maneuver an audience with Pope Pius XI! But she didn't stop there.

Mother "made" us stuff on escargots, Wienerschnitzel, goulash, linguini, sukiyaki, and borscht. She "made" us fumble in the language of the country we were visiting, to the amusement of all.

Well, that's just a starter, but you get the idea. Mother gave her absolute all in trying to prepare us for our adult lives. I only wish that now she could understand how much gratitude I feel for all the blessings and advantages. Somehow, I pulled through all that bouncing around. I came out with an insatiable love of learning — passably enlightened, sometimes frightened, but at least I never "did drugs" and never landed in jail!

Finally, some kudos to add to the above. Not only did Mother never break a promise, she never badmouthed a single soul. (This was forbidden at our dinner table.) And even though it was rough sailing for us kids from childhood to adolescence to adulthood, I can now, from a bird's-eye view, get the whole picture.

Thank you, Mother. Bless your generous heart. Never wavering in your affection for your children, truly, you were a rare and a noble soul!

Once Mother was admitted to the psychiatric ward, she deteriorated before my very eyes. Within three months she was transformed from an ambulatory patient to an obese, overdrugged, mindless, bedridden zombie. She didn't recognize me, my wife, Mirelda, or our three daughters when we visited. It was heartbreaking.

At this time, Nancy had just graduated from nursing school in Brooklyn. Here is her bitter recollection of her visits to our mother:

Soon after Mother was admitted to the hospital, she was overdrugged. The obvious symptom of overdrugging was one I had learned about in nursing school — her new habit of clutching at the hem of her dress, pulling it up to her waist, picking at it erratically. And she was roughly treated by untrained, gross-looking orderlies. Twice I saw two of them toss her into bed so roughly that she emitted a shrill scream.

Here, in this ward, the head nurse was a disaster. Welded to her desk, she chewed gum constantly. Her attitude toward her patients was one of disdain, as if they were in no way related to the human race.

This was the first time I had witnessed the case of a slow, drawn-out murder — not too strong a word — by a doctor untrained in geriatrics and by an incompetent staff. On the last few visits I made to Mother, she had bedsores all over her body. Although I protested strongly to the staff, they did nothing about the bedsores.

And then, as if Mother hadn't suffered indignities enough, her wedding ring, her diamond engagement ring, and all her other valuables were stolen.

Just one year after Father's death, Mother died in February 1969, at the age of seventy-seven. Nancy asked her doctor the exact cause of her death. "His ignorance was appalling," she told me. "Medical schools today rarely bother with geriatric education. He told me that she died of infectious bedsores all over her body. Any competent professional knows that there is not one excuse for the appearance of bedsores on any patient at any time. They are painful. With proper nursing care they are preventable."

What a tragic end for so noble a person as my mother! To this day, a lump comes to my throat when I recall the last years of her life or when I hear a snatch of the music — the Beethoven, the Bach — that she loved. Or when I come across other reminders of her, like the picture of her with that delightful dimple on her left cheek.

Rest in peace, Mother. Your busy world is hushed, but your presence in the lives of those who loved you will never dim or fade away.

Despite professional counseling, Nancy's grief has never been adequately resolved. Because of what happened to Mother, however, she made an important decision: to enter the field of gerontology, the discipline that deals with all the aspects — mind, body, and spirit — of the process of aging. Influenced as well by her upbringing in China, where "old is beautiful," she wanted to make certain that no

My sister Nancy in 1966, when her life was finally coming into focus. Here she is, looking wistful as she decides to enter the field of "creative" geriatrics.

patient of hers would ever have to suffer the pain and indignities that Mother endured.

If only Mother had lived to see what became of her daughter! Nancy became deeply involved in geriatric nursing, in writing books, and in giving seminars in almost every state. She stressed that which was denied her mother — the vast potential in the elderly for joy, creativity, and fulfillment. My sister's book, *How to Put Joy into Geriatric Care*, has become required reading for the staffs of many nursing homes across the nation. It is a subject she discusses with compassion, not just because of her mother, but as a result of her nationwide professional contacts and research.

So ended the richly tapestried lives of Father and Mother. They had brought me incalculable joys along with inexpressible pain and sorrow. In the end, they were once again in my heart, just as I had always been in theirs.

Juggling Marriage, Children, and the Job

A TEMPESTUOUS MARRIAGE

"Tempestuous." That's the best word I know to describe my sixteen-year marriage. Just how a promising, rosy romance can gradually assume the characteristics of a volcano, with 8.9 Richter-scale eruptions the rule, not the exception, I'll never be able to fathom. During these years — shaky, unnerving ones — deep-seated, permanent scars were etched on parents and children alike.

Mirelda Crowley, after graduating from the University of Toronto, taught for eight years in an Ontario public school, then earned her master's degree in English at Northwestern University in Evanston, Illinois. Tired of teaching and eager for adventure, she made a trip to New York to see if she could parlay her teaching experience and her interest in school curricula into an editorial position with a textbook publisher. She had a number of interviews, but it was World Book Company's editor-in-chief, Ross Marvin, who hired her on the spot.

It was there that I met Mirelda and we fell in love. One year later, June 1954, we were married in an Episcopal church ceremony attended by Father and Mother, Mirelda's mother, my sister Nancy, and a circle of friends. Lost in the euphoria of the moment was the question of whether either one of us was ready to be married at that time — especially to the other.

Our first home was a third-floor apartment in Manhattan. Within six years we had moved to Mount Tabor, then Summit, New Jersey, and had welcomed the arrival of three daughters, Julia, Nancy, and Laura.

Whatever problems were eventually to engulf us, Mirelda and I

Laura, six, Julia, ten, and Nancy, eight, in our Mount Tabor, New Jersey, home. (Julia is holding an infant cousin.)

had one thing in common: our unwavering love for our three daughters. All three were studious, liked people, and enjoyed a good laugh. Each, in her own way, was striking in appearance and downright beautiful when she wanted to be.

As the girls grew older, tensions arose between Mirelda and me. She objected strenuously to the amount of time I spent working at home, after business hours, at the expense of the family. Down deep, I knew she had good justification for her complaints. Nevertheless, I steadfastly maintained that I needed to spend as much time as was necessary to stay on top of my job.

Freely I admit that I was a workaholic. And for a simple reason — I had a chronic, almost pathological fear of failure. You remember how my first boss, Mr. Bryant, depicted me to company management as inexperienced, uninformed, and incompetent and how he came within a whisker of getting me fired. A consequence of that perilous period was that for years afterward, whenever I had to choose between spending time with my family and doing a job for Macmillan that was right, proper, professional, and above criticism, I almost always chose the job. As a result, the clasps on my briefcase could be heard snapping open as early as eight o'clock most evenings at home, and they seldom snapped shut again before midnight.

Taking me by complete surprise, something happened that changed my situation dramatically — an exciting promotion! I had been with Macmillan for eight years but had not realized I had done so well that it would bestow this honor upon me — the job of executive editor, second only to Bob Rahtz, the editor-in-chief. I would now be responsible for fifty editors in the fields of English, reading, literature, and adult education. The exhilarating news for me, in addition to the substantial salary increase, was that I would no longer be editing and producing books myself but would be supervising the work of other editors, thus freeing myself of all the gritty little details that were so time-consuming. For the first time in my working life, I would be able to get my work done in closer to normal working hours! The happy result of all this, of course, would be that I could call a truce with Mirelda. It was well past time to reestablish my relationship with her and really get to know the kids. Unfortunately, things did not work out as I had hoped.

Instead, we found ourselves engaged in a serious tug-of-war for the hearts and minds of our three children. My new efforts to take a greater part in family life found two adults embroiled in questions of decision-making and control. Which of us would do what, and when, in relation to ourselves and the children? Differences in personality and upbringing came to the surface and thwarted our earnest and well-intentioned efforts to fashion a workable marriage. The end result was that in order to reduce the possibilities for confrontation, Mirelda and I often left problems unattended to and decisions postponed.

In time, exhausted, I consoled myself with a stack of papers that never questioned what I did. The clasps on my briefcase could be heard snapping open every evening as I disappeared into the quiet of my study.

LABORING IN THE EDUCATIONAL VINEYARDS

From time to time, Mirelda gave vent to her frustrations by complaining about my shortcomings to a relative, friend, or neighbor: I worked too hard and spent too little time with my family, or I didn't have the knowledge of public school education that she had gained from years of teaching in the Ontario public schools.

One day I made a disturbing discovery. While up until this time Mirelda had discussed my inadequacies only with other adults, she now included our children. When I objected to this undercutting of my paternal image, she insisted that she was only telling them the truth.

But my marriage was not my only worry. The pressure at work was accelerating. I was becoming mentally and physically exhausted. By the time I boarded the 5:47 Erie-Lackawanna commuter train for the ride home to Summit, I was in sore need of a break from the paper chase as well as a bracer for whatever awaited me at home. It was then that I fell in with a trio of bourbon-drinking bridge players. They needed a fourth and, lo and behold, there I was, ready to join them. They were fun-loving scalawags who had learned the secret of how to relax after a brutal day in New York. One was a stockbroker, another the owner of a camera shop, and the third a corporate lawyer. What they had in common, aside from a passion for bourbon and bridge, was a quick wit and a keen mind.

After boarding the train, we would each pick up a drink from the bar car (theirs were bourbons-on-the-rocks, mine pink chablis) and then settle down to some serious bridge. They kidded me mercilessly about the glass of pink chablis that I kept nursing throughout the trip, but I told them, "I'm just drinking enough to qualify as a bridge player in your illustrious company." That brought on a good-natured round of jokes as well as a fresh round of drinks, and when one of them let slip that the guy who had occupied my seat before me drank grape soda, I had 'em all dead to rights. I soon won them over, and they forgot all about replacing me with a more dedicated drinker.

For almost a year, I was a member of the "Fearless Foursome," as we called ourselves. Then, in May of 1966, I received a surprise offer of a job in Evanston. It was a definite promotion: I would be editor-in-chief of the schoolbook division of Harper & Row, one of the oldest and most respected publishers in the nation. I would be responsible not only for the English and reading programs but for all the other subjects as well: math, science, history. At Harper I would spend less time on details and be able to concentrate on the broader conceptual development of the entire publishing program. What an opportunity!

My elation was dampened by the dread of another confrontation with Mirelda, but, wonder of wonders, she agreed. Recalling her years in Toronto and Evanston, she said she felt more comfortable in the Midwest than in the East. With a feeling of keen anticipation, I accepted the job.

After my final day at Macmillan, I took the 5:47 for the last time. As the bridge game neared Summit and it was obvious that the Fearless Foursome was about to break up forever, we all made a solemn pledge: the last survivor of the four was to drink formal toasts to the memory of each of the other three, in turn, until he became very drunk. As a parting gesture, the others agreed that in the event I turned out to be the lone survivor, I should be permitted to offer my toasts with pink chablis. That notion brought forth another round of jokes and a final round of drinks.

When Mirelda and I broke the news of the Chicago move to the girls at breakfast one morning, they burst into tears and for ten minutes sat at the table sobbing. Through the tears, wails, and moans, Mirelda and I could discern the main problem: "We'll lose all our friends!" After receiving assurances that they would make lots of new friends in Illinois, the girls were able to reduce the torrents of tears to a few trickles and an occasional hiccup, and by afternoon they were out plying the street, behaving like agents of the Illinois Chamber of Commerce, touting the wonders of Chicago and inviting all their friends to come out and see them.

GETTING (UN)SETTLED IN ILLINOIS

In July 1966, our family headed west to Evanston, and we purchased a home in nearby Wilmette. Although Mirelda and I were still having serious problems, the three girls seemed to fit right in at school and quickly made up for the friends they had left behind in New Jersey.

Harper & Row's schoolbook division was the former Row, Peterson & Company, the textbook firm that Harper had bought in 1962 in an effort to get a toehold in the schoolbook field. Since that time, however, the division had been ailing. In 1966 Mel Arnold, a rising editorial star in Harper & Row's New York office and soon to become president of the company, was dispatched to Evanston to shape up the division. Quick to grasp the situation, he saw that he needed a new editor-in-chief, and with the aid of a head-hunting organization in New York he located me at Macmillan.

With high hopes, I started work. Before long, however, I found myself in a painfully awkward situation. For one thing, the former editor-in-chief, a director of the company, remained in the department as an *éminence grise* even though I had been told that he would retire. For another thing, a handful of editors and sales reps — unlike the vast majority of dedicated professionals — undercut my efforts to create fresh, new programs in the various academic subjects. Un-schooled in political infighting, I found it increasingly difficult to pull everyone along. After a year, I decided to look for another job. (I should note that seven years later, Harper & Row shut down its Evanston schoolbook operation entirely.)

At that point it was my great good fortune to meet Fred McDougal, the head of the schoolbook division of Rand McNally & Company, based in Chicago. McDougal was seeking an editor-in-chief for the division, and I turned out to be his man. Rand McNally, the nation's top publisher of atlases, road maps, and tour guides, had made only a halfhearted entry into the textbook field. Andrew McNally III, the company's president, enjoyed the prestige that publishing textbooks brought to the company but was reluctant to make a serious financial commitment to the schoolbook division. McDougal, a man whose idealism had been cradled at Yale and left unscathed by Harvard Business School, had long nurtured the notion of making innovative textbooks that would instill in students a genuine love of learning. He discovered that I had the same convictions, along with the necessary experience, and he concluded that I could help him persuade Rand McNally to make a greater investment in textbooks.

At the time I joined Fred McDougal at Rand McNally, he had just returned from a tour of British educational publishers, where he had been searching for imaginative textbooks that could be adapted to American schools. "A pretty stodgy lot, those British publishers," he told me, "and that includes Rand McNally's English affiliate, which displays in its office locks of Lord Byron's hair encapsulated in a glass enclosure! But there's one company, named Penguin, that has strayed from the flock. It has just published an exciting series of paperback poetry books called Voices. Wonderful books! They make a student *want* to read, think, and write. They don't offer just the standard poems by Shakespeare, Wordsworth, Shelley, and Keats, but works by new poets who deal with real issues in today's world: war and peace, love and hate, marriage and divorce, alcoholism and drug abuse. Unheard of! British teachers using these books are ecstatic! They've seen their students' motivation soar. At the same time, they've seen their own disciplinary problems plummet."

My reaction to the books after flipping through them: "Exciting potential! If we publish an American edition, we can keep a lot of what's already there. But think of the new 'tell it like it is' *American* poets we can include!"

Together, Fred and I were able to persuade Rand McNally's management to loosen up the purse strings for an American edition of Voices.

The teacher who had developed the Voices program in England was Geoffrey Summerfield, a professor of education at the University of York and guru of teachers of the disadvantaged and disaffected. This was the late sixties, that frenzied, disconnected time when students on both sides of the Atlantic were restless and teachers needed all the help they could get to keep them in the educational fold. So now, Summerfield to the rescue.

At once, Fred and I invited him to come to America and spend the summer working with us on the American edition of Voices. He accepted the invitation. Neither one of us having met Summerfield, we naturally expected a proper Englishman who required tea at three and perhaps a spot more at four. Imagine our surprise when he showed up in jeans and beat-up sandals and sporting at his elbow a gorgeous live-in blonde who adoringly twisted his shoulder-length curls around her fingers while he expounded on his educational philosophy! When the American edition of Voices was published in 1969, it was, as we expected, an instant hit. It became the talk of English teachers across the country.

But now — total frustration! Despite the promise of Voices as an exciting new kind of teaching and learning vehicle in the schools, despite the added prestige it had suddenly brought to Rand McNally as an educational publisher, despite McDougal and Littell's further publishing proposals, market analyses, and lovingly prepared pie charts, bar graphs, and time lines, Rand McNally's managers were not in the mood for more thrilling — and expensive — adventures in educational publishing.

It was then that Fred invited me to lunch one day and sprang the big surprise: "Why don't you and I start our own company?"

My answer was swift: "When do we start?"

And so it was that three months later, in July of 1969, Fred McDougal and Joe Littell set the spark to the company that was to become one of the top half-dozen educational publishers in the nation.

I can't wait to tell you about the madcap beginnings of McDougal, Littell & Company. But first let me tell you what finally happened to my marriage. When I decided it was time for a divorce, it took almost two years to have the marriage dissolved. A few months afterward, I gave much thought to those sixteen tumultuous years with Mirelda. I had many genuine regrets. I regretted that I had not developed my Two-List System until the mid-sixties and therefore could not use it as an aid in understanding her until things had reached the point of no return. I regretted, too, that I had not taken a greater degree of leadership in getting us to a marriage counselor before things had progressed too far. Most of all, I regretted that my three children would have to grow up without receiving the daily love and nurture they deserved from both their parents.

Mirelda returned to her native Canada. She resumed her teaching career in the Ontario public schools, and word has it that she has been an enthusiastic, dedicated teacher of the deaf and the visually impaired.

FINDING A NEW JOY IN MY LIFE

One morning, when I was still at Harper & Row, a young woman was shown into my office. Her name was Joy Hartmann. I could tell at once that she was someone apart from all the other applicants I had interviewed for an editorial job. She had soft, stylishly cut blond hair and a celestial smile. She answered my questions with a quiet self-assurance and asked razor-sharp questions of her own about textbook publishing. I'm not sure exactly what it was about her that impressed me the most, unless it was everything.

"Tell me about your background, Ms. Hartmann," I said to her, "and why you want to enter the field of educational publishing."

"As a child growing up in Milwaukee," she began, "I dreamed only one dream. That was to become a concert pianist. Upon graduation from the University of Wisconsin with majors in music and English, I moved to Chicago to pursue that dream. For ten years I studied with Howard Wells and Arnie Oldberg — two world-class piano teachers — and by the end of that time I seemed to be well on my way. Then one day at Evanston Township High School, where I was giving piano lessons, I slipped and fell down an entire flight of marble stairs. The result of that fall was two back operations, a year in a body cast, and an end to my piano career.

"I then took two years of graduate study in English at Northwestern University, turned my attention to teaching English, and for ten years taught honors and advanced placement classes at Evanston Township High School. I believed that the only way to teach students to write was to have them write often and to guide their writing individually — which meant that for ten years I was often up until one or two in the morning evaluating their compositions. Exhausted from teaching huge classes of honors students every day, and unwilling to remain in a job that I considered impossible to perform properly, I decided to leave teaching. Today I would like nothing more than to be able to help create textbooks that will inspire young people not only to write but to write well."

"Good for you," I said. "You obviously care a great deal about your students. You also obviously want to create livelier textbooks. You're just the kind of person we need here in educational publishing."

For the rest of the interview I tried to hide my excitement about the huge fish I was reeling in. Two weeks later, I hired Joy Hartmann and put her to work on a new series of English textbooks.

A year passed. I left Harper & Row to join Fred McDougal at Rand McNally. In dire need of a top editor to handle the American edition of Voices, where did I turn? To Joy, of course. I persuaded her to leave Harper and come to Rand McNally. The Voices project was tailor-made for her creative talents.

From the time I started working with Joy, I thought she was someone very special. One day I felt a compelling desire to convey that feeling to her. I didn't want to say anything that committed me to any kind of relationship, preoccupied as I was with a demanding job and a collapsing marriage, so I made a photostatic copy of a love poem by Wordsworth, put it into a plain envelope, and, while she was away, placed it on her desk. The poem: "She Was a Phantom of Delight."

> She was a Phantom of delight
> When first she gleamed upon my sight;
> A lovely Apparition, sent
> To be a moment's ornament;
> Her eyes as stars of Twilight fair;
> Like Twilight's, too, her dusky hair;
> But all things else about her drawn
> From May-time and the cheerful Dawn;
> A dancing Shape, an Image gay,
> To haunt, to startle, and waylay . . .

Somehow I had expected (what egotism!) that Joy would instantly know who had delivered that poem and thank me for it. Days went by and she said nothing. That stirred my competitive juices. Did she think someone else had given her that poem? If so, who? I was apparently not the only one who thought she was marvelous — I had competition!

Now I began to realize how much I needed Joy and to wonder what my life would be like if she were to walk out of it. I sprang into action. "This time," I admonished myself, "don't do anything so silly as leaving a love poem by Wordsworth on her desk." So this time I made it one by Byron. I made a copy of "She Walks in Beauty," stuck it into an envelope, wrote "Joy" on the outside without trying to disguise my handwriting, and dropped it on her desk. She said nothing about that poem either. Henceforth, Poetry Man made no more hit-and-run deliveries.

When Fred and I founded McDougal, Littell & Company in July 1969, we hired Joy as editorial director, with responsibility for the editing and production of all books published in the field of English. With the new company consisting only of Fred, Joy, a secretary, and

Joy in the Shakespeare Garden, where Will of the Magic Quill cinched our romance.

me, and with the four of us thrown together in a tiny office in Evanston, we all saw a lot of each other. After a year or so, I discovered that I was falling pumpkin-pie, stars-in-the-sky in love with Joy. I also learned that — like me — she was in the final stages of a divorce. Joy and I now had frequent lunches together. Sometimes we drove over to Lake Michigan and walked along the beach. After such occasions I would sometimes pass her office and see her shaking little amounts of sand out of her shoe into the wastebasket.

Not long after the judge had signed my divorce decree, I asked Joy to accompany me to the Shakespeare Garden at Northwestern University — that beautiful 70-by-100-foot garden of flowers, herbs, and shrubs mentioned in Shakespeare's plays. In the enclosing double hedge of hawthorn, in the fountain and sundial and benches, it is typical of the intimate Tudor garden. The Shakespeare Garden is a place where mortals, if they are curious, can get a sneak preview of Heaven.

I wanted Joy to accompany me there because I had something important to ask her. I'm sure you know what it was, and so did she. I asked Joy my question, and she gave me her answer. We then strolled through the garden, arm in arm, among the rue and the monkshood and the wild thyme. I promised her a wild time for the rest of our lives.

Eagerly we went about making arrangements for our wedding. I very much wanted us to be married in an Episcopal church, especially in view of my background as a bishop's son, so we went to the minister of that church in Evanston to make the arrangements and set a date.

In sepulchral tones, the minister gave us the bad news: "Because you have both been divorced, I'm afraid I cannot marry you without the approval of the bishop of Chicago. That might take as long as a year."

"Well, that takes care of that!" I mumbled to myself. After we had left the church, I said to Joy, "Why don't we arrange to be married in your church — down the street? I'm more than willing to become a Methodist for half an hour."

And so, happy day! Joy and I were married in the Methodist church on March 31, 1971. Attending the ceremony were Fred McDougal, his wife, my sister Nancy, and a few close friends. After a festive celebration at Biggs Restaurant in downtown Chicago, we took off for a two-week honeymoon in the Bahamas.

Wordsworth and Byron, neither one of you guys got the job done for me with those love poems. But Shakespeare, baby, you sure came through with that garden. Thanks, Will!

15

STARTING A NEW
PUBLISHING
COMPANY

HAS IT EVER HAPPENED TO YOU? You hit upon a brilliant idea, only to have it drenched with cold water? Fred and I fielded such flak when we mentioned our plan.

"No way!" cried the naysayers.

"Impossible!" agreed the gloom-and-doomers.

"Pipe dreamers! Start your own company with no money, no capital, no collateral, no financial backers? Not even a clue as to what you will publish, let alone where? No headquarters, no employees, no payroll, no nothing! Naive! Absurd! Get real!"

The barrage got worse.

"That Fred McDougal — dead-end employee for a mapmaker! He and his balmy China-born colleague, Joe Littell — they think they can beat such odds, knowing that everyone who has tried has failed? No one in the past forty years has succeeded in starting up a new elementary and high school textbook company! To compete with the big companies, those two will have to spring full-blown with a large list of books and a nationwide sales force. Impossible!"

Unfazed, Fred and I shot back: "Remember the words of the great Lou Gehrig: 'IF YOU WANT TO DO SOMETHING BAD

ENOUGH, YOU'LL DO IT!'" Fred and I wanted it bad enough. So we did it!

Even *we* were amazed when, twenty-four years later, the firm of McDougal, Littell & Company, with three hundred employees and annual sales of $70 million, ranked among the top half-dozen educational publishers in the United States. Starting from nothing and nowhere, we became the primary tenant in Rotary International's World Headquarters in Evanston, with branch offices across the nation.

FRED McDOUGAL — POPCORN AND LADIES' LINGERIE SALESMAN

You wonder what kind of business experience qualified us for such an ambitious venture? Already you know a lot about me, but you should get better acquainted with Fred. "Go on, Fred," I urged him, "tell them your story." In his own words, he tells it:

I think I was brought up to be an entrepreneur, although I never realized it. At age nine, growing up in Glencoe, I got my start selling popcorn. I went around the neighborhood knocking on doors, announcing: "Popcorn — free popcorn samples!" Then I'd take orders for huge cans of the stuff and deliver them on my bike, which was a real logistical feat.

My dad loved popcorn — he was my best customer. He made me keep books — profit-and-loss statements and balance sheets. So I was introduced to business at a very early age, and clearly my dad, who was in business for himself, valued work. (He was in municipal bonds with a partner — a business I never understood, never saw anything romantic about, and knew I would never go into.)

I always had summer jobs. One summer I sold ladies' lingerie for the esteemed Realsilk Hosiery Company. Memories of Realsilk — ah, what fond memories! It was the summer between my sophomore and junior years in high school. We went into training for two days and learned about such things as nylon-reinforced toes and heels on their new line of men's hosiery — a major new corporate

When Fred McDougal greets you, this is the smile you'll get!

thrust, I gathered. What they failed to tell us was that all men's hosiery had nylon-reinforced toes and heels — a lesson that I learned
and remembered when training McDougal, Littell sales reps. Later
that summer, we Realsilk sales reps found ourselves in a sales contest that consisted of a horse race, in which the horses — mine was
named McDougal — moved around a track at the speed of our
sales. I started getting postcards with reminders on them that my
horse was lagging — culminating, as I recall, in the injunction, in a
later, desperate card, "Use the whip!" Anyhow, none of this speaks
to my core experience of the summer, which began when we were
given our sample kit, which consisted of various types of women's
undies, stockings, and the *pièce de résistance*, a tape measure. We
were then shown how to fill out the order form, which called for
various measurements, including bust size. I became convinced
that I would be spending a good part of my summer measuring
women's breasts, a vision that inspired me far more than any sales
contest. Unfortunately, just as they had not told me that all men's
socks had nylon reinforcing, they also did not tell me that women
already know their bust sizes, so all my summer sex fantasies went
unfulfilled. The tape measure lay idle. It was a bitter pill indeed. At
any rate, the point is that I always worked, even though my father
was doing well financially at the time.

At some point, as every English major does, I suppose, I wanted
to be a writer — until I discovered that it was hard and that I had
insufficient talent, to put it gently. At Yale there was a course called
Daily Themes, which called for a short work of fiction every damned
day. I remember laboring over my works for the first five days and
getting my papers back with a couple of W marks, also discovering
that many of my fellow aspiring T. S. Eliots also had Ws and that
none of us had any idea what W meant. It turned out to mean
"worthless," and perhaps that was my first intimation that I wasn't
cut out to be a writer. So if I couldn't be T. S. Eliot, perhaps I could
have tea with him — and that suggested becoming a publisher,
of course.

At Harvard Business School I sent résumés to New York publishers during my second year and went to New York to interview
several, but I discovered the amazing fact that you actually had to

do some job in a company, presumably one you were qualified for — that is, you had to be a sales rep or an editor or something. At business school you spend most of your time pretending to be the president of a company, so I felt that all the alternatives were very lowly. Surely a Harvard Business School graduate could not go out and call on bookstores! Then I found in the placement office that Rand McNally was looking for people to go into their training program, for one year, which would acquaint me with all aspects of publishing and printing. I suppose I assumed I would know everything in a year and become a vice-president, so I took that job.

I worked at Rand McNally for eleven years in a variety of positions, including assistant to the president, Andrew McNally III, and finally head of the school division, where I was briefly the boss of his son, Andrew IV, whom I trained so well that he ended up as president and chairman. Obviously I was not destined for further greatness at Rand McNally, so I decided that the quickest route to the top of a company was to start at the top — which I proceeded to do, thanks to a serendipitous pairing with a truly great editor-in-chief, Joe Littell. I figured that his creative genius and competitive drive would complement my relatively mundane but fairly broad talents, and that together we could succeed against all the odds and dire predictions of naysayers that it was impossible to start an elementary–high school publishing company. We could — and did. What fun!

Fred and I agreed that despite my comparatively limited credentials (I had never sold popcorn, but I *could* swear in Chinese), we should make quite a team — in fact, pull this publishing thing off with a flourish! So here we go!

THE BEGINNINGS OF McDOUGAL, LITTELL & COMPANY

Once Fred and I had made the decision to start McDougal, Littell & Company, we had to have the answers to two questions, and have them quickly: (1) What would we publish first? (2) Where would we get the money?

What Would We Publish First?

We decided to publish a soft-cover literature series based on the Voices model at Rand McNally. While Voices consisted of only one book of poetry for each grade, 7 through 12, we would produce *four* books for each grade: a book of poetry, a book of short fiction, a book of nonfiction, and a book of plays. These four types of literature made up a complete literature program and together could compete against the single, big, hardbound literature textbook offered by several major publishers. Why start out with literature textbooks rather than math or science or history? The others could take years to write, and the result could be of uncertain quality. Hemingway had already finished. And it was good.

Where Would We Get The Money?

Fred and I figured that we needed a staggering $330,000 to produce literature books for grades 7 through 12. Where would we get the $330,000?

Fortunately, we discovered that there was money available in 1969, given high ordinary tax rates and a strong stock market. Happily, the big question turned out to be not "Can we raise the money?" but "On what terms and from whom?" for we needed to have equity ourselves and had very little to put up. We were warned about various potential investors. "Watch out for doctors," we were told. "They're naturally looking for places to put their money where they can make capital gains instead of paying ordinary income taxes. The problem is that they'll prove to be pests — looking for quick returns, not understanding the vagaries of business, and wanting to get their money out on their own terms." We found that most sources of venture capital were mainly concerned with their exit — how they would get their return, how much return, and especially how soon. That meant to most of them that the company would either be sold in five to seven years or would go public. Either scenario would be extremely dangerous to an emerging company that might not be ready for either — a prophecy that certainly was borne out at McDougal, Littell.

We finally settled on Bill Handelman, Fred's Harvard roommate, who was in business with his father and three brothers investing the money of wealthy people. Handelman had no fixed timetable for getting his money out, which was ideal for us, and he had clients who could afford to take risks. One of them was Carroll Rosenbloom, who owned the Baltimore Colts and then the Los Angeles Rams, and who was known as a gambler and high roller who had speculated in such risky ventures as Broadway shows. He was our biggest investor. Another was the actress Dina Merrill. All had two things in common that endeared them to us: they could afford to lose money and they could afford to be patient.

In short, having the right original investors was a major factor in allowing us the freedom to develop the company as we saw fit and to keep the company independent until it was fully established. At that time we would be able to buy back the shares of the original investors and provide them with a good return on their investment without selling the company to outsiders.

GETTING UNDER WAY

We were on a roll! Not even a tornado could stop us once we'd made the Great Decision — what to publish first! "Nothing less," we decided, "than a whole series of literature books — in all respects original in its presentation." A whopping challenge awaited us. We'd produce those four literature books for each grade, 7 through 12 — a total of twenty-four books — and get them out by December 1970. That gave us a year and a half to do the job. For this, the creative spirit of Joy Hartmann would find its outlet while, with whatever combined talents we possessed, Fred and I would keep this tremendous project moving forward.

Our confidence soared. We could do it, for we had enough of that precious commodity, money (the root of all happiness). Enough, anyway, to get us off the ground. "So, let's go!" we told each other. "Let's get moving!"

Joy assembled the poetry books herself, and we got three creative teachers to put together the books of fiction, nonfiction, and plays. While Joy and I concentrated on the production of the books, Fred focused on the financial end of things and on gearing up for the marketing effort to come. Although Fred had the title of president and I was editor-in-chief, we took care to avoid rigid distinctions. I consulted him on editorial matters and, by the same token, he listened attentively to my opinions on sales and marketing strategies even though we both recognized that, never having sold popcorn or brassieres, I was at a severe disadvantage in that area.

Once we had opened our three-room office in Evanston, we had an important obstacle to surmount. We needed to establish our credit so that we could stagger payments to typesetters, printers, and binders. In short, it was essential that we get a good credit rating from Dun & Bradstreet. Unfortunately, the D&B investigator who came to inspect our premises could not have walked in on us at a more awkward moment — we were all wildly celebrating Fred's birthday! A prim-looking individual, he caught us sitting around a table wearing party hats, tooting horns, popping balloons, and blowing French ticklers in one another's faces. Fred looked ludicrous. He was wearing six hats, all piled up on his head, labeled "President," "Sales Manager," "Treasurer," "Office Boss," "Jolly Good Fellow," and "Accounts Payable."

Fred beckoned to the investigator and said amiably, "Pull up a chair and join us!"

Joy cut a piece of birthday cake for him and said, "Here you are — come help us celebrate!"

I grabbed an extra hat and made a label for it that read "Dun & Bradstreet." "Here's your party hat!" I said jovially.

The visitor just stood there, looking as comfortable as the pope in an abortion clinic. Finally mumbling something like "I'll be back soon," he vanished out the door, never to return. With long faces, we decided that our credit rating had vanished along with him. Luckily, our references must have come to our rescue, for soon we were surprised to receive an excellent credit rating from Dun & Bradstreet. Imagine our elation when we realized what this meant. We could now join America's most prestigious companies in their monthly performance of that most hallowed of corporate rituals: making their suppliers wait for their money.

Our new literature series was totally unlike anything else in existence. It emphasized the contemporary scene rather than traditional literature, which had little meaning for students at that time. It included war, protest, hurt, shame, lies, death, and despair — all facets of the real and often cruel world that were avoided by other literature programs. It included the best of life, too — beauty, friendship, humor, courage, forbearance, and love. It spoke both to what life really is and to what it can become. While some of the selections were by traditional literary figures, many were by vibrant new writers who had seldom, if ever, appeared in schoolbooks. They were fiction writers such as E. L. Doctorow and Flannery O'Connor, poets such as Denise Levertov and Alice Walker, nonfiction writers such as Norman Mailer and James Baldwin, and playwrights such as Tennessee Williams and Harold Pinter. The name we gave to the new series was Man. Does that sound sexist? Believe it or not, it didn't then. "Man" was still a strong, serviceable word that referred in the broadest sense to all humanity or humankind, and not just to you-know-who.

The Man books got off to a spectacular start. One of the reasons was a review that appeared in the *English Journal*, the English teachers' bible. Here is a portion of that review:

MAN. *Joy Hartmann, Editorial Director; Geoffrey Summerfield, Advisory Editor. Evanston, Illinois: McDougal, Littell & Company, 1970.*
    This is the most exciting and stimulating literature series for the secondary school to appear in recent years. All of the works in the series have emotional and personal relevance for today's secondary school students. "Jingle Bells" by Seymour Epstein, which deals specifically with one reluctant thirteen-year-old's visit to his grand-

parents, shows, by extension, the sadness and joy, relationships and gaps that exist between the generations.

"The Problem Child," by William Maxwell, is a modern Cinderella story that shows the results of the loss of mother love. "Chicken Hawk's Dream," by Al Young, is a sad but humorous story about Chicken Hawk, who went through high school half-smashed and half-drunk and had the illusion that he could play the alto sax like Charlie Parker because he had once done it in a dream.

Each of the selections is exciting to read. This is the only series in my memory that I have read through as a pleasure rather than as a chore. I think this is, above all, because of the one aspect of these books that is most amazing because it should be usual rather than so rare it must be noted — these books tell the truth. They include controversial authors and controversial themes. Obviously these courageous publishers have not used excuses such as fear of poor sales in the South as reasons for the inclusion of certain pieces of literature. . . .

As for controversial themes, just compare the following excerpt from Yevgeny Yevtushenko's "A Precocious Autobiography" with the excerpts from Pepys's Diary that are so widely used in our schools:

> All of us when we are starting out in life have our special demons who try to kill our faith in human beings, to make us doubt the very possibility of an unselfish motive in anyone, demons, with smooth, enticing hands who try to lure us forever into dark labyrinths of cynical distrust.
>
> And when I was young, I too had such a demon. . . .
>
> The demon was philosophizing:
>
> "You believe that what keeps society together is love, don't you? Well, take this woman and myself. I sleep with her though I despise her, and she hates me but sleeps with me, and, what's more, washes my feet every night. Why do we stay together? Because we need each other. I need her to sleep with and to wash my feet. And she needs me to feed and clothe her. Society is not based on love but on mutual hatred."

Does this seem like pretty strong stuff for the secondary school? Not as strong as the movies students stay out of school to watch.

Not as strong as the shootings at Kent State and Jackson State Colleges. Not strong but true.

I congratulate this new company on its first venture. If there is any material which can still help us keep our students in the schools, it will be material such as this series. . . .

— Sheila Schwartz

Fred had thousands of copies of that review reprinted and sent to English departments throughout the country. At the same time he offered to send free samples of the Man books to all teachers and school administrators who might be interested in purchasing multiple copies for classroom use. "Give 'em a free sample of popcorn," declared Fred, "and if it's really good, they'll buy a big can of the stuff." He had learned well from his experience as a nine-year-old!

We didn't need a sales force because all we had to do was make sure that teachers saw our books. The Man series was an immediate hit. With our tiny post office box stuffed tight with orders every morning, Fred, Joy, and I were ecstatic.

Our company had made a great start, but we were still apprehensive. We needed sales of $300,000 the first year in order to meet our next year's expenses for printing and binding, salaries, and overhead — or else it would be "Adios, McDougal, Littell." And so it was a jubilant Fred, near the end of the first year, who declared, "We've hit the $300,000! We've made it!"

"Hooray!" said Joy, beaming all over. "Now we don't have to spruce up our résumés and go back to work for somebody else."

"Not only that," I added excitedly, "but we can even plan what to publish next!"

A heady day for us all.

"FILE THIS CORRESPONDENCE IN THE BATHTUB IN APARTMENT E"

After a year in that cramped office in Evanston, we moved to larger quarters in Kenilworth, a suburb farther north of Chicago. Our new office, which was to be our company home from 1970 to 1982, was an apartment in a Tudor-style courtyard that resembled an English mews. It was ideal not only because of the low rent but because we were able to secure options on all the other apartments around the courtyard. The unsuspecting tenants of the other apartments would never have welcomed us with open arms had they known we had secured space that enabled us to grow for about ten years. As we did so, evicting apartment owners right and left, we ended up with quite a supply of kitchens and bathtubs. Desperately short of space for files and storage, we turned almost every bathroom into a file room. As a result, our standard means of data retrieval for twelve years was to consult tall, black vertical filing cabinets standing upright in various bathtubs. We also acquired an excess supply of toilets, which were always leaking.

Our earliest office furniture was closeout children's chairs and tables; for years we never had anything approaching real office furniture. Our truck? An abandoned meat delivery wagon. Warehouse space we acquired down the street at an industrial distributor's. And when shipments of Man books arrived from the binder, you should have seen Fred — he would go and unload the trucks himself since the union truckmen balked at taking the boxes any farther than the tailgate. Fred looked dashing in his worksuit with MAN on the back — his special uniform for unloading.

"Reflecting on it," I said to Fred some time later, "I think that some of the things we did in the early years were pretty good, necessity being the mother of invention and all that. We used part-time people effectively, including older and retired people. We employed mothers and let them work around their kids; for example, when our production manager had a baby, we let her work out of her home — all this before practices like that were common."

"Not only that," said Fred, "but we kept our costs down. We warehoused our books with other companies that had extra space. Our salespeople could work from their phones rather than being out on the road all the time. Either that, or they were part-time former teachers in a few metropolitan areas who returned home every night. I think that being lean in those years was the key to our ability to survive. And I'll never stop saying this: the decision to publish books that sold themselves was critical; our books were either hated or loved by people who saw them and needed no selling — we just had to get people to look at them."

ONE MAN'S MEAD
IS ANOTHER MAN'S POISON

By the early 1970s, sexism in language had become a big issue in the women's movement — and oops! here we were, selling a series of books called Man! I'll never forget that day — it was in Minneapolis at the 1972 convention of the National Council of Teachers of English — when the anthropologist Margaret Mead stormed over to our company's booth. She was wielding a tall staff that looked as if she had peeled the bark off it by hand. She positioned herself in front of our booth and, pounding her staff on the floor, shouted, "How *dare* you call your books 'Man'? How *dare* you demean the other fifty percent of the human race?" As she continued her tirade, Fred, Joy, and I could do nothing but watch her demonstration in benumbed silence as flashbulbs popped all around us. It was no comfort to us when a large crowd gathered around our booth to investigate the commotion. We were decidedly relieved when, after a few moments, Mead strutted off just as suddenly as she had appeared, taking with her a host of admirers.

Margaret, I think that was a bit of an unfair shot you took at us. Only weeks afterward, I came across a just-published book of yours that contained an essay called "The Immortality of Man." In that volume the word "man," used in the sense of "humankind," is sprinkled all over your pages like poppy seeds on a breakfast roll. (You're gone from our midst now, Margaret, so I'll say no more. *De mortuis nil nisi bonum.*)

By now, the Man books had run their course, and we were happy to discontinue them before Germaine Greer got into gear and Betty Friedan hit the fan.

PERSONALIZED PUBLISHING

In the early 1970s, many high schools turned away from traditional mandated courses to the elective system, in which students were allowed to choose from a smorgasbord of "mini-courses," with the result, it was hoped, that they would become more motivated to learn. Between 1970 and 1975, we published dozens of lively soft-cover books for those courses. Some of our titles were *Science Fiction, Literature of the Supernatural, Coping with the Mass Media, How Words Change Our Lives* (a book on semantics), and *The Comic Spirit in Literature*. Although they never matched the sale of the Man books, they helped feed the bulldog.

They also helped us build good relationships with teachers and students. One book in particular can serve as an example: *Learning About Peoples and Cultures* by Dr. Seymour Fersh. This textbook, still in print in a 1989 revision, is the first world cultures book to look at other cultures as insiders rather than as outsiders would view them. It is also the first to discuss other cultures without comparing them to existing norms in other countries. Fersh helps the student to realize that "each of us is tempted to perceive his or her own culture as *the* culture rather than *a* culture." Typical of his teaching methods is the way he uses the example of a Hindu wedding in rural India. The marriage ceremony, in appearance, is very much like an American one: vows by the bride and groom, blessings by the priest, and gifts from family and friends. Mention is made that the wedding takes place in the home of the bride's family. Fersh now springs the surprise: the bride and groom have not seen each other until the ceremony; theirs was an arranged marriage.

American students' reactions are predictable. Almost all of them show surprise, shock, and disapproval, because the many similarities to an American wedding gave no clue that the marriage had been arranged. From Fersh's perspective, the negative responses are not only anticipated but welcome. He now has a beginning point for students to examine their assumptions. This happens when they learn how in rural India brides often marry into "joint families" that provide survival and continuity for family members and the village itself. "This kind of lesson," says Fersh, "is essential in helping students to become self-educating."

I first met Sy Fersh at the 1972 convention of the National Council for the Social Studies. He was then education director of the Asia Society and already the author of widely used textbooks on culture regions. Previously, he had been a high school and college teacher and a Fulbright professor in India. At the McDougal, Littell booth, he told me of his admiration for our books, and our friendship was off to a quick and solid start. We shifted our conversation to the hotel lobby where, after an animated two hours, we agreed enthusiastically that Sy would write a book for us. Two years later, at the 1974 convention, *Learning About Peoples and Cultures* was on display.

Over the years, Sy and I have kept in close touch. We have not been surprised to learn how parallel our lives have been in many ways: his years in India and mine in China; his service in World War II, which helped him define his perspectives and character (he was wounded by a German sniper during an infantry battle in March 1945). Sy is now officially retired and busier than ever, writing, consulting, and traveling. He recently told me, "As someone has said, 'I hope to die young . . . as late as possible.'"

COMING UNGLUED

In the fall of 1975, we had an unexpected setback that came close to putting McDougal, Littell out of business. All of our books fell apart — literally. It happened after the national oil crisis. The glue supplier had changed his formula to use less of the petroleum base. The books were fine when they came off the binding line, but they subsequently came unglued — fell apart both in our warehouse and in classrooms across the country.

How can I forget that embarrassing day when I paid a call on the chairperson of the English Department at New Trier Township High School, just two blocks from our office, to show her our newest mini-textbooks. She had half a dozen English teachers in her office at the time, and I happily passed a boxful of books around for them to examine.

"Notice that our softback books now have the new film-laminated covers," I told them proudly. "Our books can now withstand all sorts of student abuse." No sooner had I said that than the teachers opened up their copies and all the pages fluttered out of the books and piled up around their shoes. I was speechless! I figured that if scenes like this were taking place in English departments all over the country as teachers opened up the sample books we had sent them, McDougal, Littell was done for.

Fortunately, we were able to have the books in our warehouse rebound and new books sent to the schools to replace the defective ones — all at the binder's expense. That year, however, we experienced our first downturn in sales and our first net loss. It was a scary year for all of us.

McDOUGAL, LITTELL MAKES THE BIG TIME

In the mid-1970s — to the surprise of everyone or no one, I'm still not sure which — there occurred the most sudden and the most dramatic shake-up in the history of American education. The Back to Basics movement snapped the schools back to a traditional curriculum, with its heavy emphasis on mastery of facts and skills. It was a 180-degree turn in educational philosophy. Publishers had warehouses filled with textbooks that, with their "soft" approach to learning, became worthless overnight.

Fortunately, Fred and I had noticed the growing dissatisfaction of teachers and parents with what they perceived to be an aimless, unstructured curriculum; we had witnessed their dismay at seeing students graduating from high school barely able to read and write; and we had begun to get a feeling, way down deep in our gut, that something big was about to happen. A full year before the start of the Back to Basics movement, we began to prepare a rigorous hardbound grammar/composition series built somewhat on the model conceived by Lee Deighton and me at Macmillan. With the timely publication of this series, called Building English Skills, we got a long jump on other publishers of English textbooks. Through three editions, lasting well into the 1980s, Building English Skills outsold all other English series in the nation.

In addition to publishing a companion series called McDougal, Littell Literature, we have since branched out into other subject areas: high school geometry and algebra, high school American history, and elementary reading, spelling, handwriting, and health. The company continues to focus, however, on maintaining its preeminence in the field of English. The current successor to Building English Skills is the Writer's Craft, which is in use in fifty states and in 1993 was adopted by sixty percent of the schools in Texas.

Ever since the beginning, McDougal, Littell books have had a different look, a different feel, from those of other publishers. This is so because of Joy's insistence on elegance of typographic design, on sharpness in the reproduction of photographs and other artwork, and on superior quality of paper. "When students are using a textbook," says Joy, "they should feel they are holding something of value — something they can respect, and something that appears to respect them as well." What a pleasure it is to hear a teacher say to us, "I can always tell a McDougal, Littell book at a glance!" Over the years, McDougal, Littell books have been honored with fifty-five awards for excellence in design, typography, and printing from the American Institute of Graphic Arts and the Society of Typographic Arts.

Part of Fred's dream for McDougal, Littell was to have the employees own all of the company. In 1985 we took a big step toward that end by purchasing the shares of the original outside investors for $4,950,000, half in cash (borrowed from the bank) and the remainder in subordinated five-year notes. I elected to sell my shares at the same time.

Following the purchase of the stock, Fred was essentially the sole stockholder, with the exception of a small number of shares owned by the employees in an Employee Stock Ownership Plan, which we had instituted in 1984. In 1986 Fred took a big step by selling about thirty percent of his stock to the Employee Stock Ownership Plan. This gave him some assets for the first time outside McDougal, Littell stock and, at the same time, gave the employees a significant equity interest in the company for which they paid nothing — an enormous win-win situation. The ESOP shares were in effect a retirement plan for employees — great if the company did well, not at all great if it did not.

As I noted earlier, the company that started in 1969 with four employees jammed in a tiny three-room office is now the primary tenant in Rotary International's World Headquarters in Evanston. And I'll say it again! With more than three hundred employees and annual sales of $70 million, McDougal, Littell ranked in 1993 among the top half-dozen educational publishers in the nation.

Not bad for a popcorn salesman and a mish-kid, eh?

16

RETIREMENT
AND THE SALE OF
McDOUGAL, LITTELL

MY UNEXPECTED EARLY RETIREMENT

In 1987, while I was as busy as ever producing textbooks for McDougal, Littell, a funny thing happened. I began to feel a need to take my life in a different direction. Over a period of months the feeling persisted, kept increasing in intensity, refused to go away. On my sixty-second birthday, I thought of little else.

What had prompted those thoughts — thoughts so strange for a person who had made a lifelong career of overcommitting himself to his work, who had always been confident that he would work well into his eighties like his very first boss, old Mr. Bryant?

I can only guess at the reasons: the residual effects of World War II; my incredible family stresses, first as a son, then as a husband; the pounding effects of thirty-eight years of sixty- to seventy-hour work weeks that had seized my energies, held them hostage, and clouded my ability to see the parts of my life in true relation to one another. Finally, the demons in my head simply told me to go. "Clear out," they said. "Do something else. Go!"

Strangely, too, I didn't feel exhausted or beaten down — simply disengaged, floating abstractedly above the level of close detail that I had always relished and demanded of myself.

Doctors couldn't find anything wrong with me. Taking a vacation in the Virgin Islands didn't help.

I told Joy of my intention to — retire? resign? I didn't know which. She had retired from her position as editorial director the previous year and gave me her full support. I apprised Fred of my intention to

Joy and I, Lake Forest, Illinois, 1984.

leave, and after a long period of vacillation I made my final decision. Fred didn't fully understand, but who could have expected him to — especially if I didn't understand all the reasons myself? Nevertheless, he treated my decision with consummate respect and helped to make my departure from McDougal, Littell a smooth one.

After leaving the company, I was still sorting things out. On warm days, it helped to be able to work with Joy on our two great hobbies — maintaining and enjoying our hundred and twenty varieties of roses and spending time with our devoted Irish wolfhounds, Rory and Nora. I saw more of my daughters, Julia, Nancy, and Laura. I read a stack of books I hadn't found time to read for years. Joy and I did more entertaining than we had ever done before.

A year later, I still didn't know for sure why I had severed myself from a company I had loved so dearly and from people I had admired so deeply. All I knew was that it had been the right decision. It showed in my renewed energy and in my recaptured happiness. It caused Joy to tell me: "You're not *retired* — you're *re-fired!*"

And now Fred, in his mid-fifties, was there to carry on at McDougal, Littell. How good a job would he do? By the time you have finished reading this chapter, I think you will be able to decide for yourself.

The scene now shifts to Boston.

NADER DAREHSHORI — AN AMERICAN SUCCESS STORY

Houghton Mifflin Company is one of the great publishing houses in America. Headquartered in Boston, it had its beginnings in 1832. Most of its early directors were Harvard graduates, coming from old Boston families and born to wealth and social position. Not so, the present head of Houghton Mifflin.

Nader Darehshori was born and raised in a small village in southern Iran, the son of a wheat farmer and sheep rancher. He became an elementary school teacher, then left for America to earn a bachelor's degree in education. His walk-in interview with the dean of students at the University of Wisconsin at Oshkosh revealed an earnestness and a declared sense of purpose that won him a four-year scholarship. To his teachers there, he was a brilliant student; to his fellow students, he was a Big Man on Campus and homecoming chairman! Upon graduation in 1966, he took a job as a sales representative for Houghton Mifflin's college division. From there, it was a steady rise to the top. Today, Darehshori presides over the house of Hawthorne, Longfellow, Thoreau, Whittier, James Russell Lowell, Oliver Wendell Holmes, and Harriet Beecher Stowe. As if that were not a sufficient array of talent, there later came Willa Cather, Archibald MacLeish, Bernard DeVoto, John Dos Passos, Winston Churchill, Rachel Carson, J. R. R. Tolkien, Cornelia Otis Skinner, John Kenneth Galbraith, Arthur Schlesinger, Jr., Ross Lockridge, and James Dickey.

And now there's me! Two of those Houghton Mifflin authors, incidentally, did not remain in the fold. Willa Cather, insulted when her long-time editor took the liberty of calling her by her first name, fled to another publisher. Ross Lockridge, undone by the fame and fortune brought to him by his first book, committed suicide. I intend to do neither.

Houghton Mifflin is also a leader in educational publishing, with a wide range of elementary, secondary, and college texts and assessments. And that's where Nader Darehshori comes into my story.

It was in the late 1970s that he began to keep a watchful eye on a fast-rising educational publisher in Illinois by the name of McDougal, Littell & Company.

HOW TO BUY (AND SELL) A COMPANY

The 1970s and 1980s had been years of rapid growth for McDougal, Littell, but there were clouds on the horizon. In the early 1990s it became clear to Fred that the company could not look forward to steady growth indefinitely. "Your retirement created an enormous void," he told me (a statement that still brings me occasional twinges of guilt), "and new product development slowed as we searched for a satisfactory editor-in-chief and I struggled to hold us together."

The enormously successful McDougal, Littell Literature was slaughtered in the Texas adoption by a new and extremely attractive series from Prentice-Hall. The company recovered eventually and brought out new programs that swept the next Texas adoption and helped skyrocket sales to $70 million in 1993. Meanwhile, however, McDougal, Littell had seen several states cancel or postpone their scheduled adoptions, some after the company had even worked an entire adoption with sales reps, samples, and so on.

Simultaneously, the cost of producing books had escalated tremendously. In 1969 and 1970, McDougal, Littell could publish a whole junior and senior high series for $360,000. By 1993 a new English series with its accompanying materials — teachers' editions, cassettes, software, tests, teachers' resource boxes, and so on — would cost $10.5 million.

"With those kinds of dollars," said Fred, "we had to be right all the time. Furthermore, if we had a new investment for a scheduled state adoption that turned out to be postponed, not only would our return on investment be delayed and thereby reduced, but we could end up investing even more money in marketing with no immediate return."

In short, Fred began to feel that he was gambling, not only with his own money, but with the retirement money of hundreds of his colleagues, for whom the ESOP was their only retirement security.

"At the same time," said Fred, "I was considering the company's future without me. In February of 1994 I turned sixty-three and was looking forward to doing other things. Neither Tom nor Steve [his sons] had shown any particular interest in McDougal, Littell, and even if they did, at this point it would be a long time, if ever, before either was ready to assume management responsibilities. Nancy Lauter, who had joined the company in 1974 as advertising manager and who eventually became senior vice-president of sales and marketing, leading our marketing and sales growth, became my wife in 1986, and we found our lives together constricted by her continuous responsibilities, including travel, leading to her decision to step down to a part-time role, heading up international sales and sales training, so that we could have more time together."

Fred now began to explore options to secure the company's future after and without him. His preference was to sell the company totally to the employees through the ESOP, but the debt that would have been incurred would have had the dual effect of lowering the value of the company stock and saddling the company with excessive debt-repayment obligations that would deprive it of the funds it needed to grow. In short, it would defeat the very objectives he sought — to provide long-term financial security for the employees.

He also considered going public. Over the years investment bankers had suggested this alternative many times, but he had resisted it because he and I had felt that our ability to grow was enhanced by not having to show annual growth and by being able to invest heavily in the future at the expense of current earnings. Going public still seemed a very dubious strategy.

"Finally," said Fred, "I had to face the fact that the best way to protect the employees was to find the right buyer — one who would respect individuals, let us continue to operate as much as possible as we had, protect the maximum number of jobs, and if possible add synergies — that much-abused term referring to something that rarely, I think, exists in real life. Above all, I hoped to find a company whose culture would be similar to ours. I started to make a list of possible companies I might talk with, but held back because I was concerned about the effects of rumors upon our employees. I had seen over and over what happened with other companies that were going to be sold — how customers shied away from buying from them (with considerable encouragement from the competitors' sales reps), how the best editorial and sales people began to get attractive job offers — in short, how companies started to disintegrate when word got out that they might be for sale. At McDougal, Littell we had seen it at first hand, over and over, as rumors of our possible sale had floated around — many times over twenty-plus years. I was determined to avoid that — and I held back in approaching possible buyers."

At that point, Nader Darehshori called and invited Fred to lunch.

Fred had been approached by Houghton Mifflin before at various times, along with many of the other companies, so he suspected that Nader did not simply yearn for his companionship, as pleasant a thought as that would surely be. But the timing was uncanny — this time — for in secret the top company on his list as a possible buyer that would meet his criteria was, in fact, Houghton Mifflin.

As Fred had suspected, Nader did suggest the possibility of an alliance, and he also held out the vision of McDougal, Littell as a secondary publisher under the Houghton Mifflin umbrella, with Houghton Mifflin itself as an elementary publisher. McDougal, Littell would take over Houghton Mifflin's secondary product line, sales of which were relatively modest, and Houghton Mifflin would take over McDougal, Littell's elementary sales, which were only about a third of its business. As it happened, this was exactly Fred's vision as well, for McDougal, Littell's greatest strength was middle school and high school publishing, and Houghton Mifflin's was at the elementary level. It was a logical fit and allowed for the possibility of McDougal, Littell's continued existence in Evanston, with its own sales force and editorial staff.

A major obstacle, however, was price. Houghton Mifflin's initial and subsequent offers were below what McDougal, Littell's advisers thought the company was worth — and Fred had a fiduciary and moral responsibility to the stockholders to maximize the price of their shares. He had to convince Houghton Mifflin that it had to match a potential competitive bid — without actually taking the company through the painful process of visibly putting it on the market.

The negotiations were one-on-one, Nader and Fred. Eventually they shook hands in the Algonquin Club in Boston with only a few people on each side aware of the discussions — a major accomplishment. The negotiations continued through the 1993 Christmas holidays with regard to a number of difficult issues that only lawyers and accountants can dream up, and I suspect that both Nader and Fred were truly exasperated by some of them. The outcome remained in doubt until the very end. Finally, Fred and Nader, following the approval of both boards, reached agreement at four A.M. on January 7, 1994, and Houghton Mifflin made the announcement that day. The final purchase price for McDougal, Littell was $138 million.

Unbelievably, the Federal Trade Commission held up the transaction, concerned about the small overlaps in the product lines, and made more work for more lawyers for more weeks. Fred and Nancy left for Ha aii as planned many weeks before, and while they were there — on March 1 — the deal finally closed. Hawaii was a really good place to be at that point!

As a result of the sale, more than a hundred McDougal, Littell employees ended up with stock in their ESOP accounts of more than $100,000 each — some long-term employees with many times that amount. Fred had expected to be excoriated by his colleagues for "selling out," but to his very pleasant surprise the reaction was overwhelmingly positive, thanks to the financial security people suddenly woke up to on January 7. As one colleague said to him, "Now I won't have to buy bruised fruit any longer." People also seemed to understand the risks of remaining independent and to appreciate the quality of Houghton Mifflin as a true publishing company rather than a conglomerate for which publishing was only a sideline. Finally, people genuinely appreciated the confidentiality with which the transaction had been conducted — particularly people who had been through mergers of other publishing companies.

All in all, the aftermath that Fred had so dreaded turned out, after the initial shock, to be an accolade. "I couldn't have been more surprised," he told me happily, "and I'm grateful down to my toes."

MEMORIES OF MY YEARS AT McDOUGAL, LITTELL

So many memories I cherish of those years at McDougal, Littell! Here are a few of them. To me they convey, as much as any, the essence of what made — and still makes — the company special.

The First Convention. The defining moment in our company's history may have come as early as 1969, just four months after we had started business. It was in Washington, D.C., at the annual convention of the National Council of Teachers of English. Fred, Joy, and I, as well as our secretary, were there to introduce the first five Man books that were ready. Aware that we needed to do something dramatic to call attention to our unknown books and our unknown company, we hit on a plan. The night before the convention began, the four of us ran up and down the endless corridors of those two gigantic hotels, the Sheraton and the Shoreham, where the teachers were staying, and slipped Man brochures under their doors — about three thousand of them — along with an invitation to stop at Booth 330 and sign up for a free copy of Man.

Well! For three days our tiny booth looked like a Washington's Birthday sale at Filene's Basement. By contrast, the big publishers' salespeople, in their long, carpeted, designer-created booths that looked like the top side of a royal yacht, could do nothing but stand around, bravely smiling and joking with one another, arms folded, while this near-riot was taking place at the McDougal, Littell booth nearby. Teachers by the hundreds signed up for samples of the Man books, and a good number of them, on returning to their schools, ordered classroom sets for all their students.

A McDougal, Littell editor said to me recently, "You know, that often-told story of the Washington convention still seems the perfect metaphor for what set our company apart from all the others."

The Christmas Parties. I have fond memories of our company parties. Our first party was in our warehouse in Kenilworth. Fred and I wore red vests and plaid pants each year. (The locations changed and got grander, but the pants stayed the same.) When the company was still small enough to do grab bags, each employee brought a gift for someone else. I remember the gift someone gave me one year — a two-brimmed cap that said, "I am their leader. Which way did they go?"

Special Interest Groups. Educational publishers are always criticized for "inappropriate content." It's amazing how many special interest groups we had to deal with; the religious right, the gender watchdogs, the ethnic group activists affect every chapter and every piece of artwork in every book. One school system rejected our literature books because one of them contained a photograph of a small boy hugging his pet sheep. They said it "fostered bestiality and unnatural acts." When the National Rifle Association kept our high school grammar and composition books off the approved list in Indiana because we had included an essay in favor of gun control by Boston's chief of police, employees showed up at our Christmas party toting water pistols. If you were there, you weren't helping us do proper penance for that act of lese majesty unless you had a snootful of water dripping down your face. (That essay on gun control, incidentally, was included in the book only as an example of a well-developed five-paragraph essay.)

The "Whorehouse." The fellow who ran our warehouse thought it was spelled "whorehouse" and as a result sent fascinating dispatches to the office from his job site.

The underdog. We were always the little guys taking on the giants, and we loved it. Feeling his oats one day, Fred dreamed up the ad shown on the next page and had it placed in national magazines for schoolteachers and administrators.

The implications of the ad were endless. While those other companies were being run by nameless, faceless legatees of founders long gone to their rest, teachers could still visit a McDougal, Littell booth and find a real McDougal standing right there before them, alive and well, glad to see them, ready to listen, ready to assist them in any way. Amazing! To say nothing of a real Littell, also breathing in oxygen and blowing out CO_2, also happy to see them, concerned about their textbook needs, eager to be of service. Astounding!

And there was something else about that ad. Notice the word "big" in the headline. Sure we were big — if you think that in comparison with other companies' fifty-story Manhattan sky-rises, our cozy apartment-office in a tumbledown courtyard in Kenilworth, Illinois, was big. The point is, many teachers *thought* we were big — big, old, and established — mainly, I suspect, because our company name sounded just as hoary, just as venerable, as anyone else's.

McDougal, Littell has something the other big names in textbook publishing don't have.

A real McDougal.

A real Littell.

Perhaps someday soon you'll have a conversation with one—or both—at an educators' convention.

Your comments might even influence the direction taken in some future McDougal, Littell textbook.

In any case, isn't it good to know that many of today's finest and best accepted texts are coming from real human beings, not just faceless corporations?

McDougal, Littell & Company

Publishers of more than 160 titles nationally, including elementary English, spelling, handwriting and health.

McDougal, Littell & Company, P.O. Box 1667, Evanston, IL 60204
For information, phone 1-800-323-4068. In Illinois, call collect 1-312-967-0900.

For weeks after that ad appeared, our switchboard jangled with calls for "the real McDougal" and "the real Littell." What fun we had with that ad!

What Perks? In the early years the employees had no perks — no 401K, no health care reimbursement, no bonuses — but they all cared so much about what they were doing that they worked nights and weekends and didn't mind.

Look, Ma, No Typewriters. I think we were the only publishing house in the world that refused to acknowledge the existence of typewriters. In 1985, when we moved to the Rotary International Building in Evanston and went straight to word processors, everyone nearly died of future shock.

There are those memories, and many more. They are mostly smiling memories. Some are laughing memories. A few are wistful memories. Almost all of them I have replayed over and over in my mind, and in my heart.

17

REVISITING MY CHILDHOOD IN HONOLULU

MEMORIES: WARM, WISTFUL, AND — WHOOPS!

Recently I had an experience that evoked in me certain heartwarming as well as disturbing memories. Joy and I flew to Hawaii. It was her first trip to the Islands and, all energized, I could hardly wait to show her my old haunts in Honolulu. No sooner had we settled in the hotel than we drove straight to Queen Emma Square, the site of the Bishop's House — that marvelous manse that had been my childhood home as well as command post for my scams, pranks, and shakedowns. What would I find? Even though I had already steeled myself for the shock of not seeing it there (having heard that, being termite-ridden, the house had surrendered to the bulldozer), I was in no way prepared for the trauma of finding in its place a huge, shiny black asphalt parking lot. Silently standing on the hallowed spot where my home had been, I swallowed hard as memories — a whole flood of them — washed over me.

Next stop: the cathedral. That great stone Gothic church stood, as it always had, next to the Bishop's House — or next to where it used to be. With a catch in my throat, I entered the main portal. Joy and I walked slowly up the red-carpeted aisle to the chancel. We paused at length before the stalls where, as a ten-year-old, I had sung in the choir. We then moved to the passageway in back of the altar. There we saw, set into the wall, the memorial to my father, a large stone tablet:

TO THE GLORY OF GOD AND IN MEMORY OF
THE RT. REV.
SAMUEL HARRINGTON LITTELL, D.D.
FIFTH BISHOP OF HONOLULU
BORN 1873　　DIED 1967
HE LANAKILA MA KE KEA
"VICTORY BY THE CROSS"

I stared at the tablet until my eyes became too misty for me to see it clearly. Slowly we moved on.

So far in my tour, I had experienced some sadness, some wistfulness, some joy of remembrance — all emotions I could expect on such a memory-laden tour. But the discovery I would make in just a few minutes came as a jolt.

Adjoining the cathedral was the parish house — the very place where the childlike innocence of my tour vanished. After peeking into various classrooms, we entered a particular room — the vesting room, where the choirboys dressed for Sunday services — which I had known so well. As I glanced around, a long-suppressed memory welled up in the very depths of me, for I was picturing the room just as it had been when I was a child. Standing against one wall, I recalled, were some wooden cabinets. But against the far wall stood some horizontal shelves. I stopped short. "Wait a minute!" I thought.

"That's where something happened to me as a choirboy!" Why was I getting so uptight?

Yes, right there, on the bottom shelf — I was only ten years old — that's where I had been sexually abused. Time and time again, two older youths had violated my person. One was no other than an angelic-looking crucifer, who, on many a Sunday, faithfully and with great dignity, carried the cross in the procession. The other, second in line, was a flag bearer, entrusted with our Stars and Stripes. And it was during off-hours, when the parish was empty, that those two persuaded me with a monetary bribe to lie down on the bottom shelf, where, taking turns, they repeatedly abused me.

Those boys made me feel I was being a "regular guy," doing what was expected of boys my age. Though I had a gut feeling that something here was not right, I had no one to talk to. Besides, I didn't *want* to talk to anyone about this. I couldn't very well go up to my father, the bishop, and say to him, "Look, Pop, I've just been ridden like a surfboard by two of the guys you have carrying the cross and flag in church on Sunday. They tell me there's nothing wrong with what they're doing, and they each pay me fifty cents a time — which is more than I get for singing in the choir." No, I couldn't very well have said that to my father.

Over the years I had buried that experience, keeping all such thoughts locked in a dark corner of my mind. But now, as I left the parish house, living it all over again, my mind swirled. I was angry — red-hot angry, inwardly shaking. How could those older teenagers have taken advantage of a ten-year-old, a mere child — one far too young to deal with matters of this sort? How could they — both of them churchgoers, both well regarded in the community — have told me, "This is just one of those things you don't tell the older folks"?

That night I lay awake, too angry to fall into even a fitful sleep. I vowed to myself, "I'm going right out first thing in the morning, round up those two boys, confront them with what they did, and beat them to a pulp." It wasn't until sunup that I realized that those "boys" would now be in their seventies! By breakfast time, my anger somewhat subsided, I forced my mind into more productive avenues of thought. What else could I do? What can you really do with such memories other than face them, blow your top, rechannel your energies, then come back to present reality?

Somehow I had been able to camouflage my state of mind, for Joy knew nothing about the fury that had raged within me the previous afternoon or why, through the night, I had been so restless.

A TRIP TO THE PALI

The next morning, ready for another outing, Joy and I headed for the Pali, that string of jagged cliffs that offers a breathtaking view of the north side of the island. To get to the Pali from Honolulu, we took the Pali Highway north for five miles, making a gradual ascent under a lush canopy of banyan trees. Once there, we parked at the Pali Lookout and gazed down from the top of a moss-covered cliff that plunged twelve hundred feet to the plains below. Spread out before us, to the left and right, was the view of windward Oahu that Mark Twain called the most beautiful in the world.

From the lookout, just to the right of us, I spotted the Old Pali Road, that narrow, twisting road that wound along the windward cliffs and, for almost a century, was the only means of descending the Pali before a tunnel was carved through the mountains in the 1960s. For me, that old road, now blocked by a chain barrier, was full of memories. Just taking that scary trip along the edge of nearly vertical cliffs (so reminiscent of the terrifying road to Kuling, China) had always been for me the essence of high adventure. Especially romantic to me had been that legendary enemy to the surety of safe passage, that treacherous portion of the road that lay in wait halfway down the cliff, that heart-stopping segment that suddenly doubled back on itself — the hairpin turn.

Seized by an overwhelming impulse to run down that road and see the hairpin turn, bursting with anticipation, I turned to Joy. "I'll be right back," I told her. "I need to make my last farewell — to see the hairpin turn just one more time!" Hardly ending my sentence, I hurdled the chain barrier and sped down the road. At times, the steep downward thrust pitched me forward so fast that I wasn't sure I could ever stop. I had to leap across deep fissures in the crumbling asphalt and avoid dozens of prickly bushes bursting out of cracks in the road. Halfway down the Pali, I rounded a bend in the road and there, spread out before me in all its twisted magnificence, I saw what I was seeking. It didn't look nearly as scary as it had when I was a kid, but never mind — it was the hairpin! I was in touch with my childhood again, in touch with my memories — even comical memories, like the time Father couldn't quite complete the turn and sideswiped some bushes on the cliff, loosening that avalanche of dirt and vegetation that buried Morris and me up to our waists in the rumble seat.

I kept my eyes fixed for a moment on the hairpin turn and then, with a surge of exultation that brought with it a sudden rush of energy, I headed back up the mountain — starting at a brisk walk, picking up speed, then running ever faster until, as I approached the chain barrier, I was sprinting as if to a finish line. Upon my return to the lookout, drenched with perspiration and gasping for breath, Joy greeted me with a cheery hello and a friendly smile, her face betraying not the slightest suspicion that I had just won a death-defying race with time.

I think she understood.

A VISIT TO MY SISTER'S GRAVE

On our trip back to Honolulu from the Pali, Joy and I stopped at Oahu Cemetery to see Charlotte's grave. When I was eleven years old, that beloved sister of mine, only in her late twenties, had succumbed to her troubles and suddenly taken her own life. At her gravesite, a peaceful place shaded by tall kukui trees, we stood for several minutes. Silently I read the inscription carved on the gravestone:

CHARLOTTE TAYLOR LITTELL
Born June 12, 1908 — Kuling, China
Died August 13, 1936 — Honolulu

Then, standing before her grave, I spoke to Joy, thinking of how short but how warm had been my relationship with Charlotte. "I remember how she used to save every colorful stamp she could lay her hands on for my stamp collection. I remember how she and I used to plant marigold, nasturtium, and zinnia seeds in our flower garden in the front yard. How we used to laugh uproariously as we played a silly little piano duet based on a theme from Haydn's Surprise Symphony. If only I knew why it was that a soul so sweet and gentle — and yet so alive and vibrant — had to die so early in life. I wonder, too, what she would have done with her life had she not cut it short. Would she have married, had children? And how many more people would have received her precious gifts of creativity, friendship, and love?"

And now, with a sudden flash, something hit me as I stood there before her grave. I was dumbstruck — numbstruck — by the realization that in all the years after Charlotte's death, never once, in my recollection, had my parents mentioned her name. Not once! It was as if she had never existed. How inexplicably sad! And all the sadder it seems today, in this age of open discussion of death, of grief therapy and counseling, that my father and mother kept their feelings forever bottled up inside them. The hurt must have been deep. And yet Charlotte deserved to be remembered openly and proudly for her personal qualities, her extraordinary gifts, and her professional accomplishments — her music. I left the gravesite exhilarated by my recollections of my sister but, at the same time, depressed by the veil of silence that had shrouded her memory.

In view of the stresses on my sister, I have often wondered if she and I didn't have in common a certain heartache — that is, the lack of a parent or other relative to confide in, someone who could give us guidance in our distressing passage through youth. For Charlotte to have chosen to inflict on herself the ultimate solution to her unbearable problems, with no one to talk to, must have meant pain of the most excruciating sort. I, too, know how it is to go through the tortures of growing up and to do it alone — with nobody in all those boarding school years to share my burdens. Our parents never discussed personal matters with us. They probably wouldn't have known how to relate to Charlotte, much less how to advise and console her, how to alleviate her suicidal thoughts.

As we left the gravesite, Joy put my feelings into words: "So crucial is the need for honest, open human communication — for a chance to share one's burdens with a spouse, sister, brother, parent, or friend — that its absence can cost a human life. In this case it was your sister Charlotte's."

WE MISH-KIDS:
OUR FINAL DESTINY

YOU WILL PROBABLY REMEMBER that during my father's thirty-one years in China, he sired seven children — four by his first wife, Charlotte, and three by his second wife, Evelyn. Collectively, we mish-kids had certain things in common. We were survivors of a quixotic upbringing. We were rooted, then uprooted, in several countries. We were acquainted at first hand with violence and turbulence in a country often hostile to us "imperialists" and "foreign devils."

While eventually some of us Littells were able to overcome, at least partially, the emotional, physical, and spiritual consequences of such an upbringing, others of us ended in early tragedy. Let's look at how we were affected and what became of the Littell legacy.

JOHN

John, the oldest son, was twenty-one years older than I, and I could rightly say to him, "Oh, Johnny, I hardly knew ye." He was shipped out of China at age twelve to attend Kent School in Connecticut. He then went on to Harvard, where he graduated cum laude. In eight years of absentee schooling, he was able to get back to China just twice, for two summers. His isolation from the family may have had its negative effects, for John was painfully shy — in fact, so ill at ease with people that he shunned social gatherings. To compensate for his inability to project himself, he developed a lively interest in hiking, music, and stamp collecting. His major passion was foreign affairs — a subject that laid the groundwork for his career.

While visiting our sister Charlotte at Vassar, John fell in love with her roommate, Char Stanfield. The two decided to be married in New York City, in the home of her parents. Now it happened that Char's father was Jewish and her mother Presbyterian. Apprised of that bit of untidiness, Father played the China card. He informed John and Char that he could not give his blessing to their marriage unless they came to China so that he could baptize Char in the Episcopal Church and then marry the two in St. Paul's Cathedral.

Well, Father got half of what he wanted, anyway. Char did agree to become an Episcopalian, but she wasn't about to embark on that endless, difficult voyage to Hankow. The couple committed the pardonable sin of being married in St. Thomas's Church in New York City.

John became a career diplomat. He first served as attaché in Peking, next as vice-consul in Shanghai, then as consul in Shanghai, Mexico City, and Kingston, Jamaica. Although his marriage produced a son, also named John, it was doomed from the start. Char was a vivacious New Yorker who was happiest with a crowd of people around her. Unhappy with John, she divorced him and eventually married a Britisher with more swash in his buckle.

But John's problems didn't end there. In those days the State Department would never allow a divorced person to remain in the Foreign Service. As a result, John was forced into a mid-life career switch. The next thing we knew, he was serving as an officer in the Federal Reserve Bank in San Francisco.

After a second unsuccessful marriage, John found a more reclusive partner and settled down in Tiburon, in a home overlooking the Golden Gate Bridge. Becoming more at ease with himself, he rekindled his interest in music, serving as president of the San Francisco Bach Choir. A hysterical call came in 1981 from his devoted wife to tell us of his death, at age seventy-eight. We were glad that he had found compensation for the insecurities and loneliness he had known throughout his life.

EDWARD

Like John, brother number two was sent off to faraway schools — Kent and then Harvard. During Edward's six-year stretch away from our China home, he never once returned for a visit and saw Father and Mother just once, when they were in America on furlough.

After college, Edward entered the ministry, and in the 1930s he served on the staff of Grace Cathedral in San Francisco. And that's where my fondest memories of Edward come in — memories of an eleven- and twelve-year-old. On our trips to Europe from Honolulu, Mother and I would always spend a day or two with Edward in San Francisco. The minute we had settled ourselves into the Hotel Stewart, he would show up with the next day's itinerary: two cable car rides, Fisherman's Wharf, Nob Hill, Chinatown, Golden Gate Park, Sutro Baths, Ding Hao Restaurant. In the evening, happy and dead tired, we would return to the hotel, where Edward and I would sit on a bed and play endless hands of slapjack, rummy, hearts, and concentration. "Edward," I would say to him (in the parlance of the day), "you're a good egg."

It was after Pearl Harbor that Edward really came to life. On December 8, 1941, he received his commission as an army chaplain, rose rapidly to the rank of captain, and participated in the invasion of Guadalcanal. For helping to evacuate the wounded under heavy fire, he was awarded the Bronze Star along with a citation for "acts of heroism performed in ground combat." Unfortunately, while in the South Pacific, he was bitten by a malaria mosquito and suffered the ill effects for years to come.

Edward was always there when you needed him. If you were a family member with an emergency of any sort, you didn't call 911 — you called Edward. I remember how in the difficult days following Charlotte's death he took a leave of absence from his duties in San

Francisco to answer Father and Mother's call to Honolulu, where he helped to comfort and console us all. I remember how he showed up at Fort Dix, New Jersey, to welcome me back to the States after I had been freed from POW camp. He sent a telegram to Father and Mother that read: JOE ARRIVED AT FORT DIX TODAY. LOOKS SWELL. LOVE. EDWARD. That was a lie, of course; I looked awful. It may have been simply Edward's way of reassuring the family that I hadn't lost an arm or a leg. I remember how he hurried off to western Pennsylvania to comfort Nancy when she sat in the hot seat — a prime target in that religious crossfire. So many times Edward came through for us.

In the 1970s, Edward took a parish in Hoboken, New Jersey. Not having a car, he allowed the altar boy to drive him to homes and hospitals so that he could comfort the sick, the old, and the lonely. He was much beloved by all of his parishioners.

Edward is a no-frills fellow who has managed to keep his life simple. He has always lived light, with few possessions. He never owned a car. He never smoked, drank, or married. Today he lives in retirement in his father's native town — Wilmington, Delaware. At ninety, he's still a good egg, and now just a tiny bit on the hard-boiled side, which is the way I like 'em.

CHARLOTTE

You know the tragic story of my sister Charlotte . . . how she became a concert pianist, receiving many East Coast accolades for her performances . . . and how at the age of twenty-eight, one month before she was to perform as soloist with the Honolulu Symphony Orchestra, she committed suicide in the kitchen of the Bishop's House. Her desperation, her reason for her action, has never been understood, nor has any one of us adjusted to the fact that this could have occurred. Such trauma, whether happening yesterday or decades ago, remains at the forefront of our minds. "One gets through it," said a wise person, "but one never gets over it."

HARRINGTON (HANK)

When only thirteen, with the family still living in China, Hank was shipped off to Kent School. For years he was left to his own devices — his adored sister Charlotte, then a student at Vassar, being his only close relative nearby. Somehow, nevertheless, he coped. And magnificently, too, I should say.

On the surface, he was the all-around nice guy. At Trinity College he was captain of the crew, president of his fraternity, editor of the college newspaper, voted "the Man Most Likely to Succeed." On his rare visits to our home in Honolulu, he was a charmer — witty, fun to be with, the family booster, greeter, cheerleader, social director, chauffeur — bursting with personal magnetism. And that smile! When Hank fixed that smile on you, and flashed those steel-blue eyes, you melted!

Underneath that facade, however, was a serious, brooding human being. Throughout his life, he never stopped aching inside, so strong was his sense of guilt and self-blame for the deaths of the first two females in his life — his mother and his sister.

The death of his mother came in Hankow, eighteen hours after he was born. For this, Hank felt he was to blame — certain that it was all his fault. *She* should have survived — not he. He also suffered unspeakable remorse that he had not but *should* have sensed the desperation, the gloom, that gripped Charlotte and sent her to her self-destruction. "Why," he lamented to me once, "was I not able to foresee and prevent that tragedy?"

Hank was the mystery man of the family. After serving with distinction as a naval officer in the Pacific in World War II, he took a job with the CIA (we think) and for thirty years inhabited various parts of the globe — Tokyo, Hong Kong, Frankfurt, Laos, Liberia — the whole time officially connected to the State Department, the Pentagon, or the National Security Council. He and his beloved wife, Flora, produced two sons, Harrington Jr. and Reid, who lived abroad with them for short periods of time but grew up mainly in American boarding schools. From the beginning, I learned not to ask Hank about his work and, in deference to his temper, *never* to mention those incendiary letters C, I, and A.

Never during his short visits to the States did he and I discuss politics. It was only after McDougal, Littell came into being that he gave me an inkling of his political orientation — at some long-distance expense to him! Periodically, during the 1970s and 1980s, he would telephone me at the office — one time from Lisbon, another from Saigon — to give his kid brother what-for (and how come) for including something in a textbook that did not conform to his political views. One day, through a crackling overseas telephone connection, he shouted, "Say, Joe, I think it's seditious the way you tell students in your history books that many Americans were opposed to the Vietnam War. Shame on you, old buddy!" Another time, from another part of the earth: "Say, Joe, why in Heaven's name do you include in your history books whole paragraphs on the women's movement? That's not *history!*" After one particularly lengthy call, he said with a chuckle, "Gosh, Joe, I hope you don't mind my being your transatlantic gadfly." "Not at all," I replied. "Even if we don't agree on everything, it's always great to hear from you and get caught up on your family."

Hank and Flora adored Portugal, where they bought a home in the Algarve in anticipation of retirement. But this was not to be. After a bad fall, Hank suffered excruciating back pain and was returned to the States for continuing treatment, during which time he and Flora retired to St. Petersburg, Florida. Not long afterward, Hank discovered that he had lung cancer and was forced to undergo extensive chemotherapy treatments.

In his seventies, Hank was suddenly widowed. One day he met Betty, the beautiful widow of a retired marine general, rediscovered romance, remarried, and — bright-eyed once again — survived another three years, enjoying companionship and carefree ocean cruises. Surely this new life, stress-free and rejuvenating, played a part in diminishing the physical and psychological pain he had come to expect.

Finally, there was just one more hurdle to clear before he died, at the age of seventy-nine: of all things, a toe amputation! But one had to admire his fortitude. I had to smile at the way he responded when Joy and I commiserated with him on his bad luck. "Aw, shucks, Joe and Joy," he grinned, flashing those steel-blue eyes at us, "on my left foot I've still got four great toes. Anyway, who ever decreed that a person has to have five of those darn things?"

So that was my brother Hank. Mostly congenial, sometimes withdrawn. Yet in our hearts he was ever so special. And in the Littell clan, Hank will remain forever and by far the most inscrutable.

MORRIS

Earlier I described how Morris, for many years a drifter, magically evolved as a piano impresario, enchanting his listeners in bars and cocktail lounges in New York and Long Island. It was on Long Island that he met Ann, his last big love. A cocktail waitress, she was young and good-looking, with a creamy-smooth complexion and a smile that mesmerized. Ann was a devout, almost fanatical member of a tiny fundamentalist Christian sect called the Esoteric Church of God.

Morris and Ann were married in the Esoteric Church in Hempstead, Long Island. Soon afterward, when they visited Father in the hospital, he persuaded them to let him marry them again in an Episcopal church service in the hospital chapel. He may have wanted to marry them a second time in case the credentials of the minister at the Esoteric Church were not entirely in order. Or it may be that he just wanted a piece of the action. At any rate, Morris invited me to the private ceremony, and I was happy to attend.

Facing the bride and groom in his wheelchair, Father conducted the entire service himself. His speech was blurred, but his eyes were afire. His left hand, withered from his stroke, steadied the prayer book on his lap; his right thumb and forefinger turned the pages with some difficulty but did not detract from the dignity of the service.

After the ceremony, Morris and I visited Mother in the psychiatric ward. Churning around in her bed, wide-eyed with a vacant stare, she failed to recognize either of us.

Morris died of a heart attack at age forty-nine. Could it be that, over his short span of years, his body had absorbed too much mental and physical punishment? In any event, I'm glad he had Ann. Right after his death, she had her name legally changed to Ann-Morris Littell. "I want to be forever united with Morris," she declared, "in name as well as in spirit."

Today, I still rejoice that I had such a brother. The happiest memories of him sweep over me each time I hear his own special signature song, "The Last Time I Saw Paris."

NANCY

After Nancy's tumultuous "crossfire" experience with Don's mother and priest, resulting in an unwanted divorce and the loss of custody of her two young sons as well as periods of deep depression, she decided to go into the field of geriatric nursing. Did she and Don ever get back together again? The answer is a resounding no! Even though Don's mother did pass away and his priest was relocated, Nancy put aside the trauma, needing to move on and make a life for herself. After nursing school, she met and married Professor Byron Fox, of the Syracuse University Sociology Department, who soon became chairman of the same department at Carleton College in Minnesota. Until Byron's death in 1983, he and Nancy lived together for sixteen years — her first taste of an extraordinarily "equal" and happy marriage.

After Byron died, Nancy went to China with a group of U.S. gerontologists to study Chinese attitudes and methods concerning aging and the elderly. At that time, she was at the peak of her writing and lecturing career — teaching ways of reducing depression in nursing homes and encouraging creativity and joy in the institutionalized. I could see she was right for this career, for, as she told me, "Joe, you know, it was not only because of our mother's tragic old age but also because of my admiration for the Chinese reverence for the elderly that I could convey this message on a vast scale through my books and seminars. How can I help but agree with the Oriental outlook that

> Age is the top of a mountain high
> Clearer the air, and blue:
> A long hard climb,
> A bit of fatigue, but oh —
> What a wonderful view!"

Nancy today? After seven years in Hilo, Hawaii, she now resides near her sons and grandchildren in Ashland, Oregon, pursuing the pounding of her typewriter, attending college classes, hiking, and generally practicing what she preaches — that is, trying to make an art of "aging with grace."

Recently, Nancy was married again, to an artist from Hilo. It was a brief relationship, entered into, she told me, "because of my intense loneliness in the years following the death of Byron." Incompatibilities caused the marriage to founder.

JOE

Here I am, yours truly, Joe — number seven in the family. You already know nearly all there is to know about me — last of the bunch, bottom of the totem pole, youngest of the Littell brood. Right?

Wrong. There's someone I didn't tell you about. There was one more child, an eighth. Elton was born, not in China like the rest of us, but in Honolulu, when I was seven years old. Why hasn't he been mentioned; why haven't I even hinted at his existence? Now you will understand. I wanted to convey to you the fullest possible sense of his lifelong isolation from our family.

I also wanted to depict the effects on a human being of such a lonely, separate existence.

And so, what is the story of my younger brother?

ELTON

Elton's birth came at an awkward — no, a terrible — time, a year after my parents' arrival in Honolulu. They were settling into the Bishop's House and Mother was forty years of age. Father and she were "up to here" in diocesan doings — meetings, receptions, conventions. A new baby in the house? Of all times! Not surprisingly, Elton was left to the care of a nursemaid for much of his young life — sometimes for months at a time, when our parents were in the States drumming up funds for missions. At the tender age of nine — yes, only nine — he was sent away to boarding school five thousand miles away, to St. Paul's School in Baltimore. Miserably homesick, he hated every minute of it. None of us saw much of Elton while he was growing up. When one of us did have a chance to visit him, he was quiet and withdrawn. He was a tall, wiry boy with a shy, engaging smile that he seldom had reason to display.

There was one time, however, when he was a freshman at Gettysburg College, that I visited him and found him to be uncharacteristically talkative and high-spirited. He was living in Pennsylvania Hall, a dormitory with some rare history. At different times, it had served as a hospital for both Union and Confederate soldiers during the Battle of Gettysburg. Elton enjoyed marching me all the way up to the cupola at the top of Penn Hall. "This," he told me with obvious pleasure, "is the vantage point from which General Robert E. Lee is said to have scouted the Union forces with his binoculars. But Joe," he added with equal relish, "many southern historians vigorously dispute the truth of that story. They assert that General Lee was far too principled a man to violate the rules of warfare — that he would never have used a hospital for military purposes." Elton then went on to give me a fascinating account of the Battle of Gettysburg.

"Yes, Elton seems to be doing fine," I assured myself. "Just fine. Perhaps college will be a turning point for him."

Alas, we'll never know. For now, into his life, came a calamitous twist of fate. On the opposite side of the globe, communist North Korea

*My brother Elton at the age of thirteen. Six years later, this shy,
withdrawn boy would be in the front lines in Korea.*

had invaded democratic South Korea, and the Korean War was on. Uncle Sam wanted Elton — right now. The army lifted him out of college before he could complete his freshman year, and after a period of stateside training Elton was in the front lines.

As with my brother Morris, he could not begin to adjust to the military life. The only thing we know about Elton's combat experience is that he took part in the battle for "the Iron Triangle." This, I learned from military sources, was a triangular group of hills north of the front lines in central Korea — a vital center of communications for the Chinese and their main base for supplies brought down from Manchuria. U.S. troops were suffering considerably from enemy fire directed at them from the Triangle. Then came the crucial order from General Mark Clark, commander-in-chief of the United Nations Command, to attack and capture the Iron Triangle.

For the life of me, I cannot picture my sweet, gentle, soft-spoken kid brother, Elton, taking part in that assault on Chinese positions atop the Iron Triangle. An army historian described the horrors he had witnessed in the storming of one of the ridges:

> Sweating, heavy-footed soldiers, their hearts pounding, dragged their throbbing legs up these tortuous, vertical hills. Those who succeeded in clawing their way close to the bunkers were greeted by the crump and shower of black smoke, dirt, and sharp steel as grenades were tossed down on them. Dirty, bloodied, miserable, they backed down, tried again, circled, climbed, slid, suffered, ran, rolled, crouched, and grabbed upward only to meet again the murderous fire, the blast of mortar and the whine of bullets and jagged fragments. Minutes seemed like hours, hours like days, and days like one long, terrible, dusty, blood-swirled nightmare. Many bodies, bloodied and flesh-torn, remained on those slopes after the struggle.

Somewhere in that ghastly bath of blood and flesh was my brother Elton. Wherever he was, whatever he was doing, it was all too much for a boy so sensitive, so fragile, so vulnerable. He cracked. Not long afterward, the army shipped Elton back to the States and gave him a psychiatric discharge. The army doctor described his condition as "post-traumatic stress disorder."

Just as in every new war, progress requires that you be killed in a new way, so in every new war, if you can avoid being killed while people all around you are getting their heads blown off, progress requires that a new term be invented to explain why you went bonkers. In World War I, you had "shell shock." In World War II, you had "battle fatigue." In the Korean and later wars, you suffered "post-traumatic stress disorder."

For the next twenty years, Elton was in and out of many Veterans' Administration hospitals. Nancy tried, I tried, countless times to make a home for our brother, but always our attempts fizzled. A loner, Elton could not handle "togetherness," for this meant joining us for meals, socializing, making small talk.

To Elton, money was only for "worthy" people. What he had from his pension he discarded so as not to devalue it. He unloaded it on perfect strangers in the street. He walked into a bookstore and handed the astounded proprietor a roll of hundred-dollar bills. He dumped on the desk of a church secretary his entire back pay from the army — a total of four thousand dollars — then walked out without a word. "I don't deserve money," he kept telling me. Diagnosed as schizophrenic, he referred to himself as such, thus reinforcing his irrational behavior.

Painfully shy of women, Elton never married.

By now, our parents were both hospitalized at St. Alban's Hospital in New York. Faithful as a devoted pet, Elton visited them constantly until they died, clinging to them — the only "friends" he had.

In the 1970s, when Edward was in charge of the parish in Hoboken, he took Elton under his wing. Free of unwanted social pressures and blessed with Edward's steady companionship and guidance, Elton blossomed. Although I didn't see him at all during that period, it was reported that never in years had Elton looked happier and healthier.

After Edward retired from the parish, Elton moved to Bend, Oregon, where Nancy's son Ron often invited him to holiday meals and sports events. Though ill at ease with others, Elton felt comfortable in Bend because there was always a Ping-Pong or softball game to be played. Elton's fine intelligence was evident when, with professional skill, he played chess.

A big event — the day in 1990 when Nancy persuaded him to visit her in Hawaii. Here's how she described his visit:

> Although it ended abruptly, Elton and I had a great visit with delightful rides around the Big Island, swims on the Kona coast and much munching on our delectable mangoes. I got him to write a piece on this for his friends back in his Bend therapy class. He'll be thrilled to see it in print.
>
> Soon after his arrival, I learned that he was suffering from a stress condition which he had not shared with his doctor. Nighttime incontinence. Although I approached the problem in a low key, my discovery so embarrassed him that he insisted on cutting his visit short. "I want to go back to Bend," he begged, "immediately." Well, in Hawaii, you can't get plane reservations that fast, so I got him a special medical pass in order to get him on the plane, which meant that they provided him with a wheelchair and wheeled him out to the plane. To my surprise, he got a big kick out of that — let out a belly laugh you could hear a mile away. "Am I in the invalid category?" he whooped.
>
> Despite the lump in my throat, we parted with a warm hug. But as he disappeared atop the runway, I had a premonition. Something told me that I'd never see my brother again.

Four months later, Elton was dead. His nephew Ron found him slumped on the floor, the victim of a heart attack. He'd always been a heavy smoker and hooked on coffee, never able to kick the habits. Perhaps those were his anchor to an illusive sense of security, which he so craved.

I'll miss Elton. I'll always miss his gentle, kind nature, although one cannot grieve that he is now beyond the realm of earthly suffering and inner turmoil. For a human being to sense, from babyhood, that he is unwanted, unneeded, unworthy to take up space on this planet — what could be more pathetic, more destructive to a sense of self-esteem?

Good-bye, Elton. You are precious. If only you had known it!

.   .   .

So there you have it — the Littell family roll call. Not all of us present, but at least all accounted for.

Let's face it — our family statistics are shattering. Of the eight of us, three remained single. Of the remaining five, we accumulated a sorry record of fourteen marriages and eight divorces. Sign of the times? Or was it mish-kid consequences? Some of both?

RELIVING THE BATTLE OF THE BULGE

Before bringing to a close the story of my own life thus far, there is something else I think I should reveal.

My nightmares! My countless dreams about one certain moment that is inscribed so indelibly that it remains forever in my unconscious as well as in my conscious thoughts. An event that took place fifty years ago during the Battle of the Bulge. The date? December 17, 1944. That was the day I shot and killed a sixteen- or seventeen-year-old German soldier on the snow-frozen hills of the Ardennes. I can still see that tall, gangling kid charging up the hill toward me. Wearing a wide grin, or more likely a grimace, and certainly terrified, he keeps plunging forward, rifle in hand, his green greatcoat flying, until the second arrives for him to meet my bullet. I can still see him in my rifle sights. I can feel my finger squeezing the trigger. I can see him straighten up, lurch forward, and fall in the snow, face down, his rifle falling on top of him and then bouncing off his helmet. He is dead, and it is my bullet that has killed him.

Over the years, I have had dozens of dreams about that one moment in my life. Each version, it seems, has a new twist that makes it more grotesque and more disturbing than the event as it really happened. In one dream, four German soldiers are charging up the hill, straight at me, with rifles at the ready. As they get closer, I recognize their faces — *they are all former classmates of mine at the German school I attended in 1939!* They are my four good friends, Dieter, Sepp, Horst, and Ulrich! As the boys approach my position on the ridge, they recognize me, too — as the American exchange student they befriended. Immediately they break into happy shouts of "Joe! Joe!" and, overjoyed to see me, they throw down their rifles and rush forward to embrace me. At point-blank range I shoot them all dead.

In another nightmare, the most horrible of all, I watch the parents of the soldier I shot as they open a telegram from Colonel So-and-So of the Wehrmacht: I REGRET TO INFORM YOU THAT YOUR SON HAS BEEN SHOT AND KILLED BY JOE LITTELL. As the father reads the telegram, his face becomes a hideous death mask, then quickly transforms itself into the grinning face of the boy who appeared in my rifle sights.

Even when awake, I still have occasional reminders of the incident. The actual encounter with the German soldier occurred not long before I myself was hit by a German mortar shell. When I look at the four-inch length of scar tissue on my left leg, I am reminded not of my being wounded but of that German boy plunging toward me, wearing that wide, fixed grin. When I sit beside the pool in my Lake Forest home and someone asks, "What's that scar on your leg?" I say, "I was hit by a shell fragment in the war." But all my thoughts are of that boy. My wound is merely a trigger to the memory of my deed.

What is the greatest regret of my entire life? It is this: that I have killed another human being — son of his parents, brother of his grieving siblings. It is true that I did it with the blessing of my government. I did it, in fact, with the *encouragement* of my government. I did it, indeed, at the *command* of my government, under the *sponsorship* of my government. But none of that helps, really.

Let's try this one. I did it, ultimately, because every civilized human being needed to play a part in the struggle to expunge from our planet the most vicious, the most criminal madman the world has ever known.

That does help a little bit, I think — but not very much.

19

THE NEXT
GENERATION

MY THREE DAUGHTERS

I enjoy periodic visits these days with my three daughters, Julia, Nancy, and Laura — all now in their thirties. It wasn't until fairly recently that I became fully conscious of the disquieting things that had happened to them when their mother and I were going through our divorce and they were living with her in Wilmette. Julia was fourteen, Nancy twelve, and Laura ten. During that period (and for many years afterward), I often had nowhere to see them except in public places — mainly parks and restaurants. Because they wanted to please me, they turned our meetings into happy occasions, shielding me from details of the disturbing circumstances that arose from having to cope with an absentee father and a mother who was under such stress from managing three children and a household that she was nearly at her wits' end.

In recent years, as the girls revealed the dismal details to me, I couldn't help but conclude that I had shown my children the same neglect that my parents had visited on me when I was growing up. Evidently I hadn't learned enough from my own distressing passage through youth. I should have sensed more, felt more, probed more, known more. I should have been aware that younger children are ignorant of life, inexperienced, and frequently don't know how to express their feelings and discuss their problems unless helped to do so by a sympathetic and loving person in a suitable environment. Why is it we so often learn these lessons only after the damage has been done to the children?

Over the years, Julia, Nancy, and Laura have worked out most of their anger with their parents, I think, and have replaced it with love and understanding. In their cases, there has been a lot of therapy involved; in my case, some psychiatric counseling. Fortunately, as things have turned out, the three girls have not only managed to survive their childhood traumas but have made strong starts in both their personal and professional lives. Julia is an assistant professor in the graduate school of social work and social research at Bryn Mawr College. Nancy is one of the founders and principal physicians in a Massachusetts women's wellness center and teaches at the Brown University School of Medicine. Laura has been a technical writer for the Computer Corporation of America in Cambridge, Massachusetts, and now attends Garrett-Evangelical Theological Seminary, a graduate school of theology on the campus of Northwestern University in Evanston.

As of this writing, in three months I will be a grandfather for the first time. Six whole months before the baby was due — thanks to the wonders of chorionic villi sampling — Julia and her husband, Gary, called to make the great announcement: "It's a boy!"

A LETTER TO MY DAUGHTERS

I conclude this story of my life, so far, with a letter that I recently wrote to my three daughters late one night.

My Dear Julia, Nancy, and Laura,

It's two o'clock in the morning — one of those sleepless nights when thoughts of you and of our family ups and downs swirl around in my mind. Before another day goes by, I need to share with you certain observations — three of them — that I've made concerning our father-daughter relationship, and for a good reason. For now, from my new vantage point as "middleman" on the ladder of three generations of Littells, these insights take on a greater significance than I had realized. As my legacy to you, I must pass them on. And so, this won't be a breezy "Hope you're fine — I'm doing great!" kind of missive. It will be a hard one to articulate, but my hope is that it will be the most worthwhile letter you've ever received from your dad. And as you read it, may you sense between every line the love I feel for you, Julia, Nancy, and Laura — each of you so special to me, in her own way.

OBSERVATION #1 (and here, I will generalize): Parents — all parents — simply *must* find ways to stay close to their children — ways to tap into their bottled-up thoughts and feelings. But how? It's difficult for children to expose their innermost concerns. Sure, they talk about daily difficulties, or "cool" and "awesome" happenings, but that's just tiptoeing around their real feelings. This means that many parents have no idea what goes on in their heads — don't know what they worry about, why they toss in bed, or what that nightmare was all about. And so, what should a parent do? (I grieve to think that, as your father, I missed so many chances to fill this basic need.) A parent can listen. Listen, with a capital L. We must be good listeners, uncritical, unhurried, accepting listeners. I'm sure you already know why this is so important, but let me paraphrase the psychologist Carl Faber:

> When parents listen to their children, valuing the children's feelings as much as their own, they convey a strong message: that they respect the kids' processes of responding to life. Children who are listened to can then trust themselves to deal with experience and conflict. It is this trust that helps them to move in this world — helps them to know that they, as persons, are O.K., and to feel that they can deal with whatever comes. *The greatest gift a parent can give is to help develop this trust by giving the gift of listening.*

The *greatest* gift? Yes, it has to be. For now I realize that children can be like the Sphinx, silent and aloof, when it comes to sharing with adults their perplexities and inner hurts. To unburden themselves, they need our help. How can they open up when they don't know how — they haven't the experience, nor even the vocabulary. They haven't yet developed the skills to analyze, deduce, generalize, or form conclusions.

Just as my parents were unaware of my loneliness and self-doubt, so, too, were you, my daughters, well acquainted with that kind of isolation. You may be able to relate many episodes in your lives when your parents could have listened, could have "been there" for you. Here's one from my own life — an episode so painful when I was desperate for a listener that never before have I shared it with anyone.

When I was twelve (and just because my father was a bishop), I was elected president of the CYF — the Cathedral Youth Fellowship. To me this was terrifying, for I had never in my young life had a chance to attend, let alone conduct, a meeting. Pure shame prevented me from seeking help from my father — and besides, he was too busy doing "important" things, I figured. Nor was I about to make a fool of myself in front of friends. So what did I do? I feigned illness. "Possibly fatal," I groaned to my mother. Came time for the opening meeting. Where was "President Joe"? I never showed up. Not once did I appear at any subsequent CYF meeting!

If only I could turn back the clock and start all over again! For sure, I'd be a better listener for my girls. I'd be more tuned in to your troubles. I'd be more available to you when you needed me. And even though life taught me that rough lesson, I still did not get it — still didn't grasp the fact that my girls were having problems not so different from my own.

OBSERVATION #2: This one has to do with making assumptions. Do you know that unfounded assumptions can lead to disastrous consequences? Here again, just as my parents made them about me, so I, in turn, made them about you, my own daughters. You know how miserable I was in boarding school, five thousand miles away from home, and how my parents assumed that "Joe is doing just fine!" Same thing in your case, when we lived apart. I assumed you were "doing fine." Remember, after your mother and I were divorced, how, because of her threats, we had to meet in the park or other public places? You always put on smiley faces — not wanting to put a damper on my enjoyment. But I never delved behind those smiles, never read your body language, never picked up your signals of distress. I assumed that you were doing well. It was only years later, you remember, that I woke up to the truth — became conscious of the indignities you were being subjected to. Oh, my God — I had eyes that didn't see, ears that didn't hear! And after our visits I'd kiss you good-bye, then go about my workaholic ways, uplifted by our togetherness. How opaque — how insensitive can a father be? In retrospect, I see what the poet meant when he said, "They were fired in the crucible of neglect."

However, Julia, Nancy, and Laura, isn't there a benefit — doesn't a phoenix sometimes arise from the ashes of despair? In our case, for sure, we've learned a lesson. Now we see what folly, and how dangerous it can be to make assumptions — unfounded assumptions.

Finally, my Dear Ones, OBSERVATION #3 has to do with the changing face of family relations. Have you noticed how parent-child ties can often be cyclical? How they rise and fall, ebb and flow? Attitudes toward parents are fraught with mixed emotions — such as simultaneous love and hate, or love today, hate tomorrow. There may be periods of indifference. Feelings toward one parent may be more intense than toward the other. Surely, within our own family structure, you have known these variations. Your dad certainly has. I have loved, and admittedly I have hated, my father and mother. But as they aged, and as I mellowed, I began to see that never, ever, did they try intentionally to hurt me. After years of reflection and applying my Two-List System, I saw that it went like this: in general, most parents, and mine in particular, acting within the framework of their circumstances, *did the best they could with the knowledge they had.* This was a comfort to me. And so, not wanting them to depart this earth when our relationship was in the pits, I decided to give them a gift — an intangible one, but it was the gift of reconciliation, of a happy ending to their lives, filled with love and peace. As it turned out, it was I who received the greater blessing.

A long letter this, but hold on. Just one final word. I want you to know that I am grateful, Julia, Nancy, and Laura, that today you and I have a warmer, closer relationship than ever before. I am glad, and will never forget the good times we've had together. We'll have many more. None of us will need a reminder that to keep things this way, we must work at it through open communication. As a wise person said, "Even when parents and children get along swimmingly, it is possible, at times, for an old anger to flare up, triggered by an episode or remembrance of things past. Let the anger run its course, talk it out, then let it go. Write it down on a piece of paper, then throw it away. Or burn it. But yes, let it go!"

If I had another life to lead, you already know what my goals would be. I'd become a better listener. I'd make fewer assumptions. And above all, I would love you, not only well (as I always have, deep in my heart), but more wisely.

Your affectionate

Dad

EPILOGUE

WHEN I FINISHED telling my life story to my friend, his Yorkshire terriers, LIFO and FIFO, were fast asleep at his feet. But my friend was wide awake. He looked at me thoughtfully for a moment and then said, "Joe, never in a nanosecond did you strike me as the kind of person who would be enmeshed in such a variety of escapades, and on such a global scale! In the five years I've known you, I've had no clue whatever that you'd been anything other than a reasonably bright, energetic guy who loves his wife and kids and lives in a home filled for some unknown reason with Chinese antiques. Can you understand why I'm surprised by what you've told me? Maybe 'flabbergasted' is a better word. Anyway, I think you should share with others what you've told me tonight. I think you owe it to your kids, and to their kids. Tell the story of your family and pass that heritage on to them. You need to tell the good things and the bad, the successes and the failures, the joys and the miseries — tell it all, and whatever insights you have gained — pass them on to your children and their children. They need to know who they are and who you are and where you came from. Please write your story."

Thanks to my friend, I have written it. In the process, I have discovered that writing about problems or experiences that are emotionally tearing to me has a therapeutic effect. Writing a memoir, an entry in a diary or journal, or a chapter not only enhances pleasurable recollections, but lessens the inner ache, softens the pain of certain memories. It gives the mind a needed respite from those haunting traumas of long ago and far away.

Eighteen months ago I started work on this book. I had no idea what talking to a sheet of paper would do for me — no idea that it would change my thinking, my feelings, my sensitivities, as much as anything in my life had changed me before.

How do I feel now, as I approach the conclusion of my writing?

Self-Confident

Whole

Free!

ACKNOWLEDGMENTS

Many kind and generous people had a part in the preparation of this book. My dear sister Nancy Littell Fox helped me recall half-remembered incidents, especially from the early China and Honolulu periods, and bring them to life on the page. My cousins Walter W. Littell and Jean Littell Winslow supplied family letters, clippings, and photographs. My nephew Harrington Littell, Jr., my cousins Helen Littell Winslow and Gardiner Littell, and Sally Smith Hasbrouck gave their unfailing good counsel and support.

Dr. Richard Wong, Chinese Studies librarian at the University of California at San Diego, reviewed the China chapters. Old China hands Walter Haskell, Paul Sherertz, and Mary Stone Yahnker helped me track down information and photographs.

Donald Young and Victor Breite, lifelong friends from I Company, 422nd Regiment, reviewed the chapter on the Battle of the Bulge. Dr. Richard Peterson, Pete House, and Eugene Kelch, also veterans of the Bulge, provided helpful information. Hans Kasten helped me recall some vivid details of our experiences in three German POW camps.

Fred McDougal lent his wise counsel to the project from its inception; he also gave me valuable assistance with the chapters on McDougal, Littell & Company. Julie McGee, Bonnie Dobkin, Kathy Mattox, and Carolyn McConnell provided timely help of one kind or another.

Robert Rahtz, the former editor-in-chief of Macmillan's school department, read the manuscript and gave me valuable feedback, criticism, and encouragement. Seymour Fersh kept his comments on the manuscript light and lively and saved me from some infelicities. John Valleau made helpful suggestions on an early draft. Sandy Froeming did a superb job of typing. Alvin Deutsch remained, as always, a trusted friend and adviser.

At Houghton Mifflin Company, Nader Darehshori touched me deeply from the start with his faith in this book. Joseph A. Kanon, executive vice-president for Trade and Reference Publishing, eased my passage through unfamiliar territories. Janet Silver, my editor, handled the various editorial stages with professional skill and commitment. I also wish to thank Wendy Holt, assistant editor; Luise M. Erdmann, manuscript editor; Rebecca Saikia-Wilson, manager of Manuscript Editing and Composition; and Anne Chalmers, senior designer. All of the people I worked with helped to make this a much better book than it would have been without them.

My daughters, Julia, Nancy, and Laura, read portions of the manuscript and stimulated my work with their suggestions and comments.

Finally I wish to express my gratitude to my wife, Joy, for making me believe that anything I set out to do, I can do. I also wish to acknowledge my indebtedness to her for so quickly sounding the siren whenever my efforts fail to measure up. I cannot thank her enough for her assistance in shaping this book.

CREDITS

Excerpt from T. S. Eliot's "East Coker" in *Four Quartets*, copyright 1943 by T. S. Eliot and renewed 1971 by Esme Valerie Eliot, reprinted in the United States by permission of Harcourt Brace & Company. Permission to reprint in the English language throughout the world, excluding the United States, granted by Faber and Faber Ltd. Excerpts from *A Treasury of Humor* by Eric W. Johnson, copyright © 1989 by Eric W. Johnson, are reprinted by permission of Prometheus Books. Excerpts from the review in *English Journal*, September 1970, by Sheila Schwartz, copyright © 1970 by the National Council of Teachers of English, are reprinted by permission.